REASONABLE
and
ℋOLY

D1598637

REASONABLE
and
$\mathcal{H}$OLY

ENGAGING SAME-SEXUALITY

Tobias Stanislas Haller BSG

Seabury Books
NEW YORK

Copyright © 2009 by Tobias Stanislas Haller BSG

All rights reserved. No part of this book may be reproduced, stored in a retrieval system, or transmitted in any form or by any means, electronic or mechanical, including photocopying, recording, or otherwise, without the written permission of the publisher.

Unless otherwise noted, the Scripture quotations contained herein are from the New Revised Standard Version Bible, copyright © 1989 by the Division of Christian Education of the National Council of Churches of Christ in the U.S.A. Used by permission. All rights reserved.

Library of Congress Cataloging-in-Publication Data

Haller, Tobias Stanislas.
    Reasonable and holy : engaging same-sexuality / Tobias Stanislas Haller.
        p.   cm.
    Includes bibliographical references.
    ISBN 978-1-59627-110-4 (pbk.)
    1. Homosexuality—Religious aspects—Anglican Communion. 2. Same-sex marriage—Religious aspects—Anglican Communion. I. Title.
BR115.H6H355   2009
241'.66—dc22
                                                                            2009003787

Seabury Books
445 Fifth Avenue
New York, New York 10016

www.seaburybooks.com

An imprint of Church Publishing Incorporated

5 4 3 2 1

". . . and here we offer and present unto thee,
O Lord, our selves, our souls and bodies,
to be a reasonable, holy,
and living sacrifice unto thee . . ."

THE BOOK OF COMMON PRAYER

For James

דודי לי ואני לו

Song of Solomon 2:16

Contents

A Note by Way of Introduction

What follows began as an unfinished series of blog posts at *In a Godward Direction* (jintoku.blogspot.com) but it draws on more than a third-century of reflection and engagement with same-sexuality from a Christian perspective. As such, it has been furthered by the work of many scholars and theologians who have tilled this field before me. That includes those with whom I agree and those I find to be mistaken. I have, if anything, learned as much from the latter as the former—because they forced me to wrestle with their assertions and explore the primary material they cite—often to find that assertions sometimes do not match citations. To friend and foe alike I am indebted for guidance in pointing me towards those original sources. In that process I have made a number of my own findings, some of which I am not aware of having seen the light of day before now. I may have missed such earlier observations, and apologize in advance if I should seem to be presenting a shop-worn commonplace as a novel discovery.

That being said, I am not going to lard the pages with footnotes. References are provided in concise form—and I urge the reader to check my assertions against these texts. Expansions and additional observations appear as sidebars or call-outs, rather than being consigned to small type at the bottom of the page. The bibliography, too, is intended to be helpful, and includes books not actually cited. The questions at the ends of chapters, and the dialogue that forms the substance of the final chapter are provided in an effort to stimulate discussion rather than to close it off.

As to some scholarly concerns: for the sake of brevity, and in part because it is secondary to my concerns, I take the canonical approach and refer to "authors" such as Peter and Paul, in the knowledge that much that the text attributed to them is seen today to be the work of disciples. The same can be said of the teaching of Jesus. But I am primarily interested in taking these texts *as the church has received them* prior to the rise of higher criticism—which is not to say I disregard the value of such critical methods, but that I do not find them, ultimately, to be of much utility in addressing what is a problem in moral theology, rather than source criticism.

Similarly, though I will make passing reference to the sectarian Qumran documents, the intertestamental and apocryphal literature, my primary reliance will be upon the texts that are authoritative in Christianity and Judaism—the Bible and the Mishnah/Talmud—as well as the primary texts of major formative theologians in both traditions. It is the bulk of the main tradition with which I am concerned, rather than the interesting but eccentric byways. Even the main path occasionally becomes twisted, so I hope the reader will bear with me on this journey.

Finally, when it comes to the vexed question of authority, I follow the example of Richard Hooker in thinking: "Companies of learned men be they never so great and reverend are to yield unto Reason; the weight whereof is no whit prejudiced by the simplicity of his person which doth allege it." (II.7.6) Thus, given the amount of disagreement on the matter at hand, among very many learned people, I do not seek to pile up names of those who support my views as opposed to those who don't. When I quote a source, ancient or modern, it is generally because I find it to express a thought with particular wit and wisdom, or because I find it necessary to take issue with it. It is to you, the reader, that I make my argument—which you will receive or reject, I hope, on the basis of the argument itself, rather than on the credentials of those who support it or oppose it.

Tobias Stanislas Haller BSG
The Bronx
September 2008

1.
Where the Division Lies

IN THE CHURCH'S ONGOING DISCUSSIONS AND DEBATES OVER SEXUALITY, BOTH sides have advanced their arguments. I sometimes feel the debaters are talking past each other, and that they are coming from totally different conceptual worlds. The problem appears to lie in the premises (or assumptions) that underlie the differing points of view. If we are to come to a resolution of our differences — and it is a big *if* — it will be important to begin with certain agreed-upon principles, if we can, and work step-by-step through to that resolution. So what I am attempting in this volume is to begin to unpack, challenge and revisit (and perhaps revise) the underlying premises or assumptions of the traditional view, in an effort to get behind the "reassertions." Along the way, I will lay out some of the rationale for what is sometimes called the "revisionist" view — though the *revision* may sometimes be a return to an older understanding rather than the adoption of a new one. The goal will be to see if there is any basis of agreement from which a different settlement might be reached, or if we really are thinking and working from two radically incompatible bases. I know that some will not be willing to take this journey, fully convinced of the rightness of the so-called traditional view on one hand, or the pointlessness of trying to demonstrate the obvious need and rationale for change in that tradition on the other. But I hope that a review of the tradition itself may also open up some avenues for fruitful exploration.

I will, of course, want to deal with all of the apparatus of Scripture and reason as well. I will in part be challenging the *rational* basis of a negative view of same-sex relationships, because the traditionalist assertion often goes beyond a merely religious disapproval. That is, many if not most of those who think "homosexuality is wrong" do not see it as wrong merely in a religious sense — the way, for example, an Orthodox Jew might say that it is wrong to eat pork, but not hold a Gentile to that standard — but wrong in a moral or ethical or even legal sense,

1

I may at times seem like the child who asks, over and over, "Why?" But I've seen little in the wider debate that takes a form of much beyond a differently worded, "Because." I know things have been a certain way for a length of time. That in itself is no reason for them to remain, particularly when it begins to appear that the Emperor is very scantily clad indeed.

rightly subject not only to religious reproof, but to secular regulation as well; in short, not only plainly immoral but by rights illegal. All things that are illegal are generally seen as immoral; but not all things deemed immoral by some should also be illegal for all. Theocracy is not, at least on American shores, a welcome form of government; and we learned through Prohibition the danger of legislating morals. Still, in the present case, some are urging legal or even constitutional action.

The church does influence the secular society in which it finds itself, and can often be a force for good. The concern here is for care and prudence, and the virtue of humility. If what the church is teaching is correct, then by all means it should have impact on the world. But if it is wrong—well, Christian churches of all traditions have more than a few embarrassing skeletons in their closets.

As a part of that humility concerning its moral theology, not all in the church who hold any number of things to be immoral wish or work for them to be illegal in a pluralistic society. However, in the present case, there are more than a few religious conservatives who are also willing to see (at the extreme) state sanctions against same-sex relationships, or (at a minimum) a denial of state approval in recognition of such relationships.

In order to make this case, expanding from the sacred to the secular realm, it is clear that the voices of the tradition have gone beyond a simple religious basis for their opinion. The primary evidence for this lies in the arguments often advanced, many of which go well beyond the scriptural material. Needless to say, a biblical prohibition would not, in a pluralistic society, avail to sway the state to adopt it. It is ironic, though, that even with the minimal references to same-sexu-

The civil prohibition of murder is sufficient not to require additional theological support—few, if any, would claim that murder must be illegal because the Bible says so. So the breadth of the prohibition beyond the community of believers is based on rational arguments which are not founded on exclusively religious grounds. People *within* the faith find the biblical statement on murder is sufficient, and they would abide by their conscience on this matter even were the state to allow it—as, indeed, some of them say it does in the case of abortion, an example of an area in which some within the faith community would like to see the wider world embrace their view.

For many, the texts that forbid same-sex relationships are sufficient for their own internal morality. It is apparent that these texts are *not* convincing to a number of other believers. Hence, even within the church, some feel the need to make a broadened

ality in Scripture, secular courts in not-too-distant memory held up religious teaching as a rationale for continued state prohibitions. But as we will see, from the church's standpoint, if the scriptural case alone cannot bear sufficient weight to "settle" the matter *for the church*, then appeals to natural law, a purported good for society, or assertion of the complementarity of the anatomy of the sexes (to cite three common examples of additional arguments) become necessary.

Telling Right from Wrong

I would like, then, to turn to the various specific arguments, and the premises upon which the traditional case is most often made. It is important first of all to tease apart the general from the specific by asking what is held to be "wrong" about same-sex relationships, and "right" about mixed-sex relationships.

As a starting point, most of those who oppose same-sex relationships oppose *all* such relationships, regardless of qualities of fidelity, mutuality, and so on. Thus issues rightly and widely recognized as "moral" are held to be irrelevant. At the same time, the conservative view recognizes that these values exist, and are necessary in a mixed-sex relationship; that is, as commonly put, sexual relationships are appropriate only within the context of a faithful, life-long, loving, mixed-sex marriage. So it appears that the argument from the conservative position is reducible to the irreducible fact of the sex of the couple—the sex difference *must* be present for a sexual relationship even to be *capable* of being moral, so that even if a same-sex couple possesses all of the other moral values, the lack of sex-difference still renders the relationship, and any sexual activity within it, immoral.

What this must mean, logically, is that there is some character or quality inherent in the sex-difference that is *morally determinative in and of itself,* apart from any other aspect of the persons or their relationship. There are two such qualities often advanced as premises:

---

effort to bring additional *logical* evidence to bear. Similarly, that the secular realm is less than fully persuaded by the secular arguments is evidenced in the reverse appeal to "Judeo-Christian principles," or appeals to the "religious nature" of marriage.

Yet throughout history and into the present a number of cultures and religions have instituted forms of same-sex marriage. As a fact on the ground such relationships are widespread, even when not publicly acknowledged or granted civil recognition. But same-sex marriage and/or civil unions *are* now a part of the law of a number of sacred and secular jurisdictions in the US and the rest of the world. So this is no longer simply a matter of theory. The civil world is unlikely to be persuaded in a more conservative direction by religious evidence when many, even among believers, are no longer convinced by it.

- that the purpose of sexuality is procreation, and only heterosexual sex is capable of it;
- that heterosexual sex represents a joining of two distinct complementaries.

In the next chapter I will address the first assertion.

$\mathcal{Q}$uestions for Discussion or Reflection

- *Is same-sex marriage, or any form of civil union or domestic partnership, provided for by civil law in the jurisdiction in which you live?*

- *What kinds of restrictions on marriage are in force in your town/city/state?*

- *What kind of legal restrictions on same-sex couples exist in your town/city/state?*

- *Can you think of other matters on which the state has taken a neutral view, in allowing actions you consider immoral?*

- *On the other hand, are there things that the state restricts that you think should be permitted?*

2.
Pro-Creation

*I*T IS COMMONLY ASSERTED THAT THE ESSENTIAL PURPOSE OF SEXUALITY IS PRO-creation, and that procreation (and sexuality) are limited to marriage. I will demonstrate that not only is procreation not essential to marriage, but that its relationship to sexuality is not absolute; that it can be (and is) separated from other ends of marriage—the unitive, symbolic, social, and preventative—which in themselves, and apart from procreation, can and do form a proper basis for a sexual relationship within marriage.

Ways and means and blessings

Before entering into the specifics, I want to address the language of *purpose* and *function* or *ends*. In general, although this language has a place in the tradition, it seems to reflect an overly utilitarian ethic focused on *results*. I would prefer to follow another aspect of the Christian tradition that refers to the *goods* of marriage. In this view, sexuality is not simply a function, or the use of a person (or two persons' use of each other) towards some end or goal, but an act growing out of the love between persons that is open to the good that may come. Self-giving love, rather than self-asserting need, provides the basis for the action which grows out of the love, and which is a blessing in itself apart from any result.

In addition, *purpose* in this context implies an *a priori* assumption, a social or theological one at that. There is a difference even between a *purpose* and a *function*. *Purpose* sees sexuality not merely for what it does and how it does it, but as a naturally or divinely *intended* "plan for humanity"—depending upon one's world-view—as the

> Martin Buber said the I-Thou relationship enjoys the highest ethical status. A loving relationship finds its end and purpose in the other as a person, not for some extrinsic product or result. The couple are gifts for and to each other.

5

result of a secular personified Nature or theological understanding of God. It is important, therefore, to be aware of this subtext in the secular and sacred tradition before proceeding.

Defining the goods

Avoiding both *purpose* and *function* at the outset, most people (including those outside the faith) would agree that human sexuality appears to have two principal *goods*, procreation and union. (The reflective or symbolic good, in which marriage serves as an image for the relationship between Christ and the church, or God and Israel, is solely theological. I will address union and reflection in subsequent chapters, as well as a *cause* or *end* of marriage that has dropped both from most contemporary discussions and from the preface to the Episcopal marriage liturgy: marriage as a remedy for fornication, for those who lack the gift of celibacy.)

The church has (until fairly recent times) traditionally emphasized procreation over union, but it appears that such an emphasis is not well supported by Scripture, reason, or even other elements of the tradition. In this and succeeding chapters I hope to sketch out a number of points concerning the various goods of sexuality, and consequently, of marriage.

In 1949, the Episcopal Church introduced a canonical impediment to marriage: the existence of any "concurrent contract inconsistent with the contract constituting canonical marriage." This somewhat circular impediment included the intention (by a couple capable of procreation) deliberately to *avoid* having children by mutual agreement. The impediment was removed in 1973. The Roman Catholic Church maintains the requirement that couples at least *not be ignorant* of her teaching that marriage is "ordered toward the procreation of offspring" (Canon 1096) and, of course, forbids artificial contraception. A couple who chose deliberately not to have children would contract marriage invalidly. (1101) However, neither church forbids marriage to persons who are *incapable* of procreation. The Episcopal canons are silent on the subject, and the Roman Catholic canons state this explicitly. (1084.3) The actual *ability* to procreate is not required for a valid marriage.

In the process I will demonstrate that procreation is neither essential to marriage, nor the principle good of human sexuality. I use the word *human* intentionally, in order to highlight the fact that sex and sexuality are not unique to human beings. We share membership in a species predominantly male or female, and our limited capacity to reproduce sexually, with most animals and many plants. It has been observed in the past that expending theological energy on the mere existence of the sexes and the capacity to reproduce—which is part of our animal nature—shifts the focus away from what makes us truly human and serves as locus for the image of God in human form: our capacity to love and to reason.

The witness of nature

No one would claim that sex has *nothing* to do with procreation; rather it is obvious that the existence of male and female in many species of animals and plants is a part of the natural process by which life is perpetuated. It is not, of course, the *only* means of such propagation, and many forms of life, including some vertebrates, reproduce without making use of sexual differentiation or sexual intercourse.

However, when it comes to human beings, it is trivial to observe that the existence of male and female, and their capacity for sexual intercourse, is intimately connected with procreation. The natural law tradition takes this as given. But that is, in part, why this tradition is of little use in the present discussion, as it begs the question: it assumes as a premise the very matter under discussion, that is, that procreation is the *primary* purpose for or good of sex.

The difficulties with ends-based natural law arguments in this regard, which are advanced against birth control as much as against same-sexuality, in particular those that focus narrowly on the mechanics of sexual intercourse, are well summarized by Gerard J. Hughes in *The Westminster Dictionary of Christian Ethics*.

> It is one thing to say that the natural function of the eye is to see. But even bodily organs can and do serve several functions. And if one asks of the body as a whole what its function is, the answer is much less clear. Even less clear is the answer to questions such as "What is the function of a human life?" or "What is the function of sexuality in a human life?" The way one might try to answer these questions seems quite unlike the way one might try to answer questions about the function(s) of the endocrine glands or the heart in the human body. The notion of "function" at this point becomes much more a matter of moral assessment than a scientific inquiry. ("Natural Law," 413)

Given that caveat, from an objective standpoint the following observations are telling, even in light of a functional or ends-based viewpoint:

- **Procreation is not simultaneous with intercourse,** which in humans is not the planting of a seed (as the pre-modern world imagined it) but the placement of millions of sperm in a place where they are eventually capable of reaching a single ovum, at which point one sperm may fertilize it.
- **Intercourse does not always lead to procreation.** Any couple who has experienced difficulty in conception can attest to this fact; even fertile couples experience a completely *natural* separation between capacity to have sexual relations and the capacity to procreate, and not every sexual act results in

> The church does not hold everything natural to be moral. Often it is not what is natural, but that which is acquired or develops that is moral. The moral sense itself is not "natural"—it must be developed as one matures and grows; thus we do not hold young children to be capable or responsible as moral agents.

conception. In addition, the human female does not have an estrus cycle, and unlike the females of many other species is sexually "available" at times when fertilization is not even possible.

- **Procreation can take place entirely apart from intercourse** (through artificial insemination and in vitro fertilization) and, perhaps needless to say, **apart from marriage.**
- **Intercourse can take place when procreation is impossible or avoided.** In addition to the "naturally infertile period" that is part of the menstrual cycle (which, as noted above, has no impact on ability or willingness to engage in sexual intercourse), women become infertile after menopause (this is not a "defect" but a part of the natural life process of the human female), and human beings can engage in intercourse when some other cause (intentional obstruction or incidental defect) prevents conception.
- From a sociological perspective, in looking at the question of "the function of sexuality in a human life" it is clear that **sexuality has major social and cultural implications apart from procreation,** and has taken many forms in many cultures.

At the same time, it is fair to notice the assertion (which some occasionally raise in such discussions) that every human being who ever lived is the result of sex between a man and a woman. This, however, in addition to overlooking conception via artificial means or *in vitro*, neglects three exceptions significant to the religious question—Adam, Eve, and more importantly, Jesus—which brings me to the witness of Scripture.

The witness of Scripture

There are times I have to confess that the utility of Scripture in helping us better to understand our current situation may be approaching its limit. Over the last thirty years I have seen texts tossed back and forth, twisted and stretched beyond their capacity, or shrunk to insignificance. When I consider how little the Scripture actually says about the presenting issue, and how much of what it says is in a limited vocabulary of half-a-dozen Hebrew and Greek words—some so rare they are only understood by conjecture, others capable of a range of figurative and literal application—and then take account of the energy of the debate, I begin to wonder at Scripture's ever providing us with a settlement to the matter.

Still, Scripture is a "given"—indeed it is a *gift*; but it is a gift that requires unwrapping, and some assembly, and batteries are not included. Contrary to those who assert the doctrine of *sola scriptura*, the Scripture does not (indeed cannot) interpret itself, although we may use one portion of Scripture better to understand another. But Scripture does not stand alone, apart from reason, the inspiration of the Holy Spirit, and the record of the church's wrestling with those sometimes difficult texts. As Richard Hooker put it,

The force of arguments drawn from the authority of Scripture itself, as Scriptures commonly are alleged, shall (being sifted) be found to depend upon the strength of this so much despised and debased authority of man. . . . Even such as are readiest to cite for one thing five hundred sentences of holy Scripture; what warrant have they, that any one of them doth mean the thing for which it is alleged? Is not their surest ground most commonly, either some probable conjecture of their own, or the judgment of others taking those Scriptures as they do? (II.7.8)

In the callout section titled "Principles of Interpretation," you will see a summary—drawn from traditional Anglican sources and the Scripture itself—of how Scripture is best engaged in understanding God's overarching intent for human beings: that we should come to the knowledge and the love of God. I will, in this and succeeding chapters, attempt to employ these principles in coming to my conclusions.

> It is sometimes said that sexuality is, by divine intent in Genesis 1, intrinsically ordered towards procreation. We might just as well observe that according to Genesis 2 it is intrinsically ordered towards human society. But how does one determine if something is "intrinsically ordered" towards some good, apart from seeing if it results in that good—and how *intrinsic* is it if it is equally capable of failing in *that* good or achieving some *other* good? This is especially important when a person or a couple is incapable of procreation: is not their marriage also *good*?

Back to the beginning

In spite of how important sex and sexuality are to the life of the world, the Scripture asserts and the church affirms that the most important conception in human history, that of Jesus Christ himself, took place apart from sexual intercourse between a man and a woman. This is, naturally, an article of faith and revelation, not reason. However, we are presented with this theological truth; reason can seek to understand what God may intend by it. That God should choose this means of entering upon the human scene should give pause to those who wish to make more out of heterosexuality in the scheme of *salvation* than is evidenced in Scripture. As I will demonstrate, God's choice is best seen as a reflection of Jesus' teaching on the new Creation, which is not a recapitulation of the old, but the beginning of something new.

But let us for a moment return to that beginning, to Genesis, naturally often cited in discussions of human sexuality. Note the obvious fact that Genesis contains two creation accounts, and they are not harmonious in numerous details; in several points they are contradictory. This has not prevented people merging the two accounts in various ways. Jesus himself performed such a *midrash*, though with a significant omission, as we shall see.

However, it is best to treat the two accounts with care in distinguishing the concerns each expresses. It is immediately apparent that Genesis 1 refers to procreation (both animal and human) while Genesis 2 focuses on the good of companionship and unity. This indicates how these two goods can be discussed apart from each other.

Many reasserters seem to think that Genesis offers the best argument against same-sex relationships, and regularly return to it in discussions of the subject. However, the fact that Genesis 1 presents us with the creation of male and female as ordered towards procreation (though Adam and Eve themselves were created *without* procreation) does not automatically imply a prohibition on same-sex rela-

---

∾ Principles of Interpretation

1 The Holy Scriptures of the Old and New Testaments are "the Word of God" and "contain all things necessary to salvation." *(Oath of Conformity; Article VI, Book of Common Prayer, 868)* They are called the Word of God by the household of faith, not because God dictated the biblical text, but because the Church believes that God inspired its human authors through the Holy Spirit, and because by means of the inspired text, read within the sacramental communion of the Church, the Spirit of God continues the timely enlightenment and instruction of the faithful. *(BCP, 853)*

2 The Holy Scriptures are the primary constitutional text of the Church. They provide the basis and guiding principles for our common life with God, and they do so through narrative, law, prophecy, poetry, and other forms of expression. Indeed, the Scriptures are themselves an instrument of the Church's shared communion with Jesus Christ, the living Word of God, who uses them to constitute the Church as a Body of many diverse members, participating together in his own word, wisdom, and life. *(Article XIX)*

3 The Scriptures, as "God's Word Written," bear witness to, and their proper interpretation depends upon, the paschal mystery of God's Word incarnate, crucified and risen. *(John 5:39; Article XX)* Although the Scriptures are a manifestly diverse collection of documents representing a variety of authors, times, aims, and forms, the Church received and collected them, and from the beginning has interpreted them for their witness to an underlying and unifying theme: the unfolding economy of salvation, as brought to fulfillment in Jesus Christ.

4 The Scriptures both document and narrate not only God's saving acts but also the manifold human responses to them, revealing that God's unchanging purpose to redeem is fulfilled, not by means of a coercive, deterministic system, but through a divine plan compassionately respectful of human freedom, and adapted to changing historical circumstances, cultural situations, and individual experience and need. *(Acts 11:1–18, 13:46–48)* In reading the diverse texts of Holy Scripture, the Church seeks an ever-growing comprehension of this plan and of the precepts and practices whereby believers may respond more faithfully to it, walking in the way of Christ.

5 The New Testament itself interprets and applies the texts of the Old Testament as pointing to and revealing Christ. *(Matthew 26:54; Luke 4:21, 24:27; Acts 8:35, 18:28)* Thus, the revelation of God in Christ is the key to the Church's understanding of the Scriptures as a whole. *(Article VII)*

6 Individual texts must not, therefore, be isolated and made to mean something at

tionships, any more than the pre-scientific discussion of the origin of the world, or the structure of the cosmos, need automatically rule out the teachings of physics or cosmology.

Moreover, the tale that tells of the divine establishment of X does not *in itself* require a negative assessment of Y, in particular if X and Y can be shown both to

odds with the tenor or trajectory of the divine plan underlying the whole of Scripture. *(Article XX)*

7 It must be concluded that the words of a scriptural text or texts, however compelling, cannot in every circumstance be received by the Church as authoritative. Even if the Church has no authority to abrogate "commandments which are called Moral"-unlike its jurisdiction in "ceremonies and rites" (Article VII)—the true moral significance of any commandment is not simply given but must be discerned.

8 Thus, for the Church's judgment of the morality of actions and dispositions to be authoritative, it is insufficient simply to condemn those things that are condemned somewhere in Scripture, or to approve those things that are somewhere approved.

9 Faithful interpretation requires the Church to use the gifts of "memory, reason, and skill" *(BCP, 370)* to find the sense of the scriptural text and to locate it in its time and place. The Church must then seek the text's present significance in light of the whole economy of salvation. Chief among the guiding principles by which the Church interprets the sacred texts is the congruence of its interpretation with Christ's summary of the law, the new commandment, and the creeds. *(Matthew 22:37–40; John 13:34)*

10 The Church's interpretation of Scripture is itself part of the human response to the economy of salvation, an essential means whereby the Christian faithful understand God's actions in their lives and experience, and therein know God's power and purpose to judge, redeem, liberate, and transform. *(Romans 8:15, 21)*

11 Yet precisely because the Church's members are human, their reading of Scripture is contingent and fallible, even in matters of faith and morals. *(Articles XIX)* In reading its Scriptures, the historical Church always remains a wayfaring community using discernment, conversation, and argument to find its way.

12 Interpretative security rests not in an indefectible community or infallible magisterium, but in the tested deposit of the baptismal faith and, above all, in the covenant God who is faithful to a people who err. *(Luke 24:41–49)*

13 To affirm the "sufficiency of the Holy Scriptures for salvation" *(Article VI)* is to enlarge the sphere of human liberty by acknowledging limits upon what may be required in matters of faith and morals. Taken in this way, the Scriptures do not lose their authority, but on the contrary fulfill their ultimate intent, which is to bring all people to the blessed liberty of the children of God, whose service is perfect freedom.

[adapted from *Let the Reader Understand*. New York: The Diocese of New York of the Episcopal Church, 2002]

belong to a larger category, and have more in common than in contrast. If Y can be shown to partake of some similar values, or participate in some of the same goods, as X, it is on *that* basis it should be judged, not simply because it is not X. Part of our problem in the present discussion is our tendency to see heterosexuality and homosexuality as somehow *opposed* to each other, or mutually *exclusive*, rather than as differing expressions of one overriding reality—the human capacity to love—and as solutions to the human problem of solitude and isolation.

The Genesis of the Bible

In addition, Genesis 1 is a *creation* account, an account intended to explain the *origin* of certain things. As such, it is quite natural that—as with many other creation stories the world over—it should recount the creation of the sexes. This is not to discount the divine inspiration of the text, but to acknowledge that as God interacted with those who composed the Scriptures, their culture influenced what they heard and recorded under inspiration.

Scripture is the inspired Word of God, but it is always written in a human tongue. People do not speak God's language, or have God's knowledge, so God, when speaking to people through inspiration, will be heard in the human language of the culture and time of the one inspired, in order to receive any knowledge at all. God always "talks down" to us, and our finite human capacity always limits how well we understand the infinite God and express that understanding. One cannot put the ocean in a bottle; new wineskins are used for new wine. As Jesus himself would later say, "I have many things to say to you, but you cannot

⤳ Begotten, Not Made

It is sometimes suggested that a man and woman, in coming together to conceive and bear a child, become "co-creators" with God. The act of bringing a new life into the world is a wonder, a human life all the more wonderful; and a couple can cooperate with this or seek to frustrate it. But since a new life can come into the world even when not intended, the degree of cooperation required is not fixed—a child can be conceived in spite of the intentional efforts to prevent the conception; or fail to be conceived even when that is most earnestly desired. So the language of "co-creation" is probably too strong even for a planned pregnancy. The fact that Genesis 4:1 is sometimes used as the prooftext (". . . Eve . . . conceived and bore Cain, saying, 'I have produced a man with the help of the LORD'") should be of little comfort, both on account of Eve's past and Cain's future. Both Eve and Cain assume themselves to be too much like God, the only giver and taker of life. It is God who creates all life, the One who "gives the growth" whoever it may be who "plants or waters" (1 Corinthians 3:7). It is, ultimately, God who has made us, "and not we ourselves" (Psalm 100:3).

bear them now. But when the Spirit of truth comes, he will guide you into all the truth" (John 16:12–13).

So it is not surprising that the culture and society of ancient Israel, which took little notice of same-sexuality and had no social construct to describe it, should not include any reference to it in its creation account. Contrast Genesis 1, for example, with Aristophanes' satirical creation account in Plato's Symposium: different cultures have different perceptions of "what is" and so different explanations for how they came to be.

The inspired recipients of God's word in Genesis believed the sky to consist of a dome in which the sun, moon, and stars were set, and which had windows to admit the rain stored in the pool of waters above. God, of course, knew that this was not true, literally or in any other sense, but the minds of those God inspired had no place to hold such concepts as gravity and freely floating planets, stars and moons—or that the earth was not stationary at the center of a revolving universe. They had the evidence of their senses to the contrary, and would not, as Jesus would later say, have been able to "bear" the truth. So God communicated to them in a language that did not seem outrageous to them, met their expectations, and explained and ratified what they perceived. The primary truth God intended to convey, after all, was not a literal primer on the composition of the cosmos, but the theological principle that God is the creator of all that is.

So too the accounts in Genesis 2 through 4 do not present a literal history of the first human beings, but a theologically relevant account. God's word was designed meaningfully to explain truths to people in keeping with what they perceived, within their time and place—to address the questions to which the account pro-

---

It is not unusual for a society that has a generally negative view towards same-sexuality either to ignore or deny its presence within that society. The contemporary view that "there is no homosexuality in Africa (or wasn't until the Arabs or the West brought it)" or in Korea (if we are to believe the mother of Margaret Cho), echoes the Talmudic judgment in reference to why same-sexuality was seen as a particularly Gentile affliction: "Israel is not suspected." (bKiddushin 82a) Certain communities vociferously deny the existence of same-sex relationships within their population, and either render them invisible by calling them something else ("we don't even have a word for it"), or insisting, should they become evident, that they are foreign intrusions, or an aspect of an "alien culture."

The other approach, as in the British Public School system, is to tolerate it, ignore it (and wear boots and cough as the dormitory master makes the rounds of the dormitory) and never speak of it. This is attested in C. S. Lewis' autobiography, *Surprised by Joy*, where he noted the irony of something so broadly condemned in the larger society being, in the narrower hothouse confines of the school, "the only foothold or cranny left for certain good things." (100,109)

vides the answers: small matters such as why snakes have no legs, but also the truly important questions of life, the universe, and everything: primarily, why is it that people do wrong things; why do they die; why do they marry; why should a perfectly natural thing like childbirth be so painful and life-threatening. We would no more expect the Scripture to provide a reasoned explanation for human psychosexuality than to expect it to provide us with an accurate value for *pi*.

Some say, "Genesis has to be literal history, because if it isn't we can't trust anything else in the Bible." My parents told me about Santa Claus when I was young, and when later I discovered there is no Santa Claus I didn't distrust my parents on everything else. I understood they were just trying to get me to be a good boy by telling me that someone somewhere was keeping a list and checking it twice. The fact that our earthly parents have been using such a device as a means to discipline should probably be good evidence that God did the same—as, indeed, we are assured that "the Law was a disciplinarian until Faith came . . ." (Galatians 3:24).

When the world was young, God "spoke in many and various ways by the prophets" (Hebrews 1:1) but later through the Son. Jesus, the Son, used parables—and unless one thinks these to be literal accounts, too, to a similar end. Like Father, like Son.

Beginnings and ends

So let us return to Genesis 1. Procreation—a function of the sexes both in animals and in humans (as Genesis 1 states explicitly)—is intended to fill the world with living things, even if that first generation of creatures and humans did not result from sex. But the theological import of this is, after all, only the *first* word on sexuality, not the *last*. This is an account of the *genesis* of the world, of how it came to be, not its *intended end*. The scriptural testimony may begin in a *Garden*, but it ends in a *City*, where the only marriage is that of the Lamb and his Bride, the Holy City itself. The goal and eternal plan of God is not mere restoration or recapitulation, but redemption and transfiguration. With God it is always new.

This leads to an issue sometimes raised by those who envision salvation in terms of a *return to* or *restoration of* the world of Eden before the fall, the prelapsarian world. Although Genesis 1 includes a *commandment* to procreation, Scripture does not indicate this being acted upon until *after* the fall, in Genesis 4. Procreation, in the second creation account, is postlapsarian.

The Christian vision thus portrays the life of the resurrection as prelapsarian only in this sense, as pre- or post-sexual, a new world in which there is no longer "male and female"—by which Paul (Galatians 3:28) is speaking less of an eschatological disappearance of gender than of an end to marriage based on sexual distinction. As with the other distinctions (ethnic and social), Paul points to the restoration of equality and mutuality rather than of domination and exclusion, which came about as a result of the Fall.

This harmonizes well with Jesus' description of the resurrection life as prelapsarian only in this narrow sense: a world in which "they do not marry nor are given in marriage, for they cannot die any more" (Luke 20:35–36); that is, there is no more need for "male and female" to "be fruitful and multiply" and "fill the earth and subdue it." For the old earth will have been completely subdued—not by us, but by the triumph of Christ, who has put all things under his feet—and will have passed away, and all will be made new. Procreation will be no more, for dying will be no more—but love will endure for ever in the place where we share perfect union one with another, even as God the Father and the Son are One.

> The Garden of Eden was not a place free from sin. It was, on the contrary, the setting for the first and primal sin, the effort to become like God. Thus salvation is not return to the Garden, but progress to the heavenly City, not by our own efforts to become gods, but by the grace of God who became one of us.

A change in the law

It is notable that Jesus' *midrash* of Genesis 1 and 2 (in response to challenges on divorce in Matthew 19:4–5 and Mark 10:6–9) omits any reference to procreation—he passes directly from "God made them male and female" to "For this reason a man shall leave his father and mother and be joined to his wife, and the two shall become one flesh." Omitting any reference to procreation, his emphasis is on union, and above all on its permanence through the grace of fidelity. (Those who attempt to pitch Jesus' teaching here as a condemnation of same-sex relationships, rather than in response to the question on divorce, do justice neither to their position nor to Scripture.) I will return to this passage in my discussion of the unitive good of marriage—the one which Jesus emphasized.

Jesus' rejection of the divorce statute of the Mosaic Law (given by Moses but attributed to God in the Torah) attests to another significant change in attitude towards procreation in the teaching of Christ.

The Rabbis regarded the commandment to be fruitful and multiply as universal: the first commandment given to humanity. Thus celibacy was held in low esteem or even in contempt in rabbinic Judaism, to the extent of being considered a serious moral failing.

> No man may abstain from keeping the law *Be fruitful and multiply*, unless he already has children: according to the School of Shammai, two sons; according to the School of Hillel, a son and a daughter, for it is written, *Male and female created he them*. (mYebamoth 6.6)

So important was the commandment to be fruitful and multiply that the biblical law mandated a special form of marriage which would otherwise have constituted incest (Deuteronomy 25:5–6) in order to provide for continuation of a family line ended by the husband's death before he had fulfilled the divine command. For the same reason, biblical law also allowed polygamy, and the historical accounts attest to its employment to that end. One of these incidents, however, also shows the importance of the unitive aspect of sexuality, apart from procreation: as Elkanah comforted his barren wife Hannah with the words, "Am I not more to you than ten sons?" (1 Samuel 1:8) The fact that the story of Hannah was later typologically parsed by Saint Luke in reference to Mary and the birth of Christ casts even greater significance for Christians on this episode from early sacred history.

More importantly, and perhaps related to the contrary teaching of Jesus, so important was the duty to procreate that the Rabbis *enjoined divorce* should a man find his wife to be infertile after ten years of marriage (mYebamoth 6.6). In a prescientific world, of course, failure to bear a child was most often seen as the woman's fault, as women were held to be "fertile soil" for the growth of the male "seed." Even given that, the *Mishnah* allows a woman so divorced an additional ten years with another husband just in case the fault lies with the man.

Jesus overturns this traditional understanding and emphasis upon procreation, and this may relate to and reflect the larger Divine intent in his own Incarnation apart from sexual intercourse. Whatever the source of his teaching, beginning with God's act in the Incarnation, and contrary to the main stream of rabbinic

One of the crucial problems in addressing the biblical view of sexuality is that the people of biblical times—and long thereafter—were as ignorant of biology as they were of cosmology. They no more knew how children were conceived than they could conceive the orbits of the planets. What they believed came from their observations. The man planted his seed in the fruitful (or unfruitful) soil of the woman, and the seed took root and grew, drawing for nourishment on the "soil" of the woman, much as a plant might. The semen (= "seed") represented the "active principle," and philosophers such as Aristotle believed it gave form to the raw material derived from the mother's body.

One scriptural speculation is based on the observation that the flow of menstrual blood ceased with the beginning of pregnancy, and conjectured that the fetus was made of curdled menstrual blood. (Wisdom 7:2) This belief was common until modern times. John of Damascus notes the "purity" of Jesus in that no semen was involved in his incarnation, but only "the blood of the virgin" (*Of the Orthodox Faith*, III.2) a point later affirmed by Thomas Aquinas (*Summa* III.Q31.5). Aquinas also accepted Aristotle's teaching on reproduction, and that vaginal secretions were female, and therefore defective, semen.) The biblical and post-biblical world did not know about the ovum, what was actually going on in gestation to stop the monthly flow, or the cause of menopause, though it observed the latter and assumed it had something to do with the soil being exhausted. Infertility was thus put down to something being wrong with the woman.

However, infertility at menopause is not "unnatural." It is an entirely natural conse-

thought, Jesus approves and commends celibacy (Matthew 19:12), as does Saint Paul (1 Corinthians 7:7–8).

Celibacy is, of course, a radical option, as both Jesus and Paul recognize—it is a charismatic gift of which not all are capable, but it is also an eschatological sign, a symbol for the new world in which there is no marriage.

Incidentally, this raises another argument often advanced against same-sexuality: that if everyone "practiced" it it would be the end of humanity. It is of course true that if everyone practiced *celibacy* that would also be the end of humanity—though no one, apart from an Orthodox rabbi, would thereby suggest celibacy was morally wrong. The distinctly "unorthodox" Saint Paul, in his only extended discussion of marriage cited above, actually did suggest that he wished everyone were celibate as he was—though this may be regarded as a rhetorical flourish rather than an actual intention, since he goes on to tolerate marriage in the meanwhile, even as he advises against it (1 Corinthians 7:28–31).

The witness of tradition

Finally, I turn to the testimony of the church's tradition. Although relatively recent in the body of that tradition, it is helpful to start with the preface to the

quence of the functioning of the human body. Since menopause results from the cessation of the production of a hormone, which in itself is also key to the "infertile period," there is no reason to see it as less than a part of "God's design" than any other human reality. As the number of ova formed in the ovaries is *finite* (and entirely formed as oocytes *in utero* before birth) there is no question but that infertility eventually has to take place, menopause or not. So any suggestion that fertility is a fundamental part of who women are as human persons is obviously false: an average woman is only fertile for about one-third of her life. She possesses all the ova she will ever have *before she is born*, though she cannot make use of them until the onset of puberty. One might well more accurately say that "fertility is a temporary condition caused by the action of certain hormones that affect women for part of their lives."

And that is where one of the many problems with "natural" law arises. So much of it depends on one's point of view of what is "natural." As a simple physical fact, fertility is by nature separated from sexuality, which I can read as part of God's "design" of the human creature. God "intends" grandmotherhood and grandfatherhood (a time for caring for the offspring of others) as much as motherhood and fatherhood—they are equally natural.

And the same goes for bachelor uncles and maiden aunts—who assist in the survival of genes they share with their siblings even though they do not have progeny themselves.

The Roman Catholic teaching on the licit use of the "infertile period" could not develop until the "infertile period" was discovered in 1783, and involved a reversal of the tradition that forbade intercourse during menses and for some days thereafter.

marriage liturgy in the Book of Common Prayer of the Episcopal Church. This exhortation states the issue clearly, both in demoting procreation to third place among the causes for which marriage was instituted (as articulated in the preface to the Church of England's 1662 Prayer Book), and in adding the important proviso "when it is God's will"—recognizing that not all marriages can or will result in procreation.

I note once again the disappearance of the 1662 Prayer Book's second cause—marriage as a remedy for sin and avoidance of fornication, so that those who "have not the gift of continency might marry, and keep themselves undefiled." As this is one of the biblical ends of marriage (1 Corinthians 7:8–9), its omission from our present rite is surprising. I will address this in a subsequent chapter.

Here I will note that reference to *all* of these causes or ends or goods of marriage was *entirely omitted* from the marriage liturgy of American versions of the Book of Common Prayer from 1789 up through 1928—and only made its reappearance in the 1979 edition and its immediate trial antecedents. (The 1928 edition did have an *optional* prayer for the "gift and heritage of children" and their upbringing, but apart from this there is *no reference to procreation* in the 1928 marriage rite.) Thus the American prayer-book tradition entirely omitted or downplayed any reference to procreation until the current version, where it makes a provisional appearance. (The present form of the Roman Catholic nuptial mass also places the references to progeny in parentheses.)

This is, of course, natural. For the church, unlike the Jewish tradition described above, never made procreation a *necessary* end or good of marriage, even when it gave it pride of place in its teaching or when exhorting the bride and groom. More importantly, the church has never allowed infertility to stand as an impediment to marriage, or serve as a cause for divorce (unless concealed prior to marriage). Moreover, the church does not hold marriage to end with menopause, or after hysterectomy or prostatectomy, or any other circumstance rendering one or both of the couple permanently infertile. Thus, while the church has seen "the gift and heritage of children" to be a *blessing*, it has never regarded it as *essential* to the institution of marriage. It is something to be hoped for, but has *never been required*.

There is, moreover, this promise in Scripture:

Do not let the eunuch say, "I am just a dry tree." For thus says the LORD: To the eunuchs who keep my sabbaths, who choose the things that please me and hold fast my covenant, I will give, in my house and within my walls, a monument and a name better than sons and daughters; I will give them an everlasting name that shall not be cut off (Isaiah 56:3b–5).

Perhaps the reason the hopeful Ethiopian eunuch was reading Isaiah on the road home from Jerusalem was just this promise (Acts 8:32ff). Philip became convinced there was no reason not to baptize him, although according to the Law eunuchs were forbidden to become part of the congregation of the faithful (Deuteronomy 23:1). Shall the church in our own time act in strict accordance with the Law, or in the Spirit, with Isaiah and Philip? There is so much more to "bearing fruit" than having children, as important as that is. In the same way there is much more to children, and their lives, than simply bearing them.

For the sake of the children

As the preface to the marriage rite in the BCP (1662, and again now in 1979) reminds us, sex and marriage often, and "when God wills," do involve the mechanics of conception and birth. But as these texts also show, procreation is the *beginning* of a process which includes the care and nurture of children in the knowledge and love of the Lord. In one way this reflects the same direction taken by the whole of Scripture, from Eden to the New Jerusalem, from the organic, biological beginning to the incarnate, spiritual presence of God in and with the new, transfigured City of God.

As a practical matter, same-sex couples can fulfill the intention of procreation through *in vitro* fertilization, or (like infertile mixed-sex couples) by foster-parent-hood or adoption. Surely the imagery of adoption in the New Testament is at least as powerful and as grace-filled as the imagery of birth—and we have the prime example of foster-fatherhood in Joseph himself, the patron of the Universal Church, the Body of Christ. Surely this fulfillment of the upbringing of otherwise abandoned children in the way of the Lord is a noble task commendable to all people.

Jacob Milgrom has reflected on this, in light of the rather different Jewish traditions and law, in his magisterial work on Leviticus, and suggests that adoption is one means for same-sex couples to fulfill this part of the good of procreation. Milgrom notes that the Levitical prohibition on male homosexuality does not apply to non-Jews, but in writing to Jewish gay and lesbian people, he advises that in order to fulfil the "first commandment" they ought to

> adopt children. Although adoption was practiced in the ancient world (as attested in Babylonian law), there is no biblical procedure or institution of adoption. As a result the institution of adoption is absent from rabbinic jurisprudence. Yet there are isolated cases of a kind of pseudo-adoption in the Bible . . . Adoption is certainly a possibility today. Lesbian couples have an additional advantage. Not only do they not violate Biblical law, but through artificial insemination each can become the natural mother of her children. (Leviticus 17–22, 1787)

Surely, from a Christian perspective, true religion does not lie in procreation, but in part in caring for orphans. (James 1:27) So in the broader sense in which procreation itself is the *beginning* of a process, same-sex couples (and infertile mixed sex couples) are capable of fulfilling the procreative end, or benefitting from this good of sexuality, even though their own sexual relationship does not produce the children they adopt, nurture, care for, and bring up in the knowledge of the Lord.

The state of things

It is sometimes asserted that the primary rationale for the *state* regulation of marriage was its interest in children and their inheritance rights. But various cultures have handled inheritance differently, and provision is made in the laws of various states and nations in cases where there are no children, or when there are, for that matter. For example, in Louisiana, children inherit but the surviving widow retains *usufruct*—with the right to continue to occupy the domicile for life, but without freedom to sell it. Then there's the ancient Irish principle of female ultimogeniture—an interesting adaptation to keep people waiting as long as possible to find out who the heir might be. But given this broad range of civil law governing marital relationships beyond mere procreative or inheritance issues —to say nothing of the extensive Jewish legal tradition on polygamy, enshrined in the biblical text—none of this should stand in the way of the state recognizing a same-sex relationship as easily as it does an infertile mixed-sex relationship. A couple who are biologically infertile (due to menopause, hysterectomy, prostatectomy, advanced age, etc.) are by definition *not* potentially procreative, yet the state does not forbid marriage to them on the basis that the law provides for inheritance by children. Those provisions of the law simply do not apply in their case.

There is so much more to the civil institution of marriage than protection for the children who might be born. Thus, as legal persons there should be absolutely no difference between infertile mixed-sex and the same-sex couples who, in the inter-

---

Occasionally someone will assert that even a medically infertile couple are somehow "intrinsically" capable of procreation, or of performing an "intrinsically procreative act," or an act that ethicist John Finnis calls reproductive *in kind*. Or they will assert that procreation, while not the sole purpose of marriage, "must remain as an open possibility in any genuine marriage. That is one reason why same-sex relationships, whatever they are, are not marriages and cannot be solemnized as such." (Macquarrie, 217)

But the capacity to procreate is neither intrinsic nor permanent, nor is it meaningful to talk of an "open possibility" or "reproductive *in kind*" when there is no *actual* possibility of reproduction short of the miraculous. To be infertile is, by definition, to lack the possibility to beget or to conceive.

The fact remains that neither the church nor the state prohibit marriage to perma-

est of stability and decency, should have reasonable expectation of inheritance (or at least usufruct) by a survivor, hospital visitation privileges, pension benefits, and all of the other social goods—and responsibilities—that have nothing to do with progeny. Or if there is a difference between the couples, what is it? And how should the law address it? In short, I see no compelling reason for the state not to permit same-sex marriage; in fact, it would be a positive step towards social stability.

> About this time the "Slippery Slope" argument may be forming in some minds, if not already there. This usually takes the form of, "If you allow same-sex relationships, why not polygamy, incest, or bestiality?" The answer is really quite simple. What we are examining here are same-sex relationships on exactly the same terms and with the same kinds of regulation as mixed-sex relationships: adult consent, no consanguinity, no plural spouses, permanent fidelity, and no animals except as pets.

Conclusions

Only a fertile male and female couple can accomplish procreation. But as I have shown, the capacity to procreate is neither essential to marriage nor inseparable from its other goods. This leaves us with the obvious question: What is it about males and females (*apart* from the capacity to procreate) that should limit marriage to such couples? Asked another way, What is *present* in a sterile mixed-sex couple that is *lacking* in a same-sex couple, *apart* from the difference in sex? I think the only reasonable answer is, Nothing, apart from the difference in sex.

Now, getting to this point after all the foregoing might seem ludicrous, since we know that folks approve of mixed-sex marriage and disapprove of same-sex relationships *precisely because of the sex of the couple*. The reason I have taken

> nently infertile people, even when the infertility is known. After all, fertility is a *capacity* which, though most people develop it at some point in the course of life, by natural biological processes all women and many men lose at a certain point as well. Sexual intercourse by an infertile couple is no more "procreative" or "open to procreation" or "reproductive *in kind*" (in any sense) than playing air guitar constitutes musical performance, or sitting in an automobile that lacks a motor constitutes motoring. It would be illogical to refer to these activities as "intrinsically musical" or "automotive in kind." The difference is that a car without an engine would be considered less than a car; a person miming a guitar much less than a guitarist—but an infertile person is still *very much a person*, and a couple, whether same- or mixed-sex, consists of two people. Fertility is neither essential to the human being, nor to the value of human relationships.

this course, however, is to disprove *the rationalization for this restriction on the basis of the capacity to procreate.*

To define a thing in terms of its end, as many in the tradition have done, and then switch gears and say that even if it does not achieve this end it meets the definition because of the *means* rather than the end—this is a kind of intellectual three-card monte. If the *means to the end* have value—that is, if sexual intercourse is of value even when it does not result in reproduction—then it is *that* value which we are required to examine. If the church (or the state) were willing to forbid marriage to persons past the age of childbearing, or unable to bear children for medical reasons, there might be some consistency in such a position. But failing that, as indeed both church and state rightly fail when they admit to the other values of marriage, judicious silence on the subject of same-sex relationships' inability to produce offspring would be in order.

So I will in subsequent chapters turn to the other goods of marriage (union and representation) to see if these are essential to marriage, or limited to mixed-sex couples. In short, I will address the question of whether there is something *essential* about men and women which does not include their ability, in some cases, to procreate that would distinguish their unions from those of same-sex couples.

Questions for Discussion or Reflection

- *Review the first two chapters of Genesis. What differences do you find between the two accounts of creation? What similarities? What conclusions might you draw from these differences and similarities?*

- *Do you know any couples (same- or mixed-sex) who do not have children? Do their lives and relationship appear to you to model moral behavior?*

- *How do you feel about birth control? Is the choice to make use of it warranted in any situation?*

- *Do you see any significance in the fact that people are capable of procreation only for part of their lives?*

3.
True Union

*I*N THE PREVIOUS CHAPTER I OFFERED EVIDENCE FROM THE REALMS OF NATURE AND reason, from Scripture and the church's tradition, in support of the proposition that procreation is neither essential nor intrinsic to human sexuality or marriage. Not all will be persuaded by the evidence I have presented; however, I know that some will not be persuaded regardless of how authoritative the evidence may be. Some will continue to believe an infertile couple are capable of an "intrinsically procreative act," even though they are incapable of procreation. Others may reassert that the primary purpose of marriage is the production and protection of children, in spite of the considerable evidence to the contrary. However, on the basis of all that is cited thus far, I hold that it is clear that procreation is both naturally and intentionally separable from sexual activity and from marriage. Neither church nor state forbid marriage or criminalize sexual congress between a man

It is clear both from Scripture and reason that marriage is not good in and of itself. That is, there are good marriages and bad marriages. The question is, Why? If the good things that make a marriage good can be shown to exist in another context, why can that other context not be seen as a locus of that goodness? In short, is it marriage that makes the sexual relationship good, or is it the loving, committed, faithful and monogamous exercise of sexuality that constitutes the good of the marriage? Looking at the range of forms of marriage that have been allowed and encouraged in various times and places in human history, the *meaning* of marriage is far from concrete. Biblical law, for example, allowed marriage by rape (Deut 22:28–29) and conquest (Deut 21:10–14). Yet we would not suggest this to be "good" in a moral sense.

and a woman even when one or both are intrinsically incapable of procreation. So the fundamental and intrinsic inability to achieve procreation cannot *in itself* be offered as a rationale against same-sex unions.

So I turn to a second major good of marriage: union. I will first examine the nature of union in its broadest sense (as summarized in the exhortation at the beginning of the Episcopal Church's marriage liturgy), including its moral status; and in succeeding chapters examine whether or not this good can be achieved by a same-sex couple.

The Locus of Union

> The union of husband and wife in heart, body, and mind is intended by God for their mutual joy; for the help and comfort given one another in prosperity and adversity . . . (BCP, 423)

The church gives *union* of spouses first place in its revised liturgy, the first American BCP liturgy to mention the goods of marriage at all. It clarifies that the union, while fleshly or bodily (figuratively, since the couple do not *actually* become a single physical entity), is also deeply *personal*, involving heart and mind as well as body—it is the union of *persons*, not merely of body parts. This union is ordered primarily to mutual joy (which includes but is not limited to the pleasure of sexual intercourse), and perhaps more importantly to the human values of help and comfort. Thus the good of union broadens out from physical union to embrace and enfold the emotional, mental, and social aspects of human life.

Common domicile is a major factor in the constitution of marital relationships. Some cultures make quite a point of it (the Spanish word for "married" is *casado*; the custom of carrying the wife over the threshold is a relic of a similar old Roman tradition) . We all know that to which "cohabitation" is a polite reference. The creation of a household is a major aspect of conjugal life, whether a couple have children or not. At the other end of relationships, the disposition of the domicile after a divorce is a major concern. One version of this (and a matter not far from the heart of any Manhattanite) is documented in John Guare's radio play, *In Fireworks Lie Secret Codes*. A couple (whose gender is not specified in the radio script, though it was two men in the NPR broadcast) break up while watching the Macy's fireworks display, and the first question is, "But what about the apartment?"

One Flesh: Moses and Jesus

It is important first to address the significance of fleshly union. "One flesh" is a biblical concept, but it occurs only in the context of the second creation account—all other references to this phenomenon are citations of this passage, whether in the Gospels or the Pauline Epistles. These citations will be helpful in unpacking the meaning this phrase should have for us, in that it allows us to look at how others—including Jesus himself—understood it, and how they applied it to various circumstances.

As I noted in the previous chapter, Jesus' *midrash* (appearing in Matthew and Mark) omits any reference to procreation. He jumps from the "male and female" of Genesis 1 to the "one flesh" of Genesis 2, and then adds his own conclusion: what God has joined together is not to be divided. This form of *midrash* is a rabbinic technique, finding an answer to a particular question or case ("Is it permissible for a man to divorce his wife?") by taking two scriptural passages and deriving an original conclusion from them. In this case the conclusion is all the more striking in that it explicitly overturns a Mosaic law, which allowed for divorce, as a temporary injunction to deal with hard-heartedness. If one is to draw any conclusion from Jesus' understanding of "one flesh," it lies in his emphasis on the *union* of the couple, quite apart from procreation (or the absence of procreation due to infertility, which was grounds for divorce under rabbinic law—a rather hardhearted one at that).

Jesus also mentions the change in domicile, which further locates the union of the couple in a new household, a new social structure. The union is thus not solely (and figuratively) physical, but personal and social, with an implication of the mutual help and comfort that appears in our liturgy, and with the emphasis, above all, on its permanence. The emphasis is on *joining* or *uniting* that which is not to be separated or divided.

The two Pauline references are more problematical. In these related passages (Ephesians 5:25–33 and 1 Corinthians 6:13–18), Paul is caught up in rhetorical flourishes that operate on several levels at once, so it will be helpful to tease apart the various strands in his thinking.

The "Mystery" of Ephesians

The Ephesians reference is often taken out of its context, which is disastrous for grasping the complex argument Paul is setting up. The context of the whole epistle, the primary theme, is the "mystery of Christ" which Paul describes as the *union* "of all things in him." (Ephesians 1:9–10) He develops this imagery of the mysterious union of all things in a succession of images beginning with Christ as head of his body, the church (1:22–23). In chapter 2 he describes the way in which divisions based on national or ethnic identity, of culture and clan, are abolished by the flesh and blood of Christ, in a vivid image from the Second Temple—its dividing wall separating Gentile from Jew removed—and the creation of a single new humanity out of two, in "one body through the cross" (2:14–16). Perhaps inspired by his own brief reference to the Temple, Paul veers slightly and expands on that image, in which Christ shifts from being head of the body to become the cornerstone of a Temple whose building stones are the members of the church, indwelt by the Spirit (2:20–22).

Paul returns to revealing "the mystery" in chapter 3, when he again defines it as Gentile inclusion as "fellow heirs, members of the same body . . . through the Gospel" (3:6). Chapter 4 turns to the natural consequences of being "one body"—and urges the members of that body to live in peace and harmony, through the variety of spiritual gifts with which the body is provided in each organic member, to build itself up towards the goal of more perfect union in Christ (4:11–16). He contrasts this union with the futile conflicts of the Gentiles, and offers counsel for a harmonious life (4:17–5:20).

As part of this counsel, reflecting on the orderly hierarchies of human society, he brings up three contexts of human relationship: marital (5:21–33), familial (6:1–4), and social (i.e., slavery, 6:5–9). It is in the first of these three parallel human situations that Paul introduces the language of Genesis 2. He does so by

Prongs and holes

Rabbinic tradition relied upon penetration as part of its definition of sexual congress. It also placed stress upon the male organ—to such an extent that the female genitalia were regarded as of no particular significance. This form of anatomical sexism comes to the fore in the discussion of hermaphrodites—which the Rabbis recognized as a real challenge to the notion "male and female he created them." True to the notion of penile domination, however, for practical purposes the hermaphrodite with a penis was considered male—so that "he" could marry a woman, but not be married to a man (mBikkurim 4.2). Penetration and being penetrated are the definers of sexuality in this understanding.

Scarcely more advanced in thinking on the subject, ethicist John Finnis asserts that "the union of the reproductive organs of husband and wife really unites them biologically"—which he explains as having both the qualities of procreation and friendship. But he then goes on to say that even sex between an infertile couple is still "of the reproductive kind," while denying same-sex couples can similarly "unite." This seems not to follow on two counts.

First, a married couple are not "united biologically" *when they have sex*. Speaking anatomically, the two bodies, however intimately embracing, do not actually enter into or connect *with* each other, or even one *into* the other, anatomically. It is in part a matter of topology. I raise this in response to the critique of same-sex relationships by Michael Pakaluk, who in his dismissal of same-sex relations relies on the topological fact that the digestive tract is not really "inside" a person—a topologist would say a human being is like a torus or doughnut. Human beings are, in this respect, a hollow tube, and to "enter" that tube, Pakaluk points out, is not really to be "inside."

However, neither is the uterus "inside" a woman, or the penis "outside" the man. A topologist would point out that as far as this goes we are dealing with bumps and dimples, an order of topological magnitude inferior by one to the torus or doughnut.

analogizing the mystery of human unity in and with Christ, with the union of a man and a woman in marriage. The analogy is, as it seems Paul recognizes, not quite parallel—which may explain his eventual explanation, "But I speak of Christ and of the church"—that is, he returns to his main theme of the mystery of union in Christ, though he continues to advise that men and women should be mutually loving. (5:32–33)

This passage is badly translated in the Revised Standard Version/New Revised Standard Version tradition. Clearly Paul intends to *correct* any misapprehension that his reference to the "great mystery" (which he has expounded a number of times earlier in the letter as ecclesiastical unity under the headship of Christ) might be misunderstood as a reference to marriage. Indeed, many have so misunderstood Paul's intent, in spite of his effort to clarify, and the context of the epistle

Further, contrary to Pakaluk's assertion, a man and a woman do not "reciprocally contain" each other, and they achieve no actual anatomical "union." I agree with him, when he enlarges the matter to the metaphor that "when two persons are united in love, each is within the heart of the other." (Pakaluk, 53f) But this is a romantic, not a physiological, truth. It can also be a theological truth: as Jesus noted concerning the digestive tract, what goes into the mouth passes through and out into the sewer. It is what comes out of the heart that matters (Matthew 15:17). But experience shows that this emotional unity of heart happens with same-sex couples, too. A mutual and intimate embrace is possible for same-sex couples as much as for mixed-sex couples.

Second, even though at some point, in some cases, at some time *after* having sex, a sperm might unite with an ovum—even then the fertilized ovum isn't really "inside" the woman's body, from a topological perspective. In fact, it would be very dangerous if the embryo did start to grow "inside" the woman's body rather than in the uterus: this is called ectopic pregnancy. Actually the embryo develops in the womb, where the placenta serves as a means to keep the fetal blood isolated from the maternal, even though the vessels of the placenta intertwine with those of the mother, in such a way as to allow the mother's blood to oxygenate the growing fetus' blood and provide it with nutrients. Only in abnormal situations is there any actual transfer of blood across the placental barrier. Even at this most intimate of all human interactions, the fetus and the mother are separate biological entities, though closely intertwined, and one entirely dependent upon the other.

There is no biological "union" between a mixed-sex couple apart from this uniting at the level of the nuclei of the two gametes—which can take place *in vitro* as well as *in utero*. Merely asserting that only mixed-sex couples are capable of "union" in the spiritual or emotional or human sense is just that: mere assertion, and contrary to the real-life experience of countless same-sex couples.

We should no more attribute any kind of special status to marriage itself on the basis of Ephesians 5:25–33, than we would to the institution of slavery, to which Paul also analogizes the relationship between Christ and the members of the church (6:5–9).

as a whole. Most other modern translations (JB, NEB, REB, NAB, NIV) correctly refer the "mystery" to "Christ and the church."

In any case, the main thing we can carry away from this passage for our present purpose is that Paul uses the language of "one flesh" primarily to describe union, a union as close as that between a man and his own body: "He who loves his wife loves himself" (5:28). He applies this personal union to the ecclesiastical unity of the people of God in Christ.

The ambivalent nature of "one flesh"

When we turn to Paul's other reference to this text we are on similar ground, at least as far as his concern with unity in the church as the body of Christ. But in 1 Corinthians, Paul does not see "one flesh" as an ideal, but as something to be avoided, at least when expanded in a certain direction: "Do you not know that whoever is united to a prostitute becomes one body with her? For it is said, 'The two shall be one flesh.'" (6:16) His concern is with "fornication" *(porneia)* — which, whatever the alleged breadth of meaning for this word elsewhere, here clearly refers to prostitution.

Paul understands "one flesh" to be a result of sexual congress, not of marriage. It is in this case precisely "fleshly" (a relationship with a prostitute lacking all that true human union should entail, a transaction instead of a relationship, treating the other as an "it" rather than a "thou") and in this context has no place in the life of the church. Here Paul is consistent with his usual use of "flesh" in a negative sense, as something opposed to the Spirit. (There is also perhaps an echo of the law that a priest was forbidden marriage to a prostitute, in Leviticus 21:7,14. I will say more on the meaning of *porneia* in a later chapter.)

The rabbinic literature, while deploring male same-sexuality, did recognize that it is common humanity which makes the union of persons in one flesh possible. While ruling out one man cleaving to another in marriage, Rabbi Akiba noted that becoming "one flesh" required common humanity, which excludes beasts and cattle, "that cannot become one flesh with man." (bSanhedrin 58a) As Saint Paul would observe, "Not all flesh is alike, but there is one flesh for human beings, another for animals, another for birds, and another for fish" (1 Corinthians 15:39). Only like can join with like in the creation of "one flesh."

This has application in helping to explain a possible meaning for the "strange flesh" of Jude 7. This phrase (*sarx heteras* = "different or foreign flesh") has unfortu-

The lesson we can take from these two uses—one negative and one positive—is that for Paul union of flesh is morally neutral. It is good between a married couple, but not between a prostitute and her client. It is, thus, the *context of the relationship* (the fullness of marital unity of body, mind and heart, in mutual joy and companionship) that determines the moral status of the act which renders the "one flesh" morally good. To echo another Pauline sentiment: focusing on the flesh, apart from the Spirit, leads to death, not life (Romans 8:6, Galatians 6:8) yet even so God can give life to our mortal bodies through the Spirit of Christ. (Romans 8:11).

The Nature of Union

As we have seen, the fleshly union was understood to be connected with sexual congress, but much more is needed if this union is to be seen as a moral good: which is precisely where the other aspects of heart and mind enter in. The whole person—or rather, two whole persons—are united in a variety of ways.

In the text in its original setting in Genesis these other elements are present. As noted in the previous chapter, the creation account in Genesis 1 references procreation; the account in Genesis 2 makes no mention of it, and it doesn't appear until Chapter 4, after the Fall. Rather, the emphasis in Chapter 2 is upon the non-sexual union of the man and the woman prior to their having intercourse, though that is clearly meant to happen eventually. This union finds its beginning in the flesh and bones themselves, though it doesn't end there.

This bodily reality is significant: the fact that the woman is not made *from the same substance as the man* (that is, from the soil, as were the animals whom the man rejected as unsuitable). Rather the woman is made *from the man's own substance*; she is one "like himself" (Tobit 8:6). This imagery was picked up by the Patristic church in its understanding of the Incarnation, seen as a reversal of this

nately been mistranslated in recent times as "unnatural lust." What was "unnatural" in the behavior of Sodom in Jude's view? In keeping with the mental universe in which Jude is writing—the apocryphal books of Enoch and Jubilees, together with Genesis 6:1–4—he appears to be saying that it is insult and assault upon *angels* (creatures of a different order and of being above humans, who are "a little lower" in order). So it is not that the angels are *male* but that they are *angels*—creatures with a different flesh—that is at issue.

The point—as echoed in Tertullian's critique of marriage with a non-Christian, in which he applied Jude 7—is that people are to join *with their own kind*. It is not *difference* that is important, but *similarity*.

Edenic derivation of woman: just as Eve was taken from Adam, and is of one sub-stance with him, Christ (the new Adam) was taken from the substance of the Vir-gin Mary, and is consubstantial with all of humanity solely through her. The origin of this line of thought is in 1 Corinthians 11:12, later expanded upon by the early church, and given its final form by the Council of Chalcedon (BCP, 864). We will return to these themes in a later chapter.

> In many mixed-sex marriages (and in all of them after a certain time of life) the sexual relation-ship can *only* be unitive (in its broadest sense) or only procreative in the sense of upbringing and nurture, whether of children born while the couple were fertile, or through adoption. *All marriages* of a certain duration, then, come to emphasize the unitive over the procreative. This is not just "normative"—it is virtually "universal." So the questions are: How is an infertile mixed-sex couple different from a same-sex couple, apart from the sex of the parties involved? What is the state's (or the church's) interest in allowing one union but forbidding the other?

The shift of focus away from merely bodily union towards the other aspects of human companionship is evident in the Genesis passage itself: this first human society is created because it is "not good for the man to be alone." The text points us towards other factors than the physical: leaving the paternal home to be bound to the spouse indicates a social context in the creation of a household. There are also, in Adam's effusive welcome, testimony to the *emotional* joy to be found in his having finally found *one like himself* with whom to join. This likeness—the primary emphasis of the passage—is significant in addressing one of the argu-ments often raised against the recognition of same-sex unions, that a person of the same sex cannot serve as an appropriate "other." I will take this assertion up in the next chapter.

$\mathcal{Q}$uestions for Discussion or Reflection

- Consider other kinds of "union" with which you are familiar: the union of the states in a nation, the union of workers for their common benefit. What might these "unions" have in common with the union of persons in a mar-riage? How do they differ?

- Working backwards: what are the primary sources of disunion you can iden-tify, and how do they place stress upon unity in marriage or other contexts?

- How does this relate to the question of the unity in the church? In the Trinity? In the union of the divine and human natures in one person, Jesus Christ?

4.
Double Vision

*I*N THE PREVIOUS CHAPTER I EXAMINED THE BIBLICAL CONCEPT OF "ONE FLESH" using the Bible itself in an effort to unpack this ambivalent phrase. Fleshly union is not good in and of itself, but only within the context of a loving relationship, including union of heart and mind as well as flesh.

As few (I hope) doubt that persons of the same sex can enjoy unity of heart and mind in companionship with each other, the question remains as to whether a same-sex couple can experience bodily union. Some of those opposed to any recognition of same-sex relationships argue against this possibility, largely on the grounds of what they refer to as the "complementarity of the sexes." It is variously held that the divine image in humanity is somehow incomplete without both male and female; or that an individual is somehow less than complete if not joined to a person of the "opposite" sex. I now begin to examine these assertions.

Complementarity defined

First, I note that the definition of *complementary* and *complementarity* often shifts in the course of these discussions. The Church of England study document, *Some Issues in Human Sexuality*, for example, drifts in its understanding and application of these words. It is sometimes spoken of as "differences between men and women . . . intended for the mutual good of each" (1.2.9), and elsewhere as "equality in difference" (5.3.38).

In normal English usage, however, "complementary"—when applied to two things—means that one makes up what is lacking in the other, or that both together make up what is lacking in each. In mathematics we say that a 60-degree angle is complementary to a 30-degree angle, because together they make up a right angle.

There are two faults with applying this concept to human beings and their relationships. First, it requires that the individual human being be seen as *lacking* something—as essentially incomplete or *defective*. Secondly, it implies an *essential* difference between men and women, whereby a man and a woman uniquely and jointly compensate for what is lacking in each other, or—as I think is more commonly held—one of them (the man) makes up for what the other (the woman) lacks.

You look simply divine

> Both in the Old Testament and in the New Testament the understanding of sex is rooted in the conviction that the divine image in humanity is incomplete without both man and woman.—The House of Bishops Theology Committee Report, 1977 (Journal of General Convention, 1979)

> So when the Priestly writer said, "In the image of God He created them; male and female He created them," I believe the writer was saying that the human opposites male and female complement each other into a wholeness which reflects God's nature and purpose . . . This principal is basic in Scripture: It takes maleness and femaleness, masculinity and femininity, coming together to reflect the image of God.—Bishop Andrew Fairfield, Minority Report in the Righter Decision, 1996

In these two passages, separated by nearly twenty years, Episcopal bishops made the assertion that God's image in humanity is incomplete without male and female. This belief echoes a convoluted passage in Karl Barth's *Church Dogmatics* III:

> The grace of God has this particular form; that it is in the differentiation and relationship of man and woman, the relation of sex, that there is this repetition . . . This creaturely differentiation and relationship is shown to be distinct and free, to reflect God's image and to prove his special grace, by the fact that in this particular duality (i.e., to the exclusion of all others) he is alone among the beasts and in the rest of creation, and that it is in this form of life and this alone, as man and woman, that he will continually stand before God, and in the form of his fellow that he will continually stand before himself. Men are simply male and female. Whatever else they may be, it is only in this differentiation and relationship. This is the particular dignity ascribed to the sex relationship. It is only creaturely, and common to man and beast. But as the only real principle of differentiation and relationship, as the original form not only of man's confrontation of God but also of all intercourse between man and man, it is the true *humanum* and therefore the true creaturely image of God. (III.1.41.2, 186)

That is certainly a difficult passage to grasp—no one ever said Karl Barth was easy to understand. But he appears to be saying, and may be a source for, what the bishops referred to above: that there is something about a man and woman together that reveals or completes the "image of God in humanity." A similar sentiment was expressed by Pope John Paul II, in his series of meditations on the *Theology of the Body*:

> Few go so far as to follow Paul's opinion on this. His assertion, "a man . . . is the image and reflection of God; but woman is the reflection of man," (1 Corinthians 11:7) must be one of the most widely ignored passages in the Pauline corpus.

Man became the "image and likeness" of God *not only* through his own humanity, but also through the communion of persons which man and woman form right from the beginning.—John Paul II, General Audience, November 14, 1979; "By the Communion of Persons Man Becomes the Image of God"

This papal reflection, in the words I've italicized, reveals part of the difficulty with Barth's and the Episcopal bishops' statements: for surely the image and likeness of God is present in each individual human—male or female. To assert, however, even as the pope does, that there is something *additionally* revelatory of the divine image—as if it were quantitative—in the union of male and female will not stand up to close examination.

Genesis proclaims that God made humanity (singular) "in his image and after his likeness," and that God made *them* (plural) male and female. The orthodox teaching derived from this text, in Judaism as well as Christianity, is that each human being bears the image of God *in spite of*, not *because of*, individual differences of sex. Applying an Anglican rule of biblical interpretation (understanding one passage of Scripture as illuminated by another), we can look to the text in Genesis 9:6 to offer the clarification: "Whoever sheds the blood of *a human*, by a human shall that person's blood be shed; for in his own image God made humankind." Note the singular: one need not murder both a man and a woman in order to defame the image of God in humanity! Each person is precious in the sight of God, and each reflects the divine image. It is not clear that two together add to that image—and I have already addressed the error in the suggestion that the ability to procreate reveals the image of God. Procreation is not creation, but part of it.

Of course, when it comes to *"the* creation" (as opposed to God's act *of* creation) many images are used in Scripture to portray God and God's activities—but never simply as a man and a woman together: even in the New Testament the married couple is not analogized to God, but to the relationship of Christ and the Church, as in the Hebrew Scriptures to God and Israel. The idea of God being a joining of "opposites" of male and female, common as it might be in Taoism or Gnosticism, is absent from the canonical Scripture. Moreover, Scripture reflects the image of God in all sorts of things that are *neither* male nor female: rocks, storms, fortresses, winds, fires, volcanoes; and even where the image suggests sex it isn't necessarily the sex that is emphasized. It is *never* (apart from the misread Genesis 1:27) asserted that male and female *together* are the image of God.

The attempt thus to hypostatize the largely cultural, behavioral or attitudinal differences between the sexes—when united—is unwarranted even when applied to people; to apply them to God in anything other than a poetic way is misguided if not blasphemous. And to read poetry and take it as prose is just plain silly. As I believe Luther once said, when we say we shelter under God's wings, we don't mean we believe that God is a bird.

Again, we can look to the text for a better understanding. Genesis 1 shows us that as there is nothing particularly or uniquely "human" in sex, neither is there anything particularly divine. In Genesis—and in reality, for what it's worth—creatures were created male and female before humanity was. If God had wished sex to be particularly reflective or characteristic of the divine nature, it would have been better to reserve it for the only creature that God declared was made in God's image.

Which is why the church did in fact come to understand the divine image as having to do with some human attribute. As Aquinas would put it (echoing Augustine's *De Trinitate* XII):

> The image of God, in its principal signification, namely the intellectual nature, is found both in man and in woman. Hence after the words, "To the image of God He created him," it is added, "Male and female He created them" (Genesis 1:27). Moreover it is said "them" in the plural, as Augustine (*Gen ad lit.* iii, 22) remarks, lest it should be thought that both sexes were united in one individual. (I.Q93.4 repl obj 1) . . . Therefore we must understand that when Scripture had said, "to the image of God he created him," it added, "male and female He created them," not to imply that the image of God came through the distinction of sex, but that the image of God belongs to both sexes, since it is in the mind, wherein there is no sexual distinction (I.Q93.6. repl obj 2).

Each individual human being—endowed (as the Episcopal Church's Catechism states) with the capacity to make choices, to love, to create, to reason, and to live in harmony with creation and with God—reflects the divine image, and it has nothing to do with his or her sex. Logically, one cannot simultaneously affirm that each individual is made in the image of God (which is what the church affirms) and then say that the image is somehow lacking without at least one man and one woman—as Barth and the Episcopal Bishops said.

More seriously, this notion also contradicts the church's teaching on *the* image of God: Jesus (Colossians 1:15). He was a celibate male and the express image of God, and though he had social intercourse with women, there is no indication of any sexual relations. There is no reason to believe that a man and woman together show forth God's image any more than each does alone; and we should learn to see that image in any single one of the least of Jesus' brothers and sisters.

For As in Adam

It is sometimes asserted that one is not a complete human being unless coupled to a person of the other sex. But human beings are not complementary in this sense; and to assert so is a defective anthropology and a misreading of Genesis. It also flies in the face of the doctrine of the Incarnation.

"It is not good for the man to be alone" has led to significant pressure, even in our culture, against singleness and towards marriage. Such pressure may not have the force of law, but many societies exert significant social pressure towards marriage — ironically while usually denying the same privilege to same-sex couples. In spite of the church's historic (though somewhat recently abandoned) claim that celibacy represents a "better and more blessed" state of life (*Catechism of the Council of Trent*, Session XXIV, Canon X), it remains the exception rather than the rule. The cultural norm of marriage has won out in most of the world. Some years ago the Anglican Franciscans had to shut down an effort at starting a community in Africa because the social pressure against celibacy in that cultural setting was so high; they were told that a man who is not married "is not a real man," and few were willing to take up the vocation of celibate life in community.

There is, of course, a distinction between celibacy and loneliness. A celibate need not be lonely, and can maintain social intercourse even while forgoing sexual intercourse. In some cases celibacy can be an advantage, to allow work with others without sexual pressure entering into the equation. At the same time, it must be recognized that celibacy is a charism, a supernatural gift (no less than *love*) and that very few people are authentically called to that state of life. Its arbitrary enforcement can lead not only to psychological, but also to social damage.

Karl Barth was aware of this difficulty, but ironically — and somewhat paradoxically, given his respect for Scripture, although perhaps understandably from his Reformed perspective — argued strongly against celibacy-in-community, and in favor of the notion that human identity as man or woman

> can take shape only in their fellowship with each other, and their humanity can consist concretely only in the fact that they live in fellow-humanity, male with female, and female with male. Every right of man and woman stands or falls with the observance and maintenance of this rule, and every wrong consists in its con-

Adam and Eve were of different sexes, but (necessarily) of the same ethnicity ("flesh of his flesh"). Should this (continue to) be read (in keeping with other scriptural injunctions against marriage outside the people of God—both Israel and the church) as opposition to miscegenation? The answer is a resounding no. We simply do not apply the text in that way.

travention. . . . As against this, everything which points in the direction of male or female seclusion, or of religious or secular orders or communities, or of male or female segregation—if it is undertaken in principle and not consciously and temporarily as an emergency measure—is obviously disobedience. . . . That such an attitude is all wrong is shown symptomatically in the fact that every artificially induced and maintained isolation of the sexes tends as such—usually very quickly and certainly morosely and blindly—to become philistinish in the case of men and precious in that of women, and in both cases more or less inhuman. . . . (*C.D.* III.4.54.1, 165f).

Here Barth sweeps aside centuries of tradition, and dismisses even the possibility for celibate life in community as anything other than freakish and dismal. Sorry, Benedict, Francis (of Assisi and de Sales), Teresa, Clare, Dominic, Ignatius Loyola, and countless others—and Jesus, and Paul!

The danger here is that from a theological perspective, pressure against solitude or loneliness, and the recognition of the importance of society, creeps over to a denial of the dignity of each individual, who has the right to choose a celibate life in community, and indeed may be called to it. Philosophy ratifies the concept of the dignity of the human person in acknowledging that an *individual* human being is a *complete* human being. Individual human beings may suffer from loneliness, and human society provides a number of compensations for that human need. But loneliness is an emotional state, not a defect of personhood or humanity, or the lack of an essential attribute of the human person. Solitude, and the loneliness to which it gives rise, are situational and circumstantial, not essential.

This does not mean that isolation is not a real problem for human beings. The second creation account in Genesis 2 assures us that Adam's solitude was the only thing "not good" in creation. The intent of Genesis 2 is to tell us why it is that "a man leaves his father and mother and is joined to his wife"—a recognition that this is the primary way in which human beings overcome the pang of solitude. But if marriage were the *only* way to counter solitude, then celibacy-in-community would have to be ruled out, as Barth does, as an approved state of life—and few are willing to make such a departure from the tradition, and from the implicit teaching of Jesus and Paul that celibacy is a gift, a charism, and can serve the church.

In its analysis of Genesis 2, however, the Church of England's *Some Issues in Human Sexuality* falls into this same diminishment of humanity in its effort to unpack complementarity: that "from now on neither is complete without the other. The man needs the woman for his wholeness, and the woman needs the man for hers" (3.4.53). Echoes of Barth, once again.

This way of seeing things was not, of course, original with Barth, but was a predominant view in rabbinic Judaism. As Rabbi Hertz bluntly puts it, "celibacy is contrary to nature." Jewish tradition holds that "he who has no wife abides without good, help, joy, blessing, or atonement" (Hertz 9, 931). Celibacy, then, from this perspective is believed to be gravely defective, not only because it fails to implement the commandment to be fruitful and multiply, but because an unmarried man is "incomplete." It is thus fair to acknowledge that this passage presents us with the only text that might be conceived to speak of "complementarity" of the sexes. Rabbinic tradition holds that Adam's incompleteness is only healed by marriage, based on Eve being created by a partial removal from Adam.

> The idea that Adam and Eve are halves of a complete whole shares some features with Aristophanes' satirical account of the origin of the sexes and sexual desire—although Aristophanes includes the origin of *homo*sexual desire as well—in Plato's *Symposium*.

There are challenges to that point of view, even within Judaism. The Rabbis used Genesis 2 as the source for the full and complete dignity of the *individual* human being as well, "A single man was created in the world to teach . . . that whoever saves a single life it is as if he saved the entire world" (mSanhedrin 4:5). Moreover, the "completion" of the man by the woman, even in rabbinic Judaism, is not understood along the lines of Aristophanes' dyads, or the Taoist concepts of *yin* and *yang*—it is not about a synthesis of opposites, nor even simply the restoration of something previously divided—for Adam and Eve remain themselves even after they have joined. There is a new creation in their union, without the abrogation of the old creation. It is *supplementary* and not *complementary*. Above all, it cannot be understood as a marker of an essential, as opposed to a situational, defect in the human person.

A return to the original text is helpful: God created Adam as a solitary gardener, and first tried to assuage his loneliness by making animal companions for him. Only after Adam rejected the animals did God take something from him later to restore it in "built up" form as the Woman he could receive as flesh of his flesh and bone of his bone, as someone *like* him (as opposed to the animals, who were *unlike* him, even though made from the same substance). This is not about complementarity, or the union of opposites, but of *similarity* or *identity*. Eve is a human being; as a later church synod (Douzy, 860) would say, *Eva ipse est Adam*: Eve is herself Adam.

Finally, the church later corrected a narrow reading of Genesis 1 as well, where the rabbinic interpretation required procreation, in order to give due honor to celibacy. "The single state"—an "estate" like matrimony—is honorable, though having no more ontological significance than marriage. As Aquinas pointed out

Jesus himself affirms that his
birth, while important, is just
the beginning of the process
of salvation. When the woman
in the crowd shouted out,
"Blessed is the womb that bore
you and the breasts that nursed
you!" he responded, "Blessed
rather are those who hear
the word of God and obey it!"
(Luke 11:27–28)

(contrary to the Rabbis), the commandment to be fruitful and multiply was addressed to the whole species, not to individuals (*Summa Theologica* II.2.Q152.2), and it was thus allowable for *some* individuals to respond to the calling to celibacy.

So also in Christ

Moreover, the church affirmed that the New Adam, Jesus Christ, is also fully, completely, and individually human, and that this full humanity derives entirely from the Virgin Mary. She could not bestow upon him that which she did not possess, so she must have possessed the fullness of humanity as well. So it is clear on this basis that maleness and femaleness are accidental particulars to each human being, and not essential to human nature. That is, one's sex is a personal attribute of each individual, like height or hair color. The doctrine of the Incarnation makes clear that the *humanum* is complete in the individual person, for whom sex is simply one quality of each individual. Human *nature* is something each human possesses entirely. (Otherwise Jesus or Mary could not be "fully" human on their own.) There is no "complementarity" at the level of human nature.

In addition, human society (even apart from sexuality) does not necessitate complementarity. To assert its necessity not only effectively denies the possibility of same-sex partnerships, but of periods of chastity between married couples, the goodness of friendship, and the fellowship of celibate partnership in community evinced in the cenobitic life. There is more than one good in human society.

Thus I am forced to reject the notion that individual human beings are only completed or constituted into human or social reality by sexual relationship with a person of the other sex, and to reject interpretations of Genesis 2 along those lines. A marriage based on this notion of defect—in which one person completes the other—will only lead to disappointment when the other is found wanting, or judged to have failed to fill the existential gap in the individual. This can only lead to a perpetual quest for an unreachable self-satisfaction, an ultimately selfish movement towards completion, making use of the other, rather than as the true union of individuals whose joining is more than the mere sum of parts.

This brings me to the second assertion, that there is some complementarity of male and female which renders such pairs *uniquely* capable of pairing. In the next chapter I will respond to two questions: *Are men and women actually complementary on a physical basis?* (we have already seen that they are not complementary on a human, theological, or moral basis) and *Is complementarity a necessary component of a committed sexual relationship?*

Questions for Discussion
or Reflection

• What is it about human beings that you think most reflects the image of God?

• Make a list of things that come in pairs—how many of them are two of the same, and how many are in fact different from each other?

• In what ways do a couple come to be more than the sum of themselves?

5.
Pairs and Mates —
Two are better than one

*T*wo are better than one, because they have a good reward for their toil. For if they fall, one will lift up the other; but woe to one who is alone and falls and does not have another to help. Again, if two lie together, they keep warm; but how can one keep warm alone? — Ecclesiastes 4:9–11

In this chapter I turn to two questions: *Are men and women actually complementary on a physical basis?* and *Is complementarity a necessary component of a committed sexual relationship?*

Vive la différence

There is no difference between a man and a woman as far as their each being fully human, and each capable of being the image of God. This is not, as some might think, so obvious when one looks to a tradition that had no difficulty following Aristotle in referring to women as "defective males" (*De Gener. Anim.*, II.3). Aquinas applies this to individual women:

> As regards the individual nature, woman is defective and misbegotten, for the active power in the male semen tends to the production of a perfect likeness according to the male sex; while the production of woman comes from defect in the active power, or from some material indisposition, or even from some external influence, such as that of a south wind, which is moist, as the Philosopher observes . . . (*ST* I.Q92.1).

It is true Aquinas allows that in the *collective* women are not defective, but rather "part of nature's intention directed to the work of generation"—which he believes to have been the sole purpose for the generation of woman *qua* woman. As he says earlier in this same article:

> It was necessary for woman to be made, as the Scripture says, as a helper to man; not, indeed, as a helper in other works, as some say, since a man can be more efficiently helped by another man in other works; but as a helper in the work of generation.

At this point some might be moved to raise the question, Why should we pay any attention to a moral theology based almost entirely on the defective science of Aristotle, enshrined in the church's teaching through the reasoned speculations of Aquinas? It is a very good question—since, if people cannot be trusted in earthly things, how are they to be trusted in heavenly things? And if their moral vision is bound and confused by defective worldly knowledge, why should anyone trust their moral theology? (John 3:12)

The reason I bring this up is the remarkable persistence such erroneous notions seem to have. Even with advances in science, and a better understanding of the actual nature of human reproduction (which, contrary to Aristotle and Aquinas, has nothing at all to do with moist south winds) there still persists in many circles a kind of archaic folk sexuality functioning alongside scientific knowledge, and often displacing it when moral questions are brought to the fore. This is not unlike the strange tendency even on the part of contemporary biblical scholars suddenly to treat portions of Genesis as *literal* rather than *figurative*.

To put it bluntly: *Men and women are only complementary in the archaic view of an ancient world innocent of the rudiments of biological science, or at the sophomoric level of "tab and slot."*

The creation account in Genesis 2, in its suggestion of partial complementarity (woman being derived from man and restored to him), is a part of that archaic

---

Mistaken notions concerning the biology of the sexes were still in play in the modern era. For example, even the invention of the microscope did not dissuade some from seeing sperm as the vital principle in generation, and the Royal Society received papers on the amazing miniature horses and humans one could see nested in the spermatozoa of the appropriate species recently made visible by that wonderful invention. (Schmidt, 116–117) As late as the turn of the nineteenth century, Erasmus Darwin was still teaching that women provided nothing more to the process of procreation than a nest for the nourishment of "the embryo," which derived solely from the male and not by union of male and female (*Zoonomia*, 1794).

world view. We should no more feel bound fully to embrace a literal view of Genesis 2 on human biology than we do Genesis 1 on cosmology. To over-literalize either creation account is to fall into the disciples' error in thinking Jesus' warning about the "leaven of the Pharisees" was in reference to bread (Mark 8:16), or Nicodemus thinking that to be born again he would have to re-enter his mother's womb (John 3:4). The inability to understand poetic or figurative language as poetry or figure, or to accept the fact that even in divinely inspired Scripture God's message is conditioned and constrained by human limitations, creates a huge obstacle to an understanding of the moral principles involved—and risks making the faith irrelevant to the world by being bound up with notions the world knows to be false.

We need constantly to be reminded, it seems, that the female of the human species was not actually created from a man's rib, or from a moist south wind, or defective semen. Taking Genesis literally instead of figuratively is an over-reliance on the limited knowledge of the pre-scientific world. It labored (as we still labor) under boundaries to the understanding of reality itself: we have passed beyond what limited their knowledge only to have reached our *own* limitations and unknowns. But while it is foolish to ignore our own limits, it is even more so to push the span of human knowledge *backwards* further, and limit ourselves to what was known in the Bronze Age, or the flowering of Hellenism, or the Middle Ages. We do know more about biology than Solomon, Aristotle and Aquinas, and that knowledge should inform us and lead us into better understanding. Above all, we should not be deriving *theological* principles from the limited *biological* knowledge of the past. We go far enough astray when we draw theological insight from the scientific errors of the *present*—errors of which we become aware only in succeeding generations.

We can, however, look backward with some accumulation in our total knowledge, and make course corrections accordingly. The ancient world did not know much about sexuality beyond the crude mechanics of "the way of a man with a woman"—and even there the Scripture attests to human ignorance (Proverbs 30:18–19). They knew almost nothing of the actual reproductive function.

The prevailing view was that the male seed (*zara'*, *sperma*, *semen*) was planted in the receptive female where it took root and grew. But the seed itself was the source of the person that would be born, the "vital principle" that would then draw upon the mother for nourishment and building material. Some observant naturalists of the ancient world, noting that the menstrual flow ceased once pregnancy became obvious, believed that the embryo was compacted from the menstrual blood, rather like cheese curdled by rennet. This view is reflected in Wisdom of Solomon 7:2.

It was commonly believed that human semen contained miniature human beings. This view is reflected in Hebrews 7:9–10: "One might even say that Levi himself, who receives tithes, paid tithes through Abraham, for he was still in the loins of his ancestor when Melchizedek met him." This is, of course, wrong. Only half of the genes that went to make up Levi were even in Jacob, and half of his in Isaac, and so on backwards to Abraham—only a fraction of whose genes (including the persistent Y) actually ended up in Levi, and no more came from Abraham than from Sarah!

These are just two examples of the profoundly limited archaic view of sexuality. It made sense in those times, but to maintain these views in spite of better knowledge to the contrary is unwise.

So, given that much of the understanding of sexuality from biblical, patristic and scholastic times was based on errors of fact—and hence we must call into question some of the conclusions reached—to what might a better understanding of human sexuality lead us?

Not complementary but mutual

First of all, Aquinas is correct about one thing even if he phrases it infelicitously. Procreation *is* one of the reasons for the existence of the sexes as such. I cannot join Aquinas in proclaiming it to be the *sole* reason for the sexes (or, as he would say, for the existence of "woman *qua* woman"); nor can the general principle be held as binding on particular cases, as I laid out in the earlier chapter on procreation. There I demonstrated that sex and procreation are not *necessarily* bound up with each other—that they are, on the contrary, actually separable both by purpose and by nature. Aquinas, of course, did not know this—he was unaware, for example, of the naturally infertile period during menses—or failed to take what he did know seriously, and apparently did not read any significance into menopause, of which he was surely aware (Genesis 18:11). This ignorance in itself raises serious questions about many of his conclusions, and of subsequent moral theology following his line of thinking on matters sexual.

Maleness is genetically determined by the presence of the Y-chromosome, which contains a number of genes for the production of male-sex-specific hormones, which induce male characteristics both in the womb and after birth. Other genes similarly govern such things as hair or eye color. They may even govern behaviors. That the sex-difference is important for the survival of the species *overall* is of no significance to the *individual*, for whom his or her given sex is simply an "accident" (as the Philosopher would say), a particular characteristic of the individual, no more necessary to life than the ability to manufacture other hormones or proteins that govern individual life.

Whatever the extent of differences between men and women, they come down to a chromosome and its related genes, proteins, and hormones.

However, with our better understanding of human reproduction, we can affirm that even in procreation the process is not complementary, but *mutual*—the man is not "completed" by the woman, nor the woman by the man, but rather *each* contributes an identical number of chromosomes—one from each set of pairs they possess, so that a half-set of chromosomes from each can pair up with their mates in the fertilized ovum. Thus men and women *are different*, but not by any means *complementary*—male and female do not contribute to or complete *each other*, but mutually contribute to the generation of *the new human being*. The only place complementarity enters into the picture at all is *within* each chromosome, in the DNA molecules themselves—but this has to do with truly complementary base pairs, not with male and female, as is true even in species that do not reproduce sexually.

It is pointless to seek to find a moral good in what is, after all, an animal function. Animals are not moral, though we may project upon them all of the failings and virtues of human beings and make symbolic use of them as fearful hare, proud lion, or crafty fox (as did Aesop and countless moralists since). Still the moral function lies in the human *use* of nature, and morality lies within the human sphere, since human beings have the capacity to choose and to act upon their choices.

Still, in spite of this fact, people will fixate on the crude schoolboy image of tabs and slots, as if this represented the true locus of sexuality—or indeed as if these were the only tabs and slots with which the human anatomy is provided.

What, after all, are the "sexual organs"? Surely the genitalia—the only parts of the sexual paraphernalia even remotely "complementary" in that crude sense of tab and slot—are *not* the source of sexuality. One might well say that the *brain* is a sexual organ; and when one looks beyond the gonads, themselves part of a larger complex of organs, one sees that between men and women there is remarkable *congruence* rather than *complementarity*, even when the function of a corresponding organ is no longer essential to or involved in procreation—so

It is also important to note, lest anyone try to "rescue" Aquinas by suggesting that the "lack" of a Y chromosome in the sperm is what leads to a female embryo: the individual sperm each carries only one of the two sex chromosomes in any case. Each sperm only has half of the father's component of chromosomes, including either the X or the Y. Thus, a sperm carrying the X does not "lack" a Y any more than one with a Y "lacks" an X. It is not a matter of defect or lack, but of design.

If anything is missing, it is in the Y chromosome itself, which appears to have evolved from the X by a process of reduction, so that it now has only about 86 genes left—important ones, to be sure.

far as we know. The male breast or the female glans and prostate (clitoris and Skene's glands) have functions as much geared towards the erogenous as the procreative.

There comes a time, as Saint Paul said, to "put aside childish things." We are still not perfect in our understanding of human sexuality, but surely we do know things now that place some of the beliefs of the ancient world and the later church into the same realm as tales of the stork or the cabbage patch. Until we set aside some of the fables of the past, we will not be able effectively to address the concerns of the present.

In his likeness

> Every beast loveth his like, and every man loveth his neighbor. All flesh consorteth according to kind, and a man will cleave to his like. (Ecclesiasticus 13:15–16, KJV)

Even given its limitations, much can be learned from our sacred source material, as long as it is read as sacred text rather than as literal history or science. So I would like to return to Genesis for a moment to address another common assertion of the heterosexualist agenda: that the "difference" between men and women is crucial to the licitness of sexual love.

Genesis 1 (with its emphasis on procreation) partakes of the archaic and anatomical distinction of the sexes. The words for *male* and *female*—*zakar* and *neqebah*—derive, the etymologists speculate, from the concepts "worth mentioning" or "pointed" and "has a hole in it." Genesis 2 moves towards a more unified view of *man* and *woman* as taken from man (*ish* from *ishah*). Even though this represents a folk etymology (and a folk biology) the emphasis in Genesis 2 is not

---

The slow pace by which scientific learning penetrates a culture is in part due to sexism. Sexism in the world of medicine has caused physical harm to many women over the years. It is only in this generation that the (until recently) male-dominated medical profession finally acknowledged that women suffer from heart disease in the same proportion as men. Even more appalling, though Skene's glands (the periurethral glands in women) have been known to correspond to the prostate in men for some time, it was apparently only recognized in the early years of this century that women can suffer from the same sorts of conditions as men (the equivalents of prostatitis, benign prostate hyperplasia, and prostate cancer) and with much the same symptoms—but that these symptoms and underlying disease processes had been largely dismissed. Sexism is harmful, and sometimes lethal.

on the *distinction* of the sexes but on the *likeness* of the man and the woman. It is their similarity, not their difference, that is important. While Genesis 1 emphasizes the likeness of the couple *to God*, Genesis 2 highlights the likeness of the couple *to each other*.

As I have noted in previous chapters, God's "intention" in Genesis 2 seems to be at least as much based on Adam's needs as on God's "plan." God's intent or plan, in Genesis 2, is to address Adam's solitary condition, and God only chooses to create woman after the initial effort with the animals proves to be unsatisfactory. Adam requires *human* companionship—the help of one *like himself*.

> You made Adam, and for him you made his wife Eve as a helper and support. From the two of them the human race has sprung. You said, 'It is not good that the man should be alone; let us make a helper for him *like himself*.' (Tobit 8:6)

In short, the man and the woman form a *pair*; they are *mates*; and it is clear that both of these words apply to two things *like* each other as much as to two things *unlike* each other, and in Genesis 2, the emphasis is on the *likeness*. In this sense, far from being complementary, the man and the woman are like the two blades of a *pair* of scissors—which work together *only* because they are the same as each other.

Most importantly, the relationship they form is mutual, like joining with like—much as one joins right hand with right hand in the sociable interaction between two people, and in the marriage rite itself—the *same* hand, not the *opposite* one—in a pledge of mutual joy, in which the mutuality is as important as the joy. Their mutual union does not imply the literal disappearance of the two persons here any more than it does in the love of neighbor. It is instructive to compare the similarity of two bits of Pauline advice:

> Each of you, however, should *love his wife as himself*, and a wife should respect her husband. (Ephesians 5:33) The commandments, "You shall not commit adultery; You shall not murder; You shall not steal; You shall not covet"; and any other commandment, are summed up in this word, "*Love your neighbor as yourself.*" (Romans 13:9)

The mutual union is the beginning, not the end, of a life-long relationship, in which the other is loved *as* oneself.

So it seems clear that not only is there no true complementarity between the sexes, but that the relationship of the sexes, apart from procreation, is not based solely on the differences that do exist, but at least as much upon the similarities.

Finally, to respond to the accusation that a same-sex couple are not "different" enough from each other, we can observe that, after all, *all* people are different from each other. Thus two men or two women supplement each other in bringing to their relationship something that makes that relationship greater than the mere sum of parts. People will sometimes quote what they think is a smart remark in saying, "God made Adam and Eve, not Adam and Steve." But in fact, God did create Adam, Eve, and Steve too—and each James, Tom, Suzie, and Jan—and *all* the men and women who *each* have come to be through God's grace—each and every one of us; and it is in how we treat each other that we find ourselves realizing God's intent for each of us and all of us.

Becoming entangled in the Genesis accounts, and applying them to questions they were not designed to answer, can obscure our vision of our real live flesh and blood brothers and sisters, each of them made in the image of God.

Further considerations

In the following chapters I will take up the remaining ends or goods of marriage—the reflective (or symbolic) and the preventative ("as a remedy for fornication"). I will also address the question of whether a same-sex couple can experience the same mutual joy in unity as mixed-sex couples.

It will be noticed that I have "backed into" this discussion of same-sexuality from the point of view of marriage, rather than beginning (as is the usual course) with the alleged biblical or social prohibitions. I have nonetheless touched on some of them, and will address those concerns more fully in subsequent chapters; but my initial intent has been to challenge the presuppositions surrounding sexuality itself before engaging with the rather better-traveled paths.

〜 The story of the Frankenstein monster, particularly in the film versions (*Frankenstein* and *Bride of Frankenstein*) by the gay director James Whale, provides a modern parable with a good bit of relevance to the discussion. The creature desired to have a companion *like himself*—not for the purpose of reproduction, but for companionship—a friend. Other aspects of the films served as parallels to the life of a gay male of the early twentieth century: the maker's rejection of the monster as a form of internalized homophobia; the monster's first acceptance only by a blind man as a commentary on the closet; the monster as child-murderer and disturber of the peace of marriage; the monster crucified by the mob; the monster moved by beauty but incapable of being beautiful himself—it is a rich mine of psychosexual and psychosocial angst. Of course, the original novel, by an unconventional and liberated woman author, also serves as a social commentary on an earlier time—and the fate that befalls a New Prometheus who challenges the gods of his day.

$\mathcal{Q}$uestions for Discussion
or Reflection

- *What are the chief differences you see between men and women? To what extent do you think these are based on physical differences? Cultural or social influences? To what extent does biology determine destiny?*

- *Have you ever had the task of explaining sex and reproduction to a child or young person? Did you feel comfortable doing so? Why or why not? What, if any, do you think was the source of your anxiety? Did you use analogies, and if so, what? Or did you use a more clinical approach? How did you frame the subject morally?*

- *Referring back to your list of pairs of things: What are those that are like each other? What about ones that are different? How do they differ? Are they different in form, or orientation—that is, do they have the same or a different shape, or are they mirror images?*

6.
Clash of Symbols

*I*N THIS CHAPTER I TURN TO AN ADDITIONAL FEATURE OF MARRIAGE: ITS USE AS A metaphor or symbol for the relationship between Christ and the church (or between God and Israel). This includes a reflection on the nature of symbolism, the extent to which reliance on such symbols can be helpful as well as misleading, what it is about marriage that serves as a symbol of these relationships, and whether that quality can be applied to same-sex relationships as well.

The ambivalent nature of symbols

Much has been said and written over the years about the nature of symbols, and their relationship to what they symbolize. Part of this discussion involves sacramental theology. It is fair to say that all sacraments are symbols, but not all symbols are sacraments. Beginning with the broader category, a symbol is something that stands for something else. Symbols have some likeness or relationship to what they symbolize, and/or some common context which allows them to be understood as signifying something other than themselves. Thus, a monarch and her royal authority can be symbolized by a crown, a crest, or a throne—though none of these would be *effective* as symbols in a society that had neither monarchs, crowns, crests or thrones, or had not heard of them. The degree of relatedness between a symbol and its object—for example, between a monarch and her headgear—can be quite remote as long as the culture understands the connection between them. But outside of the culture in which a symbol makes symbolic sense, it may be unrecognizable, or require explanation—and thus be ineffective *as* a symbol.

Moreover, a symbol may have a different or even contrary meaning in another culture, and other cultures may have different symbols to represent the same concept. One need not go as far afield as the Cargo Cults or the mysterious soda-bot-tle of *The Gods Must Be Crazy* to find examples of ambivalent symbolism. It is well known that hand gestures (as a form of active symbol) are just as variable as language—and a gesture that is acceptable or innocuous in one society can be obscene or offensive in another. For example, the American "thumbs up" is the Middle Eastern "Up yours!" and the American "O.K." is "money" in Japan and an obscenity in Brazil. Symbols are as often conventional (not "natural") as they are ambiguous (not "clear").

A sacrament, for the purpose of this discussion, is a symbol that does more than effect mental recognition in the observer, but actually effects a real change. Thus, it must at the minimum be comprehensible and understood to relate to that which it symbolizes."Natural likeness" is not essential for a symbol, or for a sacrament to do its work—wine *is* visually more like blood than bread is like flesh, yet both serve in the sacrament of the Holy Eucharist. Yet in some cultures bread is an unheard of novelty rather than a daily staff of life, and wine may be an exotic substance. As an ecclesiastical wag once put it even in his Western context, "I have no difficulty in believing that the eucharistic host is the Body of Christ; but I do have difficulty recognizing it as *bread.*"

Picking up the royal imagery above, and recalling all of the fuss and bother concerning its misplacement, in *The Prince and the Pauper*, the Great Seal of England in a real sense embodied a kind of *sacrament*—the real, present power of the monarch in an efficacious manner—yet the Pauper used it to crack walnuts! The crucial note here is that even with a sacrament, its sacramental nature must be *discerned and understood in a shared context.* Even so-called "natural" symbols can be misunderstood apart from a cultural context, through which they are invested with efficacious power.

This is not to suggest a form of receptionism—in which the sacrament is only valid for those who believe it to be so. It is rather to say that a person ignorant of the nature of the sacrament will also be ignorant of the grace it imparts—which it may still impart in spite of their ignorance, but about which they will remain unknowing. I am speaking here of our *understanding* of the sacraments, not their ultimate *reality.* Thus, the Great Seal was still the Great Seal even when used to crack walnuts.

Nor is it my concern here to debate the question of whether marriage is or is not one of seven sacraments or a sacramental rite (as variously construed in Roman Catholic and Anglican teaching), but rather to reflect on the *function* of the marital relationship as a *symbol* for the relationship between Christ and the church, or in the Hebrew Scriptures, between God and Israel. Whether a sacra-ment or not, it is a powerful symbol. I think at the very least we can recognize that unlike the bread and wine of the Holy Eucharist, a marriage does not *effect* the real presence of the relationship between Christ and the church. Rather, the grace of marriage concerns the love and fidelity of the couple, which is *analogous* to or *metaphorical* of the love of Christ for the church. This is at least a poetic symbol, and it may be a sacrament—depending on how that is defined.

Finally, it must be acknowledged that symbols—even sacramental ones—have clearly defined limits. Even in the undoubted sacraments, we do not believe that *all* bread and wine is holy because *some* bread and wine are the means by which we experience Christ's *anamnesis*. I raise this as a preventative to any suggestion of idolatry, in which the symbol comes to supplant what it symbolizes. Idolatry, as someone once said, is treating things like God and God like a thing. I would also suggest that idolatry can consist in treating things about people as if they were divine, and treating the truly divine image of God in humanity as if it were merely a thing. In the present context, it is possible both to make too much of marriage, and too little.

Marriage as ambivalent symbol

Several biblical authors use marriage as a symbol for the relationship between God and Israel, and Christ and the church. But, as with many of the issues surrounding sexuality, the picture is far more complex than mere equivalence. Not only is marriage only one of many symbols for this relationship, but the marriage symbolism itself is ambivalent, capable of standing for both good and bad relationships between God and God's people.

There are many earthly phenomena—and Jesus assures us (Matthew 22:30, Mark 12:25, Luke 20:35) that marriage is an earthly phenomenon!—that the biblical authors use in addition to marriage to represent the relationship between God and Israel or Christ and the church: monarch and people, tree and branches, father and children, shepherd and sheep, master and slaves, head and body, cornerstone and building. These symbols all depend on the cultural understanding of those to whom they are addressed. The Letter to the Ephesians collects and intertwines a number of these symbols, in addition to marriage. As Paul himself recognizes, his blending of these symbols gets a bit confusing, as he spins out the various cultural themes of leadership and authority, the relationship of one to many, the nature of organic or bodily union, and love and care.

Thus the Scripture does not single out marriage as a unique symbol for the divine/human relationship, and one can carry the analogy or symbol too far—as some have suggested Paul does—as if women should literally treat their husbands as if they were God. Nor should one carry away from this symbolic usage the notion that because marriage is a symbol for the divine/human interaction, it is therefore in itself divine—it remains, according to Jesus, a terrestrial phenomenon (Luke 20:34–35). So to confuse the symbol with what it symbolizes is a category error. More than a few Christian theologians have of late wandered off in a direction more suggestive of pagan notions of *hieros gamos*—the sacred marriage whereby the eternal opposites of spirit and matter, or heaven and earth, or any

other imagined or real polarities, are united—than is warranted by strictly orthodox theology. This includes suggestions addressed in the previous chapter, that
the relationship of a male and female somehow more perfectly embody the
imago dei than either does individually. Much as I may disagree with him on
other points (especially when under the undue influence of Aristotelian science),
this is a matter on which I concur with Aquinas (*ST* I.Q93.6d).

It is also important to point out that in addition to the multiplicity of symbols
for the relationship between God and people, Scripture uses all *sorts of marriages*
as analogies for equally various divine/human interactions. While Paul uses the
marital relationship and the love and care of a husband for his wife ("as his own
body") in Ephesians, there are less positive images to be found elsewhere.

Perhaps most importantly, the prophetic literature uses polygamy as an image
for the relationship of the one God with many worshipers, or multiple nations.
Thus God is portrayed as a Middle Eastern "Lord" (Ba'al = Lord: to which the
Hebrew root for a woman being married, *beulah*, is related; explicitly contrasted
at Hosea 2:18 with "my man"). As such a Lord, God is portrayed as having more
than one wife in Jeremiah 3 and Ezekiel 23. These relationships, as well as
Hosea's relationship with Gomer and the (possibly other) woman of Hosea 3,
reflect the failure of God's people in the failures of these various relationships.

So close is the affinity (in the Hebrew mind) of idolatry with harlotry that it is
on occasion difficult to tell when the text intends literal harlotry rather than figurative. (Note the very frequent use of *zonah*—the root for *harlot*—in the Old Testament as symbolic of or in connection with idolatry.) We ought also to note that
the putative author of the Song of Solomon was notorious for the range and number of his sexual interests—yet that did not prevent the Rabbis and medieval
churchmen from spiritualizing the account into a rhapsody for the devoted soul's
love for God. The male in this analogy is free (as he was under Jewish law) to
have multiple female partners, but each woman is to be singularly devoted to her
husband. In the medieval Christian adaptations of this text, it was not found at all
strange for men to cast themselves as "The Bride" of Christ. Symbols can sometimes be more flexible than people.

The use of this symbol

The question is: Given that heterosexual relationships can be used as such multi-
valent symbols, positive or negative, single and plural, and even with a degree of
sexual ambiguity, can faithful, monogamous, life-long same-sex relationships also
serve in a symbolic capacity—towards good? I will explore the negative imagery
in later reflections on Leviticus and Romans, but will note here that the same
kind of linkage between idolatry and harlotry that we see in Jeremiah, Ezekiel,
and Hosea is made between idolatry and male same-sexuality. But what might a
faithful, loving same-sex relationship (as opposed to the cultic activity described

in Leviticus or the cultic and orgiastic in Romans) stand for as a symbol—not in the cultures of those times, but in our own?

It is clear that the prevailing biblical symbol for heterosexual relationships is intimately connected with the assumption of male "headship"—thus the related analogies (master and slave, head and body, and so forth) *assume* a cultural notion of male authority, likened to the authority of Christ over the church or God over Israel. So powerful is this imagery that men become "feminine" in relation to God—as C.S. Lewis noted in his emendation to the conclusion of Goethe's *Faust*, where Lewis portrays God as the wholly masculine who confronts his bride.

> A vision of heaven: Donald Trump washing the feet of the Filipino maids and cleaning women who serve in his hotels and office towers.

But what of Christ—who voluntarily (and temporarily) assumes the position of a subordinate—not only in the great *kenosis* of the Incarnation, but in the symbolic act of the Maundy footwashing—while remaining Lord and God? When Jesus assumes the position of a servant to wash his disciples' feet, he is also assuming the position of the woman who washed *his* feet with her tears. It is no accident that Jesus uses this powerful acted symbol to show his disciples the danger of assuming the position of *authority over* rather than assuming the position of *service to*. (It is perhaps ironic that in the Roman Catholic Church only men are to take part in the Maundy ritual as either foot-washers or as those whose feet are washed. How much more powerful a symbol would it be if a male bishop were to wash the feet of women?)

Jesus is secure in his knowledge of himself, yet is free to set aside the role of authority to assume the role of a slave, a role played elsewhere in the passion narrative by a woman. As is obvious, in a same-sex relationship there are no stereotypical sex roles for the partners. They are, like Jesus, free to take upon themselves, in a dynamic interchange, various opportunities to love and to serve. This flexibility is no doubt one of the reasons same-sexuality is seen as a threat to entrenched systems of automatic deferral to culturally established hierarchies, in which "the man" rules. Like Christianity itself, same-sexuality "turns the world upside down" (Acts 17:6) by challenging the so-called *natural* roles that in reality are *cultural*. Same-sex couples are thus capable of being truly natural symbols for the mutuality of equals, free from the traditional roles assigned by culture to men and women. Whether the culture sees this as a threat or a promise will depend upon those who benefit from the *status quo*.

Further, as procreation is not an end for same-sex relationships, the relationship *itself* becomes the locus for its intrinsic goodness: that is, it is not dependent on a result that comes from the relationship, but on the relationship itself. Thus the partners do not serve as *means to an end*, but as *ends in themselves*—all being done for the good of the other, in mutual submission and love, in realization of the principle of "I-Thou." Thus same-sex unions can be symbols of mutual dedi-

Not all sexual relationships can fulfill the end of procreation, but all faithful and loving couples can submit themselves to the moral mandate, and bear spiritual fruit.

cation of each partner to the beloved, rather than as utilities geared towards some other goal or end. In this sense, same-sex unions function analogously with celibacy as signs of an eschatological end to "how things have always been"—upsetting the old dichotomies of "slave or free, male and female."

Nothing in this is to suggest that all same-sex couples are successful in this kind of mutuality, or that a mixed-sex couple is not equally capable of it (when they are willing, like Christ, to set aside the presumptive roles granted or assigned by their culture). My purpose here has been to show that, as with marriage, it is the *quality* of the relationship, not its mere *existence*, that serves as a symbol.

We find the locus of that symbol in the *moral* purpose of sexuality, which resides in mutual joy and respect, and the enhancement of society both between the couple and in the larger world. This is an enactment of the human moral mandate towards love and fidelity, mirroring the love and fidelity of God; and this is a moral value of which same-sex couples are capable. Procreation, on the other hand, does not have any moral value in and of itself, though it can be accompanied by the moral values I have just elucidated. But in itself it is a biological process, not unique to human beings. Procreation alone—divorced from its moral context as part of a loving human relationship—does not symbolize anything of moral value.

Thus the symbol we have before us—the union of a loving couple regardless of whether they are fertile or not, or of differing or the same sex—is consistent with the Gospel, with its mandate to love one's neighbor as oneself. As this mandate can be applied to marriage (Ephesians 5:28) so too it can be applied to faithful, monogamous, life-long same-sex unions. Such unions can be symbolic forces, and bear fruit for the upbuilding of society based upon this divine mandate. It is to that upbuilding that I will turn in the next chapter, as I examine the final traditional "good" of marriage.

Questions for Discussion or Reflection

- *What other symbols for God can you recall from Scripture? What about the relationship of God with humanity?*

- *What qualities of a mixed-sex marriage do you see as missing from a same-sex marriage? Why? Does any such quality apply to all mixed-sex marriages?*

7.
Remedial Reading

PREVIOUS CHAPTERS HAVE EXAMINED THE VARIOUS "CAUSES" (OR GOODS OR ENDS) of marriage, as laid out in the preface to the marriage liturgy in the Book of Common Prayer, and how these same goods might conceivably find a place within the context of a faithful, life-long, monogamous same-sex relationship. I have argued that such a relationship and union is capable of providing mutual joy, comfort, and human society no less than a mixed-sex marriage. Such a couple is also capable of fulfilling some of the ends of procreation, certainly no less than an infertile mixed-sex marriage, through adoption or the upbringing of the biological children of one or the other partner, or of unwanted or orphaned children, or through vocations that support and nurture other families. Such care and concern for others was esteemed by James as "religion that is pure and undefiled" (1:27). In the previous chapter I addressed the symbolic weight assigned to marriage in the Christian tradition and explored a number of ways in which similar symbolic value can be borne by a same-sex relationship that is equally loving, permanent, and faithful.

I have noted that our present Prayer Book marriage liturgy reintroduces these *raisons d'être* for marriage—rationalizations which had been removed in the 1789 revision (the prevailing rationalism of the day rendering it "self-evident" that a supporting case for such an almost universal human phenomenon was unnecessary). However, one of the "causes" from the 1662 version (in use at the time of our ecclesiastical and civil independence) was *not* restored in 1979. This is ironic, because it is a "cause" with an explicit scriptural basis, playing a significant part in the most extensive biblical reflection on the institution of marriage, and offering a rationale for the continuance of an institution to which Paul gave otherwise only lukewarm endorsement.

This is marriage as a "remedy for fornication"—as described in 1 Corinthians 7:1–9, which I cite here from the Authorized Version:

> Now concerning the things whereof ye wrote unto me: It is good for a man not to touch a woman. Nevertheless, to avoid fornication, let every man have his own wife, and let every woman have her own husband. Let the husband render unto the wife due benevolence: and likewise also the wife unto the husband. The wife hath not power of her own body, but the husband: and likewise also the husband hath not power of his own body, but the wife. Defraud ye not one the other, except it be with consent for a time, that ye may give yourselves to fasting and prayer; and come together again, that Satan tempt you not for your incontinency. But I speak this by permission, and not of commandment. For I would that all men were even as I myself. But every man hath his proper gift of God, one after this manner, and another after that. I say therefore to the unmarried and widows, It is good for them if they abide even as I. But if they cannot contain, let them marry: for it is better to marry than to burn.

This passage is significant for a number of reasons, not least for the way Paul describes celibacy as a gift not all possess, contrary to his wishes. Paul recognizes that sexual desire is not only powerful, but that it has an appropriate outlet for those who lack the gift to contain themselves in celibacy: marriage. It is in large part in light of this biblical source that we see marriage described in the Anglican tradition (Articles of Religion XXV, XXXIII) as a state of life *allowed* in Scripture. The purpose of the authors of the Articles of Religion was not to find scriptural *validation* for an institution that had existed in most human cultures in one form or another (validation was dealt with in the expansive Preface to the marriage rite); rather it was to *distinguish* marriage from the Two Sacraments of the Gospel directly instituted by Christ, and to assert that marriage was *permitted* to clergy.

Paul similarly explicitly permits marriage, rather than commending or commanding it, and clearly wishes all could be celibate as he is. But he recognizes it is inappropriate to demand celibacy of those incapable of living within its constraints.

From the Pauline perspective, then, marriage is, among other things, permission to have sex. It is the solution to the problem of desire, framed and confined within appropriate limits. It authorizes doing something within limits outside of which it would be sinful. It is, in short, for the vast majority of people who approach the altar as former virgins, a way of blessing sin—and thereby removing its sinfulness. They are permitted to perform (or continue to perform) an act that before would have been (or was) sinful. *Thus, the sinfulness does not reside in the act, but the relationship of the actors.* Marriage may not cover a multitude of sins, but it covers at least one: fornication (loosely, and from a biblical perspective rather incorrectly, defined as "sex outside of marriage").

This marks a development in moral thinking from late Jewish tradition into the early Christian era. Under the older biblical law, a man was permitted plural wives, resort to prostitutes, or concubinage (an arrangement midway between marriage and prostitution). A man was

> Under biblical law a man could only violate another man's marriage, a woman only her own.

not judged to have committed adultery by having a sexual relationship with a woman to whom he was not married—unless, and only if, she was betrothed or married to someone else. Prostitution was restricted, and a crime for certain women, but for men it was an available outlet for sexual tension. However, rabbinic Judaism, as well as sects such as that at Qumran, began to develop a distaste for this, and to see polygamy as falling short of an ideal (though not explicitly judged impermissible in mainstream Judaism until the tenth century, in a ban attributed to Rabbi Gershom ben Judah).

In the same period leading up to the beginning of the Christian era, prostitution as well came to be seen as a moral failing. This view is reflected in the teaching of Jesus, who also extended the concept of adultery to men violating their *own* marriages, even to the level of "adultery in one's heart."

Stopping the allowance

Marriage, for Paul, was among other things a remedy for desire, an appropriate channel for sexual energy for those unable to "contain." So can we in our present day make a similar allowance for same-sex relationships? Some will at this point say that same-sex relationships cannot be permitted *now* because they were not "allowed" in Scripture *then*. They hold that the prohibitions on homosexuality render such an approbation permanently impossible. I will address these negative texts more extensively in what follows; here I want to deal with the absence of approbation rather than the purported prohibition.

To understand the biblical (especially the Pauline) view, we must recognize that marriage was a civil institution, a civil option for Jews and Christians. Paul, in particular, recognizes it as the civil option as well as the moral one, as it counters promiscuity and prostitution (both legally permitted though regulated under Roman law, yet also widely held to be moral failings). Paul *allows* participation in this civil institution of marriage even if he does not encourage it.

Same-sexuality fell into the same category as prostitution under Roman law—regulated and in some cases permitted, but seen, especially by Stoics and other moralists, as a failing. Same-sex *marriage* was not a civil norm in the cultures amongst which Judaism and Christianity came into being. Although same-sexuality existed in many cultures of the ancient world with which Judaism and Christianity were familiar—including, in spite of the protests, Jewish cultures—the phenomenon of lifelong and exclusive same-sex relationships was very rare (or to be more precise, rarely recorded, so that there is little evidence of it—we have no way of knowing how common it may have been in reality). Civil recognition in the form of marriage was even rarer. Mixed-sex marriage, on the other hand, was a recognized institution—and although the differences between Jewish, Roman and Christian marriage customs were in some conflict (as Jewish law allowed polygamy and divorce, and Roman law forbade polygamy though it allowed concubinage and divorce), the early Christians accepted the Roman rule and Jewish ideal of monogamy, but frowned upon concubinage and divorce, largely following the opinions of the more moralistic philosophers and legislators of the time.

Thus the marriage of which Paul speaks is marriage as it existed in the civil state, under Roman hegemony, which in the time of Augustus and Tiberius exalted values of hearth and home—even if the emperors themselves and their immediate families often failed to live up to the principles in practice. There was, in Paul's time, no equivalent for same-sex marriage, even had he been of a mind to recognize it.

Applying old advice to a present situation

So it is very unlikely that Paul understood or grasped the possibility of people wanting to live in a life-long same-sex union. Some have suggested that Paul was aware of sexual orientation, but there is little evidence to support even this claim, let alone any awareness of whatever informal same-sex marriages might have existed. There are still, after all, numerous skeptics around even today who deny that sexual orientation exists, or who say that there is no need to grant "special" recognition to same-sex relationships since all people are free to marry a person of the other sex. (It is especially ironic that the reasserter community will on one

---

⁀ Saint Paul may have been aware of Aristophanes' satirical creation story in Plato's *Symposium*, but that is very unlikely, as Plato was long out of fashion by Paul's time, and collections of his work were not something one could pick up at the local Barnes and Noble. Even so, this misses the satirical twist in Aristophanes—whose tongue in cheek "praise" of adult politicians who love other men is a comical take on the fact that most Athenians found such behavior to be as *perverse* as Paul would. Athenians thought it *natural* for men to love boys and young men; but not for grown men to love other grown men, particularly if they took the "submissive" role reserved for boys or women. The Athenians despised effeminacy in any man. (For more on this see Dover or Greenberg.) It is far more likely Paul had seen, and been scandalized by, Greek pottery painting—particularly of the satyrical sort. The scene he describes in Romans 1 resembles this more than anything like "same-sex marriage."

hand deny same-sex orientation exists and on the other posit that Paul knew about it and rejected it.)

Regardless of such dismissals, many others have recognized that homosexual orientation, and the desire to which it gives rise to express a love for a person of the same sex in a physical way, is not any more likely to be combined with a gift of celibacy than it is for persons of heterosexual orientation.

> Some claim that homosexual men are "by nature" *more* promiscuous than heterosexual men. Their evidence is largely anecdotal, or based on old or discredited research studies, some of which—such as Bell and Weinberg's *Homosexualities*—derive their sample base from ads in underground newspapers, gay bars, bathhouses and personal contacts of other sample volunteers. Such a sample is unlikely to produce anything *other* than evidence of promiscuity; particularly when compared to a heterosexual sample obtained by random methods. (Bell and Weinberg, 29–38.)

But many have noted—even among conservatives who reflect upon this issue—that it is irrational as well as unjust to suggest that gay and lesbian persons should be held to a standard in effect stricter than the one applied to heterosexuals; that is, to demand permanent celibacy (or what can only be for both parties a less-than-happy heterosexual marriage) for all gay and lesbian people, especially while tolerating less than punctilious observance of the same biblical standard by mixed-sex couples, many if not most of whom engage in premarital sex, occasional affairs, or serial monogamy through the unbiblical provision of divorce. However, even if many or even most people *are* promiscuous, there are others who wish to be faithful, or attempt to be faithful.

A more tolerant view within church or state does not necessitate the recognition of same-sex relationships as either marriage or matrimony, that is, as either civil or sacred in exactly the same way and to the same extent as mixed-sex marriage. But some form of recognized permanent commitment can be seen to be appropriate as an application of Paul's teaching that "it is better to marry than to burn" to a situation which Paul himself may well have found inconceivable. Some, such as the Rev. Fleming Rutledge, have reflected on the question in this way:

> I have great respect and reverence for people who maintain celibacy if they are unmarried, divorced or widowed. This certainly remains the classical Christian standard. However, I do not believe that many people are granted the gift of celibacy. Even St. Paul, who put a high value on celibacy, recognized this in his teaching on marriage. I therefore believe we must find a way to support healthier lifestyles for Christian gay people who are beset every day by invitations to participate in the anonymity and promiscuity of the street, the bathhouse, the bar and

the club. We will do well, I think to make an honored place for the devoutly Christian gay people who sincerely want fidelity and stability in their lives insofar as that is possible for them. These couples are in the distinct minority and it seems to me that we should support them in their wish to carve out a more responsible style of life. I therefore agree (I think) with those who say that we should be discussing the possibility of some sort of blessing for gay couples who fit this description not because the culture is demanding this, but because the church has been thinking about this for some time now. (From a December 2003 presentation to a parish facing division on the issue of homosexuality.)

Although she stops short of supporting same-sex marriage, Rutledge is willing to recognize the human damage caused by unreasonable expectations or requirements, and the moral danger of a double standard, as evidence shows only a "distinct minority" of heterosexuals actually adhere to the rules of chastity before marriage and stability and fidelity within it.

However, if "marriage" can be understood in the many forms the institution has taken (some of which would now be held to be immoral if not illegal) it appears to me that it is quite possible to apply Paul's allowance — "If they cannot contain, let them marry: for it is better to marry than to burn" — to a situation he would likely not have been capable of imagining, at least in his own time.

WWSPD

What would Saint Paul do—today? Is this a reasonable question, and to what extent are speculations about what Paul might have thought or done—apart from what we actually know he said or did—relevant to the present discussion?

We do not know what Saint Paul would say today, assuming he were supplied with all the relevant information concerning human sexuality and psychology of which he was ignorant. It is highly unlikely that Paul, in his own culture and time, would have applied his rule of "let them marry" to same-sex couples. There is no evidence that he had any awareness or understanding of sexual orientation. Still, some argue that Paul knew about homosexual orientation expressed in life-long, loving, monogamous relationships, and intended explicitly to reject it. Those such as N.T. Wright and Robert Gagnon, who argue that Paul must have been familiar with Plato's *Symposium*, have little definite proof to offer, and Paul's writings reveal little or no familiarity with Plato—who, outside of Alexandria, was out of fashion in the philosophical world with which Paul *was* likely familiar— including that of the Stoics, whose thinking is consistent with (though not necessarily a source for) what Paul concludes in Romans 1. There we find Paul's sole extended comment on male same-sexuality, which describes it as attendant upon idolatry, and part of the collapse of all good order in the Gentile world, in an orgiastic setting which has nothing to say about loving monogamy.

The missing lesbians

You will notice I particularly mention *male* same-sex activity. Paul is echoing the understandings of his tradition and culture, quite apart from any possible influence or reaction from or to the Hellenistic world. As I noted earlier, there is no mention of female same-sexuality in the biblical legal code, and Leviticus explicitly states that "you shall not bed a male with the beddings of a woman. It is abomination" (Leviticus 18:22; cp 20:14—in a close to literal translation). Paul uses the word *arsenokoitai* twice in his writings (1 Corinthians 6:9, 1 Timothy 1:10) and it appears to be, as Robin Scroggs has pointed out, a Greek version of the rabbinic turn of phrase for male same-sex activity, itself based on the language of Leviticus 18/20: *mishkav zakur*. Both mean, essentially, "male-bedding"—and in the biblical text refer as well to men bedding women, as in Numbers 31:17–18. But nowhere is there a biblical reference to women-with-women.

I say this in spite of the work of Bernadette Brooten, who has done extensive research into the biblical and patristic material, as well as the relevant classical material on the subject. I have no disagreement with her conclusion that Paul would have been aware of lesbianism. I also agree that he would have looked askance at it. Where I disagree is in her taking Romans 1:26 as a reference to lesbianism.

First of all, she acknowledges that the text is not clear, and is capable of more than one interpretation. The interpretation that I find most reasonable in the context of Paul's world and concerns, and the flow of the logic of the passage, does not involve lesbianism. In short, looking at the same evidence I come to a different conclusion. For example, Brooten notes that Paul's contemporary Philo, in his *Special Laws*, covers much of the same ground as Paul in Romans. But she notes, for instance, that although Philo uses the phrase *para phusin* = "against nature," unlike Plato (*Laws* I.636) he does not apply it to lesbians but to sex during menstruation, sex between a man and a boy, and sex between different species of animal, noting he uses a similar phrase to condemn sex with an infertile woman (Brooten, 247). These are, of course, Philo's elaborations on the Jewish law, are perfectly congruent with the rabbinic judgments, and reflect the Jewish concern with procreation. Brooten's response to Miller's essay on the subject argues that he fails to apply the rabbinic material; on the contrary, I think the rabbinic material supports his interpretation, as I will elucidate below.

The Rabbis, of course, were *aware* of female same-sexuality, but did not treat it with the same severity as male same-sexuality, and it is very unlikely they would have thought of these matters as related. Male sex, as Philo said, was about the proper planting of seed in a fertile place. Women's sexuality was understood in terms of desire and satisfaction (erotic in a rather modern sense) since they believed women contributed nothing to the process of generation apart from raw material, and were merely the fertile field. So women could not, under this understanding, really "have sex" with each other, since sex was understood in terms of seed and penetration. There could be no "intercourse" without these factors.

But the Rabbis (as well as the Greeks) were also well aware of men making use of women in non-procreative ways. In fact, it is from the proof-text most often cited concerning men, Leviticus 18:22, that they derive an important teaching on the subject. They had noted, of course, that the text refers to the "beddings" of a woman, in the plural. They observed that

> This phrase, "the beddings of a woman" comes to teach us that there are two ways to bed a woman. And the passage, while it comes to teach one thing, actually teaches two things. (bSanhedrin 54a, bYevamot 56b)

That is, the law, while explicitly about male same-sexuality, also teaches something else. And what was that? Rashi clarifies: "The 'two beddings of a woman' . . . are equivalent as far as culpability concerning forbidden sexual relations (i.e., incest); the usual way and the unusual way." So the law was held to clarify, for example, that a man who committed incest with a woman, even by the "unusual way" was still guilty. The "unusual way," of course, being nonprocreative intercourse: the insertion of the penis in an inappropriate place.

While Paul was likely aware of the existence of female same-sexuality (from literature but more likely from murals or pottery), he is, in Romans, (like the Rabbis in their reflection on Leviticus) dealing with Gentile women ("their females") who have "abandoned the natural use" by their husbands having made use of them in "the unusual way." The men, enflamed, as Paul says, with lust, then turn upon each other and, abandoning women altogether, begin to use each other *in the same way*. The "likewise" or "in the same way" here refers not to categories of sexuality (a notion Brooten [249n] advances based on the *Testament of Naphtali's* comparison of the sins of the Watchers and of Sodom, as in Jude 7, which has nothing to do

---

⤳ According to the Talmud (bYevamot76a) Rabbi Huna said that women who are "lewd" (*mesolelot*) with each other are harlots, and thus disqualified from marrying a priest. But Rabbi Eleazar said that when a bachelor sleeps with an unmarried woman without any intention to marry her, he indeed makes her a harlot, but that this does not apply in the case of two women. It is not harlotry (*z'nut*) but lewdness (*prizut*). Maimonides would later clarify this position in his monumental *Mishneh Torah* (Issurei Bi'ah 21:8): Women are forbidden to be lewd with one another; and flogging is not imposed because there is no specific commandment against it, but because a married woman who does this is disobedient. Thus it is equivalent neither to *mishkav zakur* nor to adultery.

with sexuality but species) but to the use of the "unusual way" between a man and a woman, and "in the same way" two men. This gives a particular punch to the notion that the men thus receive a punishment "in themselves."

The Rabbis recognized that just as there was no Torah prohibition on lesbianism, there was also no Torah prohibition on men making use of their wives in an "unnatural" or "unusual" way, which is referred to as "turning the table." Still, this does not mean they approved of it, particularly if the woman derived no pleasure from it. When a woman complains, "I set a table for my husband, but he overturned it" the rabbinic response, delivered with a note of some regret, is, "As Torah permits it, I cannot help you." (bNedarim 20b)

Brooten notes (as I point out in the call-out text) that the Rabbis do not condemn sex between a married man and woman in the "unusual way" (*ibid.*). But I would also point out that *neither does Paul explicitly condemn the women here*—only the "males with males" receive a "penalty" and the women appear *as a means* to explain why men would do such an unnatural thing *with each other*, a thing which Paul sees as a punishment in itself. If there is any echo of Genesis in this passage, it is Genesis 3, not 1–2: the women of the Gentiles, by allowing their men to make use of them in this way, lead them astray from what is "natural." This is consistent with the later "Pauline" resistance to women teaching, based on Genesis (1 Timothy 2:15).

This is also where the language of "exchange" becomes so important: the exchange in the use of what is natural in the women (by the men), leading to an exchange by the men of their own partners. It is true that Brooten argues that some early texts support the use of *para phusin* to mean sex between women (i.e., Plato); but these usages are by far the exception rather than the rule. Most often, in the extant literature, the phrase is rarely used in a sexual context at all, and is most common in the general sense in which we would use it today, to refer to what is natural or unnatural to things or actions, most of them quite foreign to sexuality.

One source in particular is often cited: Plato's *Laws* I.636, where "The Athenian" actually mentions sex between women and between men as being *para phusin*. However, the context of the discussion is actually good order in society, and the wisdom of having *gymnasia*, and whether their virtues outweigh the vices to which they give rise. In the same way, the Athenian observes, there are few things which are not somewhat mixed in terms of benefits and deficits, and the *gymnasia* have begun to corrupt the pleasures of love. The Athenian observes that whether one is serious or joking, when male and female come together for procreation, the pleasure is "according to nature"—for humans as well as beasts. But when male joins with male or female with female, the pleasure is "against nature." (There may here be a sense in which *para phusin* means something akin to "contraception.") In any case, it seems unlikely that this is a text Paul would have had in mind—even if he were familiar with it—as he is entirely uninterested in the question of sexual pleasure, and tends to use language of obligation rather than joy, and the avoidance of desire rather than its enjoyment, when describing it (1 Corinthians 7:1–6).

However, it is equally clear that a man indulging in anal intercourse with a woman is also acting "against nature" in this sense, and that this, rather than a passing reference to Plato, is more likely Paul's meaning in Romans 1:26. As an example of a similar usage, the word *sodomy* as it appears in most present day law codes and common parlance is a broad term referring to almost any "unnatural" sexual acts. Most importantly for the present discussion, it certainly includes a man having anal intercourse with a woman. No one has any trouble understanding this usage, in spite of the more narrow reference only to men.

So my view is that Paul is referring to the practice of men using "their females" in this way. For those used to hearing this passage described as an indictment of "homosexuality" or of lesbians and gays, this may come as a surprise, or be treated as a novel interpretation. On the contrary, this is the way the passage in Romans 1 was understood at least by some in the early church. Clement of Alexandria, for example, cites this passage in *The Instructor* II.87.1 (II.X in the ANF series, in Latin). Even as late a theologian as Saint Augustine would, in (a) *On Marriage and Concupiscence* 2.20 [in some editions numbered as 2.35], and

---

ᖇᖇ Some, such as N.T. Wright, see Romans 1 as a recapitulation of Genesis, in connection with the language of creation, and of male and female. However, if Paul is referring to Genesis, it is primarily through the lens of Jewish tradition, particularly as enshrined in the Wisdom of Solomon, which documents the issue of early conflicts between Judaism and Hellenism. In particular, chapters 12–16 similarly describe the perils of idolatry and its effect upon the Gentile world. (See especially Wisdom 13:1–10; 14:8–14, 22–30; 15:6–8; 16:1.) Paul refers to "creation" in two senses: the temporal: "from the time of the creation" (1:10), and the physical, the "created world" in which God could be perceived even by Gentiles, if they had not been corrupted by idolatry and worshiped the creature rather than the creator. (1:25)

Romans is not, then, about the *rejection* of "what is natural" or "the creation"—it is on the contrary about an *embrace* of the creation *rather than* the Creator. A contemporary version of this would be the exaltation of any part of the creation to a quasi-divine status; and I suggest that this happens when people try to convert heterosexual marriage into some kind of more perfect exposition of the image of God.

So Romans 1 is not about "the Fall"—Paul doesn't really get into his Fall argument until later in the letter. He is really doing what later came to be called "natural theology," echoing the argument of Wisdom of Solomon. Those who have failed to perceive God properly through God's self-revelation in the natural world, ironically turn to images of

(b) *On the Good of Marriage* 11–12, address Paul's description of "their females" who have "exchanged the natural use for the unnatural" as they "suffer" their husbands to use the opening that is "alongside the natural" i.e., the generative one; the husbands then, having abandoned what is "natural with females" turn on each other and "similarly" take advantage of this newfound versatility:

(a) As regards any part of the body which is not meant for generative purposes, should a man use even his own wife in it, it is against nature.

(b) [The Apostle] allows as a matter of "pardon" that sexual intercourse which takes place through incontinence, not only for the begetting of children, and, at times, not at all for the begetting of children; and it is not that marriage forces this to take place, but that it procures pardon for it; provided, however it be not so in excess as to hinder what ought to be set aside as seasons of prayer, nor be changed into that use which is against nature, on which the Apostle could not be silent, when speaking of the excessive corruptions of unclean and impious men . . . Whereas that natural use, when it pass beyond the compact of marriage, that is, beyond the necessity of begetting, is pardonable in the case of a wife, damnable in the case of a harlot; that which is against nature is execrable when done in the case of an harlot, but more execrable in the case of a wife . . . When the man shall wish to use the member of the wife not allowed for this pur-

other created things, and worship these idols. As in Wisdom, this leads to all sorts of disorders, including disorders in marriage.

In light of the language about women exchanging their natural "use" (*chresis*) for the one "alongside" or "against"—or as in the Jewish tradition exchanging the "usual way" for the "unusual way"—Wisdom 15:7 makes use of this rather rare word in reference to "vessels" (also a euphemism for "women" in 1 Peter 3:7) used for clean and unclean purposes, as the maker decides. This verse is echoed in Romans 9:21, so it was clearly in Paul's mind as he composed this letter.

In short, Romans 1 represents the standard Jewish argument against idolatry, as attested in Wisdom and the rabbinic sources as well: male homosexuality is a Gentile problem, to such an extent that Gentiles are always suspected of it (Kiddushin 82a).

More importantly, in terms of the ultimate message of the whole letter, Paul is using this passage as a rhetorical device designed to convict his hearers when he lowers the boom on them at the beginning of Chapter 2. The point of Romans as a whole is that both Gentile and Jew are doomed if they try to achieve righteousness apart from the grace of God—whether they turn to the creation, or to the Law.

Romans 1, a description of the total collapse of good order among idolaters, has no application to the question of faithful, monogamous same-sex relationships between Christian men—and says absolutely nothing about such relationships between women.

pose, the wife is more shameful, if she suffer it to take place in her own case, than if in the case of another woman.

This is how Clement and Augustine read the passage, and although others such as John Chrysostom read it differently, in support of their reading I suggest it to be highly unlikely for a biblical or rabbinic Jew—and Paul was both—to think lesbian sex and gay sex are "similar" not only in terms of punishment (the former was subject on rabbinic grounds to chastisement, the latter on biblical grounds to capital punishment) but in terms of the way in which they understood sex and its mechanics and purposes, and men and women in general.

Paul was likely aware of female same-sexuality, and probably disapproved of it, as did the Rabbis. But there is no certain passage of Scripture to support that conclusion. Similarly, Augustine was aware of female same-sexuality, and while he considered it a moral failing he regarded it (typically) as less serious than male homosexuality. In Letter 211.14, the source of the Augustinian Rule for convents, he refers to women's "shameful frolic and sporting with one another" as unseemly for married women and thus much more out of place in nuns. The parallel to the rabbinic treatment is striking.

Back to Paul

So Paul did not intend, in this passage, to condemn "homosexuality"—as is often claimed. Given that the Hebrew Scriptures are silent on lesbian sexuality, and the New Testament as well, it is inappropriate to continue to assert, as many do, a "biblical condemnation of homosexuality." We will return to the further significance of this fact in a later chapter.

"Homosexuality" as a category including men and women is, after all, a relatively modern invention; the Mediterranean cultures of the ancient world regarded

---

The underlying principle in Paul's teaching concerning marriage is that it "is not sin" (1 Corinthians 7:28). Paul does not portray marriage as good-in-itself. Rather, he is arguing that marriage is "permitted"—perhaps against those who would later "forbid marriage" in a kind of hyper-asceticism (1 Timothy 4:3). But in 1 Corinthians, marriage is neither mandated nor particularly praised. It is "better" to marry than to burn with unrequited passion; and certainly better to marry than to resort to prostitutes (= porneia). Marriage is acceptable and approved for those incapable of remaining celibate. At most, it might be said to be good-for-them rather than good-in-itself. This is what the church has understood Paul to be saying and taught until very recent times, when, perceiving the institution of marriage to be under assault in the secular culture, it began to idealize marriage and to some extent idolize it.

lesbian sex as in quite a different category altogether from male homosexuality—as, indeed, these cultures regarded *women and men* very differently in most aspects of life. In particular, a Pharisee, such as Paul was in his youth, would never put these activities into the same class—or think of them as "similar."

Rather than making questionable surmises about what Saint Paul *might say*, given his particular gifts and limitations, we should instead look to him for the moral value of what he actually *said* concerning the role of sex within the context of the only kind of faithful, life-long sexual relationship with which we *know* he was familiar, as a means to cement the relationship and prevent wandering outside it: as what the old marriage rite referred to as "a remedy for fornication."

Moreover, now that *we* have a better and more accurate understanding of the reality of sexual orientation (quite apart from whether it is genetic, which is actually irrelevant to the discussion—after all, being *male* or *female* is genetic!), it makes more sense to apply the *underlying principles* of Paul's teaching accordingly when we can discern them—much as we apply other underlying principles of scriptural wisdom to changed cultural contexts. It is not so much for us, as productive as we might think the exercise to be, to imagine what Paul would say in the twenty-first century, but to apply *what he said* in his own time to *what we know* now: that same-sex couples are capable of forming loving, life-long, faithful and monogamous partnerships, and that

> the fruit of the Spirit is love, joy, peace, patience, kindness, generosity, faithfulness, gentleness, and self-control. There is no law against such things (Galatians 5:22–23).

It is better for the church, and for society, to encourage the recognizable biblical virtues of love, fidelity, and mutual support in same-sex relationships, than to hold all gay and lesbian persons to a rigid standard few heterosexuals are able to maintain.

Paul would very likely have seen same-sex marriage as deeply inappropriate, in his day and in his culture. We have no way of knowing if he'd change his mind on this (as he did on other things, as we know from his Damascus Road experience) were he to be around today to address the matter, with the advantage of the understandings of human nature that have accumulated since his time.

It is worth noting, however, that all of Paul's negative comments about male same-sexuality are linked with idolatry—either explicitly as in Romans 1, or by the use of *arsenokoitai*, the Greek equivalent to the Levitical prohibition tagged as *to'evah* in the anti-idolatry rhetoric of the Jewish law.

It is very likely that Paul's critique was addressed to what he perceived as approved among the Gentiles: either the orgies of the idolatrous cults or male pederasty; that is, the Greek idealization of the "normal" upbringing of a young man under the erotic tutelage of an adult. The Greeks did not approve of life-long sexual relationships between men, which were conceptually mapped against mixed-sex marriage or prostitution. The idea of a grown man taking the passive role was deeply offensive to the culture. There may well have been covert relationships based on equality rather than mapped against the uneven male-female marriage relationship in Graeco-Roman society—but these rarely rose to public awareness. In his time, Paul critiqued what the Greeks approved: orgy and pederasty.

That he would have joined them in condemning a male who persisted in the "passive" role may be what he was alluding to in his use of *malakoi* (1 Corinthians 6:9) is certainly possible. But Paul did not directly address the concept of life-long, faithful, mutual, monogamous same-sex relationships between adults.

Moreover, Paul is not with us at this moment, and the responsibility falls upon us to make the best use of what we have not only inherited from him, but accumulated in the centuries since he wrote.

A *summary*

Thus far I have examined the traditional rationale for Christian marriage and sought to examine the ways in which this rationale can be applied to same-sex relationships. There should be no doubt that from the secular perspective, the state has no compelling interest in prohibiting same-sex marriage any more than it would have in prohibiting mixed-sex marriage in which the couple is incapable of having children. On the contrary, the civil interest in a stable society represents a positive rationale for same-sex civil marriage, as a preventative to promiscuity (to the extent, of course, that people remain faithful to their vows: no covenant will of itself *cause* obedience).

When it comes to children, there is no indication (on the basis of many studies and meta-studies) that same-sex couples are any less able to raise their own, adopted or foster children than mixed-sex couples, regardless of any biological connection with the parents. Society provides ample role models apart from biological or foster parents—and in any case many children spend much of their childhood and infancy under the care of adults other than their parents. Clearly an increase in the number of stable same-sex couples could be a boon to finding loving homes for unwanted or orphaned children.

When it comes to the religious and moral values imputed to marriage, I have shown that the ability to bear children is universally held to be optional—that is, no Christian tradition of which I am aware requires fertility prior to marriage, or childbirth within marriage as a condition for its continuance. Procreation is thus not an essential element of marriage.

I have demonstrated that the concept of fleshly union is ambivalent, and that the argument against same-sexuality from a purported complementarity of the sexes is specious; and that same-sex couples can enjoy a mutual union that expresses joy, delight, and the self-giving love that is the object of marriage. I have shown that such relationships are capable of bearing symbolic weight in reflecting the goodness of God in relationship to the church, but more importantly the ideal of Christian love *within* the church. Finally, in this chapter, I have reflected briefly upon the stabilizing influence that the recognition of same-sex relationships might provide within ecclesiastical as well as social contexts, as well as the principle of *equity* in not requiring more of some than of others.

Although I have touched upon some of them, there are other purported scriptural objections to same-sexuality which remain to be addressed, and there is more to be said even on the texts upon which I have already commented. In the next chapters I will address the content and force of the scriptural case—both against and for same-sexuality—at greater length.

Questions for Discussion or Reflection

- *Do you think it would be either right or fair (or both) for the church to forbid anyone to marry an unbaptized person? A person of another race? To marry a second time after a spouse's death? To marry a second time after divorce?*

- *What about the state, in similar cases?*

- *What moral principle, if any, do you derive from this?*

- *Read through Wisdom chapters 13–16 and Romans 1. What similarities do you notice?*

8.
Scripture and its Witness

IT SOON BECOMES APPARENT IN READING THE WORK OF MAJOR OPPONENTS TO ANY change in the church's accommodation of same-sexuality that they are seeking to frame a larger argument, rather than merely citing the usual proof texts (as well as a few not-so-usual ones): a kind of Grand Unified Theory of sexuality that will cover all of the various sexual offenses listed in Scripture. There are, however, two primary problems with his approach.

The first is that the general attitude can be summarized as, "*Why* does the Scripture condemn homosexuality?" It is often said that the proof texts have made the basic case, which authors such as Robert Gagnon have laid out in exhaustive detail. But in the broadest sense they have not: contrary to their assertions, the Scripture does not "condemn homosexuality," or even "homosexual behavior" *in a general or absolute sense.*

As I have already noted in previous chapters (and will return to again) the primary missing factor in a "general condemnation of homosexuality" is the lack of any reference to female same-sexuality in the Law of Moses, and the fact that the one verse alleged to address this in Romans (1:26) very likely refers to something else. So the Scriptures (definitely the Hebrew Scriptures and very probably the New Testament—at least as they were widely understood in the first three centuries of the church) neither condemn nor penalize "homosexuality." Rather, the Law of Moses explicitly refers to one male homosexual act, and Paul may be alluding to this in a few places, including Romans 1.

The second problem is that the larger argument is often not based on the explicit language of the Law, but on a reading of the figurative language in Genesis—held to be permanently determinative in establishing God's plan for human sexuality. The "reasserter" critic, such as Robert Gagnon, sees predominantly through that lens, relating Leviticus (and Romans itself) back to Genesis at every opportunity. Gagnon, for example, relies on Genesis for an understanding that "difference" and "complementarity" are key to licit sexuality. In addition to applying this to homosexuality, he also seeks to draw the incest prohibitions in Leviticus 18 under this same rubric—that is, incest is illicit because the partners are not *different* enough from each other:

> Incest is wrong because, as Leviticus 18:6 states, it involves sexual intercourse with "the flesh of one's own flesh." In other words, it involves the attempted merger with someone who is already too much of a formal or structural same on a familial level (Gagnon 2007, I.B.).

Gagnon produces an essentially tautological definition—incest is wrong because it involves sex with a relative. This is rather like saying murder is wrong because it involves killing people.

Responses to this view

The first response to this theory is that it does not fit all (or even much) of the evidence. If, for example, *difference* were the defining requirement for licit sexuality, female homosexuality would also have been explicitly ruled out in the Law of Moses. It isn't. If *difference* were of primary importance, exogamy would be the preferred marriage structure under Jewish law. It isn't; in fact, marriage outside the people of Israel is condemned. Nor, as Gagnon recognizes but doesn't address, are all forms of incest explicitly forbidden, and more importantly some of those that are forbidden have nothing to do with consanguinity (the flesh of one's own flesh), but rather affinity—in which there is no fleshly connection between the parties (a father's wife not one's own mother, Leviticus 18:8; an aunt by marriage or daughter-in-law or sister-in-law, Leviticus 18:14–16.) One might go further and observe that if *difference* were in itself the basis for licitness, then bestiality would be permissible—after all, what could be more different? Needless to say, it isn't.

◠ Another kind of sodomy

The marriage of Christian to non-Christian is contrary to Scripture (1 Corinthians 7:39, perhaps 2 Corinthians 6:14—"do not become *heterozygountes*"—yoked to someone different; the provisions for "unbelieving partners" at 1 Corinthians 7:14–15 relate to marriages contracted *before* either party was baptized). Tertullian borrowed an expression from Jude's reference to Sodom—"strange flesh" (Jude 1:7)—to oppose marriage of a Christian with one unbaptized (*To His Wife* 2.2). So it is striking that the Episcopal Church should have embraced such a departure from the church's traditional teaching on marriage with so little notice being taken of it, through the amendment to the mar-

SCRIPTURE AND ITS WITNESS

It is important to note that once we get beyond issues of sexuality it does not appear that *difference* is a hallmark of the Levitical code in any respect; on the contrary there appears to be a strong bias towards *likeness* or *similarity*. Immediately following the commandment to "love your neighbor as yourself" (Leviticus 19:18) — in itself an appeal to like loving like — is the commandment not to allow animals to breed with different kinds, or to sow a field with two different kinds of seed, or to put on a garment made of two different materials. (Leviticus 19:19; see also Deuteronomy 22:9). Similarity, rather than difference, is emphasized.

Similarity also plays a part in the second and more significant response to the assertion concerning *difference*. Such a theory leads to greater difficulty with what Genesis 2 has to say, for the creation account in Genesis 2 simply does not emphasize Eve's *difference from* Adam, but as noted in an earlier chapter, her *likeness to* him: she *is* flesh of his flesh and bone of his bone. Adam rejects the animals (which though made from earth as Adam was, are fundamentally *unlike* him) as unsuitable partners and chooses instead the woman, who is made from his own substance, *the one most like himself*. That this is the correct reading is shown by Jesus' use of this passage as the cornerstone for his doctrine of the indissolubility of marriage: what God has joined together (capable of proper joining not because *different* from each other, but because of the *same* flesh and bone) is not to be put asunder. The couple *become one flesh* because they *already share that flesh*. That is what Genesis says, and that is how Jesus applies it. Interestingly enough, even Pope John Paul II came to the same conclusion (though he would go on to apply it very differently):

> In this way, we find ourselves almost at the heart of the anthropological reality that has the name "body." The words of Genesis 2:23 speak of it directly and for the first time in the following terms: "flesh of my flesh and bone of my bones." The male-man uttered these words, as if it were only at the sight of the woman that he was able to identify and call by name what makes them visibly similar to each other, and at the same time what manifests humanity (4).

riage canons in 1946. This amendment permitted marriage in which only one of the parties was baptized. In examining the General Convention *Journal* for that year, it appears that this anomaly slipped through with almost no debate (*Journal* 1946, 442f). Those who objected to the change in 1946 did so on the grounds that it is "implicit in the nature of Holy Matrimony that it be solemnized only for baptized Christians" (White & Dykman I, 414). This is clearly the position of the Eastern Orthodox who regard marriage with an unbaptized person to be incapable of liturgical celebration in a eucharistic context (Meyendorff, 29f). The idea of "Christian marriage" seems strained when one of the partners (who are understood to be "the ministers of the sacrament") is not a Christian.

So this attempt to find out a "reason" for the prohibition on a male same-sex act (not all homosexuality, as is claimed) fails. A Grand Unified Theory that will explain why some sexual acts are forbidden under Jewish law while others are permitted is perhaps possible; but we can rule out the theory of difference and likeness on these two grounds.

Other theories

More consistent efforts at this involve either the concept of a divine command which is to be obeyed quite apart from any reason for it (a view favored in classical rabbinic Judaism), or the more anthropological approach (favored in present-day Jewish reflection on the subject) which sees the various laws as deriving from social constructions in a particular society or set of societies, constructions which may explain and unify some of the various laws, or at least demonstrate the process by which they came to be. Thus the prohibition on incest with one's sister-in-law, Leviticus 18:16 (and its mandated violation in the case of a childless widow, Genesis 38:8, Deuteronomy 25:5) is not based on a purported concept of sameness or difference, but on concerns—both in the prohibition and in the mandate—about kinship and inheritance and avoiding the entanglement of multiple relationships.

Another important aspect of the sexual laws in general is that, far from representing a recognizable *moral* framework (in which all people are treated as essentially equal moral actors), the Mosaic sexual and marriage laws are strikingly asymmetric with regard to men and women: not only in the lack of the prohibition on female homosexuality, but (for example) in defining adultery. Under the Law of Moses a man can only violate another man's marriage; a woman only her own. That is, a man could have licit relations with a harlot, or take a concubine or a second wife, but not have intercourse with another man's wife. Similarly, the Law considers it a serious crime for a man to remarry his divorced wife if she has married another man in the interim. (Deuteronomy 24:1–4). I doubt anyone today would give such a rule any notice—they might even encourage it as a restoration of the original marriage. This actually happened with my paternal grandmother, yet there was no objection or outcry in the family, church, or state. Yet the Law of Moses opposes such a remarriage in very harsh terms, applying to it the same expression (*to'evah* = abomination) that is attached to a male same-sexual act in Leviticus 18:22. Again, it would appear that the primary concern is not *moral* but has to do with the entanglements of kinship and inheritance rights, seen almost exclusively in terms of preserving the integrity of the male line and security of the father's identity, which might be in some doubt in such a case—with a related purpose to preserve the holy *land* and the *inheritance* bestowed ultimately by the hand of God. Hence, most of these laws (as well as many others) refer to the land and its sanctity as a possession to be handed down everlastingly. This is the language that rings through the Torah, the promise to Abraham and his seed forever: that they should have a land that was holy to them and to God.

If a Grand Unified Theory is to be sought, it more likely lies in the direction of understanding the sexual and marriage laws in relation to the separateness of Israel from the nations, their distinction in being deliberately unlike those nations, charged with preserving the holiness of the land and the inheritance rights that guarantee it. Biblical scholars such as Jacob Milgrom (*Leviticus*) have written extensively in this quest, and this approach has the virtue of explaining much more than the employment of Genesis 1–2 as a touchstone for understanding sexual morality.

Applying these theories

This may help also to explain why female homosexuality is not mentioned in the Law. If it were true that Genesis offers the key to understanding human sexuality, based on the union of differences, then we would expect to find both male and female same-sexuality equally prohibited, just as incest and bestiality are forbidden to men and women alike, and all in the same chapters of Leviticus (18 and 20) dealing with a male homosexual act. What does the Law actually say and what can we learn from it in seeking an explanation for the omission?

There is only one explicit reference to any form of same-sexuality in the Law: the act is described at Leviticus 18:22 and the penalty at Leviticus 20:13. It first says, "With a male do not bed the beddings of a woman." The wording of the second passage is slightly different: "A man who beds a male the beddings of a woman" followed by the penalty for both. In both cases the word *to'evah* (abomination) is used to categorize the offense. I will address this passage at greater length in a later chapter. For the present, I want to consider why there is no reciprocal prohibition (or punishment) for a woman who "beds a woman the beddings of a man."

The plural "beddings of a woman" refer to "the usual way" and "the unusual way." But no plural would be used in the context of female-female sex—nor even the singular. For from a Hebrew perspective there is no way for a woman to "bed" another woman, usual or unusual, as least as far as the Rabbis were concerned, since for them sex was about the insertion of the penis— the organ that defines what a man is. When the phrase "bedding of a male" is used, it always refers, in the singular, to a woman who is no longer a virgin—who has been "bedded." This is "knowing a man by male bedding"—*yoda'at ish l'mishkav zakar.* (Numbers 31:17,18,35; Judges 21:11)

I think the reason is quite simple, and it tells us a good deal about how Hebrew culture saw sex, which supplements the notion of male primacy and inheritance. Put simply, sex is about something males "do" and females "allow." As the language of Romans 1 suggests, men "use" women. The wording of the bestiality prohibition is indicative: men "lay" or "bed" an animal, but women "stand" or "lie down" before an animal to "present" themselves to it. The biblical vocabulary is different for men and women, reflecting the difference between what a man or a woman would do with an animal. This distinction is preserved in the Talmud, where the Rabbis do address the question of male active and passive bestiality at bSanhedrin 15a. But when they come to address how men "use" an animal, they refer to "natural" and "unnatural" bestiality—that is, *using* a female animal in one of the two "ways"—and women are still referred to as allowing an animal to *make use of them* in either way (bSanhedrin 55a). So the lack of an equivalent prohibition on female same-sexuality is based in part on the inability (from the Hebrew perspective) of a woman to act as a man towards another woman.

This also explains why, as we saw above, that later rabbinic law holds that a woman who engaged in sexual relations with a woman outside of marriage (since the matter was not addressed by Scripture and there was no explicit commandment against it) was not judged to have committed adultery or harlotry, but rather was punished for disobedience.

So it would seem that there are ways to understand the asymmetry in the Law within its own context and without appeal to Genesis: as the Rabbis would see it, lesbian sex isn't sex (there is no intercourse or "bedding"), because sex requires a male.

In conclusion

This, of course, leaves us with what appears to be a clear biblical prohibition on at least one form of male homosexual activity, and a penalty of capital punishment. Obviously the church no longer demands the latter as much as some in it deplore the former. But is this a proper attitude to take towards this text, and the other texts which appear to cast male same-sex behavior in negative terms? In the next chapters I will address how we might best engage this and other texts, and the Scripture as a whole.

Questions for Discussion or Reflection

- *How might you explain the relative comfort many heterosexual men have in thinking about (or even observing pornography portraying) lesbian sexuality, compared with their discomfort in thinking about or being exposed to male-male sex?*

- *Read through the incest prohibitions in Leviticus 18. Do you see anything missing? (It might help to draw a "family tree" or diagram.) Compare this with the prohibitions in Leviticus 20. How might you explain any omissions or inconsistencies between them, or modern incest laws?*

9.
Perplexity and Guidance

The Argument

In spite of claims and calls to order our life in accord with the Bible, no one actually does so—at least not completely. Scripture contains contradictions, or at the very least tensions, between various commandments; there are corrections, revisions, expansions, and terminations to what is required; there are commandments no one *can* follow because of changes in circumstance and history; there are commandments few would defend in our day, or which have fallen to disuse, which were norms in former times. In short, all people pick and choose the commandments to which they accord authoritative status, either for themselves or for others.

Many criteria are offered for the choices made, but the criteria can be as arbitrary or perplexing as the laws and customs to which they are supposed to give order. My purpose in this chapter is to begin to explore some of these criteria.

◌ A Contradiction Close to Home

Anglicans became embroiled in a conflict over incest, introduced by the biblical prohibition (Leviticus 18:16) and mandate (Deuteronomy 25:5) concerning a man marrying his brother's widow. This caused a good bit of trouble for Henry VIII. Is there a "rationality" to prohibiting a man marrying his brother's widow, while, at the same time allowing him to marry his wife's sister after his wife's death? (Leviticus 18:18) At what point do we acknowledge that cultural influences are at play, and in some cases, dominant?

The dilemma

Scripture says a great many things about a great many topics. But what it meant to those who first recorded it and what it means for us may not be the same thing. This distinction is of importance if we are to be serious in our claim to see in Scripture not only the revelation of historical faith, but a present guide to holy living—for while we believe it to be both, the two are not necessarily the same. There are subjects about which Scripture says little or nothing explicit, yet which we feel to be very important (abortion, for example); there are topics about which Scripture says a good deal but with which we are scarcely concerned today (such as the consumption of meat that has not been completely purged of blood.) Acts which Scripture forbids or demands with lapidary clarity and considerable force are commonly committed or neglected today with scant hint of impropriety, or even awareness. There is at work some less than clearly defined process by which Scripture is put to use in framing a way to live what the believer holds to be a "biblical" or holy life, in spite of these inconsistencies in practice.

ᗡ Is All Scripture Inspired?

Second Timothy 3:16 is offered as a proof text that all of Scripture is inspired by God. Leaving to one side the self-referential objection Hooker noted long since, as to "what Scripture can teach us the sacred authority of the Scripture" (III.8.13), we are left with the question of what Paul was referring to when he wrote to Timothy.

For instance, does "all" scripture refer to its individual parts; or to all scripture taken as a whole? (As has often been said, "the Bible is the Word of God and not the words of God.") A more likely possibility is that Paul is referring to the scriptures mentioned in the preceding verse—the ones Timothy grew up with, that is, the text of the Bible as it was in Timothy's youth, which clearly would not have included the New Testament. Even the "Old Testament" was not as settled in Timothy's day as we find it today—the Bible of the early church (the Septuagint) included books that were later disallowed by the Rabbis and removed from their canon of Scripture.

Christians valued that Bible primarily because, as the gospel attests, and as Paul may be referencing, it was believed to prophesy Christ's coming—and to teach "unto salvation" in Christ. The value of the Law and the Prophets rested primarily in this instructive capacity, much like John the Baptist (himself analogized to the prophet Elijah) who points to the Christ and then steps aside as a good bridegroom's friend will.

So, noting that there is no verb in verse 3:16—not that the Greek requires it—we might better translate verses 14 through 17 as a single logical thought:

This exposes one of the weaknesses of a so-called Divine Command ethic (one species of deontological ethics, which focus on duty or obedience). This is particularly problematic for those who wish to see Scripture and its commands to be the Word of God in a literal and particular sense, for it immediately becomes a question of *which* divine commands will be obeyed. For, as noted above, no one "lives by the Scripture" in all its detailed instructions. This was documented recently by A.J. Jacobs, in his well-titled *The Year of Living Biblically: One Man's Humble Quest to Follow the Bible as Literally as Possible*. He found, for example, that there are any number of biblical commandments with which compliance was virtually if not actually impossible in the present day. As he noted in a radio interview, the closest he could come to carrying out the mandate to hold slaves was to hire an intern. Thus something the text said *to others in ancient times and circumstances* had to be adapted in order to be fulfilled *by Jacobs now*.

The effective impossibility of attaining perfection in or by following the Law was a primary issue for Paul in his Letter to the Romans. (Those who use the first chapter of Romans as a proof text have underestimated the significance of this

> But continue in the things which you have learned and been assured of, knowing of whom you learned them; and that from youth you have known the holy scriptures which are able to make you wise unto salvation through faith which is in Christ Jesus—every scripture given by inspiration of God, and profitable for doctrine, for reproof, for correction, for instruction in righteousness—so that the man of God may be perfect, thoroughly furnished unto all good works.

Every seems to be a better translation here than *all*, and this emphasizes that Paul may not be talking about the Old Testament as a whole, or its individual parts, but in particular texts that related to salvation in Christ. This is in keeping with a similar turn of phrase from the gospel, where Jesus, "beginning with Moses and all the prophets," interprets to the disciples "the things about himself in *all the scriptures*" (Luke 24:27).

If we are to take the Scripture seriously, it is important that we understand it, not only in its intent (so far as we can construct it), but even more in how we apply it. There is a huge difference between asserting as a matter of fact, "All Scripture is inspired by God," and taking, "Make use of the scripture you read in your youth, every God-breathed Scripture useful for teaching . . ." as a piece of advice to young Timothy (and by extension, to us in the church). This goes for all of the other Scripture as well: both the "God-breathed" parts and those portions that Hooker referred to as "merely historical," or those that are plainly legal and, even if God-spoken, restricted to the time, place, and people to whom they were delivered, and subject to change and reinterpretation by God in Christ and the church.

aspect of Paul's argument.) In practice, Scripture as a whole serves as a resource to the church, which, in making use of that resource, accords certain portions a higher and more authoritative status on the basis of their coherence with the needs of those to whom the text has been delivered, as it were, second hand—since none of us is the recipient of direct revelation, but only the inherited revelation committed to the church and passed along to us by means of Scripture.

And that revelation, fixed as it is in a written text, itself a rich collection of various documents composed at different times, to different ends, by different people and for different hearers, will have to be engaged by the faithful of the church in each generation, who will find themselves facing the task of receiving the revelation, and resolving the contradictions and tensions manifest in the Scripture itself.

Wait . . . Contradictions? . . . in Scripture?

Many, particularly the more conservative among us, would like to believe there are no contradictions or tensions in Scripture. After all, if it is the Word of God, how could God contradict himself?

The truth of the matter is that even such as are most ready to deplore making "one sentence of Scripture repugnant to another" will do exactly that when faced with a dilemma. For example, when it came to "the King's Great Matter," Cranmer & Company found it convenient, under significant monarchial pressure, to hold that the mandate of Deuteronomy 25:5 (the Levirate law, that when a man's brother dies childless he is to take the widow as his wife—something the monarch had done in the case of his brother Arthur's widow, Catharine of Aragon, with the express permission of the pope) was to be overturned in favor of the prohibition in Leviticus 18:16 (in accord with the monarch's troubled conscience and the failure of his brother's widow to produce a male heir). He even appealed to Leviticus 20:21, which stated the divine penalty for a man taking his brother's wife to be childlessness—an example of the elasticity in applying the text, since, of course, Henry and Catharine were not childless, though she had not produced a male heir.

One can indulge in such Anglican Fudge as much as one likes—and Cranmer may be credited with the first recipe for this rich, chewy ambiguity. But there is no use pretending that these texts are *not* in tension with one another, capable of creative interpretation in a tendentious cause, that the King's Men were at pains to resolve the tension, and that other solutions would have been possible. An example of the latter would have been to take the Levirate law as a specific legitimate exception to the general rule against incest-by-affinity, eminently applicable in Henry's case as the pope had agreed, since inheritance was at issue. Of course, that isn't the finding the monarch wanted; and as Upton Sinclair once observed, "It is difficult to get a man to understand something when his salary depends on his not understanding it." Unfortunately, it was also impossible to convince the pope that he had erred in granting an exception to the church's long-standing rejection of the Levirate law. Even had the pope been so inclined, the political issue rendered calm theological reflection quite beside the point.

Even in the midst of similar tensions of ecclesiastical power and politics, our task is still to make decisions on how we are to address the questions we now face, in order to make reasonable and holy choices about how to live—one hopes, avoiding the pressure from political considerations, lest, like the deer in the proverbial headlights we never reach the cooling springs of grace but end up on the grill and windshield of judgment. It is up to us, as the church, to use the tools at our disposal to find our way to discern the applicability of the many, and sometimes difficult to reconcile, commandments with which Scripture presents us.

The basic tool: Reason

In this interaction within the church, through the Holy Spirit, the Scripture comes alive in every generation. Every society, culture, and church that embraces the Scripture thus also exercises a form of selective critique of that Scripture, even while seeking to a greater or lesser degree to conform to the view of Scripture thus organized and understood.

Richard Hooker attested that the Scripture is neither self-authenticating nor self-interpreting: it must be approached through and by means of Reason—which is more than deductive reason (though it includes it) and involves notions we would understand as "common sense" or "rationality."

> Unto the word of God . . . we do not add reason as a supplement of any maim or defect therein, but as a necessary instrument, without which we could not reap by the Scripture's perfection that fruit and benefit which it yieldeth . . . If knowledge were possible without discourse of natural reason, why should none be found capable thereof but only men; nor men till such time as they come unto ripe and full ability to work by reasonable understanding? (III.8.10f)

Hooker also recognized both the misapplication of proof texts (which are often mis-translated or removed from the textual and contextual position that might help a more accurate understanding) and the sweeping generalizations which make Scripture appear to say more than it does. Such claims do no credit either to the claimants or to the Scripture. As Hooker noted,

> . . . As incredible praises given unto men do often abate and impair the credit of their deserved commendation, so we must likewise take great heed, lest in attributing unto Scripture more than it can have, the incredibility of that do cause even those things which indeed it hath most abundantly to be less reverently esteemed. (II.8)

So a sifting process is at work, by which any given culture or society or church, even while embracing the Bible as a whole, also separates out portions of it based on various modes of division and distinction. This process can be conscious and reasonable, but it can also happen under the influence of culture or external events.

The "Classical" Anglican Distinction

The traditional Anglican distinction between moral, civil, and ceremonial laws, while having the virtue of a kind of common sense to it (as some of the commandments are clearly related to ceremony, and others clearly to morals, and still others to civil matters) does not bear close examination if one is to take the next Anglican step and say that Christians *are not bound to follow* the civil and ceremonial laws, but only the moral ones. For, while Jesus and the Apostolic Church, as recorded in Scripture, did specifically set aside certain ceremonial and civil laws, and the course of history made some of the Hebrew laws incapable of enforcement (the destruction of the Temple rendering all of the laws pertaining to Temple worship beyond compliance), the Hebrew Law itself does not distinguish between these various sorts of commandments on this basis; all commandments alike are to be obeyed; there is no suggestion that some are *moral* and others "merely" *ceremonial*. Read through Leviticus and you will find things you will identify as high moral principles cheek by jowl with distinctly ceremonial or ritual requirements. Just to give one example my eye literally happened to light upon as I glanced at the page at random: the death penalty for a daughter of a priest who prostitutes herself is immediately followed by prohibitions concerning the priest's hair (or headgear) and vestments. (Leviticus 21:9–10) The whole passage is intimately connected with *holiness*—and so raises the question, is holiness moral or ceremonial—or both?

So the "classical Anglican" distinction, in this case, does not well serve—in particular because some of the very matters under discussion in our present debates arguably involve ritual, civil and ceremonial dimensions (ordination and marriage) as much as they do moral ones.

For example, even though Hooker explicitly refers to the Decalogue as "the moral law," I very much doubt a contemporary moralist would see idolatry as a *moral* issue; I would imagine that even in the height of the missionary efforts of the nineteenth century, few would have held that Hindus were *immoral* on the basis of their iconography, even if held to be mistaken in their beliefs. Idolatry, to our minds, is not a *moral* issue but a *doctrinal* one. But this distinction obviously cannot be made within the context of the Decalogue, the Prophets, the Wisdom tradition or Romans 1: idolatry is, in fact, the root of all immorality!

Similarly, if we take a few steps more into the Decalogue: few would consider Sabbath-breaking a major *moral* issue today, though they did in the nineteenth century, in spite of the fact that, in one sense, Christians have been deliberate Sabbath-breakers from the time the church mandated observing Sunday, the Lord's Day, rather than the Sabbath, and criminalized observance of the Jewish Sabbath (Council of Laodicea, Canon 29). For Hooker it was, of course, still a moral issue, though he separated the morality from the specificity of *which* day was to be kept free from labor, in itself a neat rationalization of the church's earlier decision with no explicit scriptural warrant:

> The moral law requiring therefore a seventh part throughout the age of the whole world to be that way employed, although with us the day be changed in regard of a new revolution begun by our Saviour Christ, yet the same proportion of time continueth which was before, because in reference to the benefit of creation and now much more of renovation thereunto added by him which was Prince of the world to come, we are bound to account the sanctification of one day in seven a duty which God's immutable law doth exact for ever (V.70.9).

In this we see a supposedly "immutable" law reinterpreted in such a way as effectively to set aside the specific form of the original law, which was to observe a day of rest at the end of the week (in imitation of God's rest after creation) rather than at the beginning. One wonders why similar flexibility in addressing our present debates on same-sexuality are so difficult—if the common factor can be understood as loving permanent relationship, transferred, in this case, not from one day to another, but from one couple to another.

Lest anyone note that male same-sexuality was harshly condemned in the Law, need I add that treating the Sabbath *as any other day* was a capital offense, and merely doing work on it entailed excision from the holy people (Exodus

---

⌣ To be cut off

A number of crimes under Jewish law, including some of the sexual crimes—those involving incest and sex during menstruation (Leviticus 20:17,18)—as well as eating fat or blood (Leviticus 7:25,27), or Molech worship or resort to mediums (Leviticus 20:3–6), all entail the punishment of being "cut off" (*karet*). This is no small matter, and was considered to be a very serious penalty. It could mean exile, though some authorities interpreted it to imply the death penalty (and in the case of Molech worship, included it). Others felt that it meant a punishment only God would impose, whether by shortening one's life or in being cursed to die childless, and thus without heritage. More seriously, some held *karet* to imply a "cutting off of the soul in the future life, in the hereafter," the consequence of a crime in which "unlike all others, death does not serve as an expiation . . .; hence, the culprit has no share in the world to come" unless some physical punishment is added. (Goldin, 40–41)

31:14); the text is abundantly clear, yet few in our day would consider violation of either Saturday or Sunday to be serious moral failings. In short, this distinction between moral and non-moral appears not to be a very profitable avenue, if we are to attempt to deal with the text itself, rather than suppositions about "What is really moral?"—which, depending on the answer, tends to beg the question, "it is moral because I think it so to be."

A *better way*

There are, in the text itself, various distinctions between and among the various laws. I would like to begin by highlighting some of these divisions, and suggest that these categories are actually useful in determining the applicability of the texts raised in the present discussion.

Some might accuse me of a "deconstructionist" approach in this, by which they mean something like "breaking it down to undermine its authority." On the contrary, I am proposing a careful and objective analysis in examination of the various parts, in order to come to a better and more accurate understanding of the whole Scripture and of its authoritative claim upon us, and to explore reasonable grounds upon which we might justifiably say—since we do say, and I hope with some justification—of portions of Scripture, "This no longer applies," or "This applies only to certain circumstances." The use of reason and reliance on the authority of the church as an appropriate interpreter of Scripture in this exercise is evident. The church does, in its explication and application of Scripture, effectively limit the scope of the sacred text.

We have already seen that no one observes the law in its entirety. The question is, Do we choose the parts we obey out of conviction, or out of mere convenience? Or worse, Do we selectively find ways to avoid laws that apply to ourselves, while imposing strict observance of laws that apply to others? There is, in all of this, a need to recall the requirement for honest weights and measures, and that unequal dealing is an abomination to God. To put a thumb on the scale when judging others, while making light of one's own offenses, is in the long run a costly course.

Labels, labels, labels

Some might well observe that the law on male same-sexual activity is serious because it is referred to as "abomination." That is certainly a weighty word, and we would be wrong to think that this meant it was a trivial matter, simply on the basis of the fact that it is also applied to things we might *now* consider trivial—such as the eating of certain foods (Deuteronomy 14:3) or the remarriage of a man to a wife he divorced but who since married another man (Deuteronomy 24:4).

However, by looking at the range of offenses to which this label is attached, we may see a pattern emerge, and by looking at the *other* laws that bear this label, see to what class the offenses belong. Here is a list of occurrences of *to'evah* in the Hebrew scriptures. I invite you to look them up to see the areas of concern. Here I will italicize those referring to ritual or cultural matters having to do with diet or idols or idolatry, and boldface those having to do with sex. (Some are very general summaries referring to all that has gone before, and these I leave unmarked.)

- In the Books of Moses: *Genesis 43:32; 46:34; Exodus 8:22;* **Leviticus 18:22,** 26f, 29f; **20:13;** *Deuteronomy 7:25f; 12:31; 13:13–15; 14:3f; 17:1, 4; 18:9–12;* 20:18; **22:5; 23:18f; 24:4;** 25:14–16; 27:15; 32:16;
- In historical books: **1 Kings 14:24;** *2 Kings 16:3; 21:2, 11; 23:13; 2 Chronicles 28:3; 33:2; 34:33; 36:8, 14; Ezra 9:1, 11, 14;*
- In the Psalms and Proverbs: Psalm 88:8–9; Proverbs 3:32; 6:16; 8:7; 11:1, 20; 12:22; 13:19; 15:8, 9, 26; 16:5, 12; **17:15;** 20:10, 23; 21:27; 24:9; 26:25; 28:9; 29:27 (Most of the uses in the poetic books are figurative expansions; though Proverbs, following Leviticus 19:36, really has it in for dishonest weights and measures);
- As to the Prophets: *Isaiah 1:13; 41:24; 44:19;* Jeremiah 2:7; 6:15; 7:10; 8:12; 16:18; *32:35; 44:4, 22;* Ezekiel 5:9, 11; 6:9, 11; 7:3f, 8f, 20; 8:6, 9, **13, 15,** 17; 9:4; 11:18, 21; 12:16; 14:6; **16:2, 22, 36, 43, 47, 50f, 58;** *18:12f* (including lending money at interest), 24; 20:4; 22:2, **11; 23:36; 33:26,** 29; 36:31; 43:8; *44:6f, 13;* ***Malachi 2:11*** (throughout the prophetic writings there is a strong linkage of idolatry with harlotry and infidelity, usually marked with the label *to'evah*).

As this list makes clear, the dominant meaning of "abomination" (*to'evah*) has to do with matters of ritual and cult, in particular anything to do with idols, idolatry, or wrong worship. The connection of harlotry (*z'nut, porneia*) with idolatry also figures prominently in this list, and the two were strongly linked in the minds of the biblical authors. We will return to this connection later in examining Romans 1 and looking at the meaning of *porneia* in the New Testament.

In the meantime, it seems clear that the prohibition on male same-sexuality in Leviticus 18 and 20 is marked with a rather clear label, *to'evah hi* = "It is abomination." Is this then to be understood as a moral wrong absolutely, or, in keeping with the normative meaning of *to'evah*, as ritual transgression, primarily associated with idol worship?

It might be helpful to look precisely at the primary law, as articulated in the Decalogue, against idol worship itself:

> You shall not make for yourself an idol, whether in the form of anything that is in heaven above, or that is on the earth beneath, or that is in the water under the earth. You shall not bow down to them or worship them (Exodus 20:4–5a).

As Jewish tradition developed, this law came to be understood not as a pro-scription on visually representative art—as it is still understood in portions of Islam, and was briefly understood by some Christians during the Iconoclast movement (which arose at the beginning of Islam's Golden Age). In the Jewish tradition, it is not the *making* of images that is the problem, but *bowing down to worship them*. (A similar distinction was made in the settlement of the Iconoclast controversy.) The thing in itself is morally neutral—as Paul would later affirm, "An idol is nothing"(1 Corinthians 8:4, 10:19)—but to *worship* an idol is a grave sin. So it may be possible to read the prohibition in Leviticus 18 concerning male-male intercourse as binding to the extent it is connected with the idolatrous cult, understanding the two clauses as linked by an implicit "when"—"You shall not lie with a male as with a woman when it is *to'evah*, i.e., connected with idola-try." That is, it is as part of the pagan "world" that the act is condemned.

Some have suggested that this is supported by the references in Deuteronomy 23:18–19 concerning the "hire of a dog" (understood by some to mean "a male prostitute"—though the Rabbis thought it meant a *literal* dog and a reference to bestiality at bTemurah 30a-b—as an offering not to be brought to the temple) or those in 1 Kings 14:24 (and 15:12, 22:46, and 2 Kings 23:7) concerning the "male cult prostitutes" (*qadeshim* = "Sodomites" in the KJV, but better understood from the root meaning as "dedicated ones" or "votaries"—dedicated to *what* a matter of considerable conjecture). The Talmud records R. Ishmael using the latter verses to prove that the Levitical prohibition concerned both the active and passive parties in a male same-sex act (bSanhedrin 54b). More recently, some scholars have chal-lenged this traditional identification of the figures in Deuteronomy 23 and the his-torical books as either male or female cult *prostitutes*, and express doubt about

ꙮ Is *to'evah* a moral absolute?

The moral valence of something labeled as *to'evah* appears not to be absolute, but related to the context. It is subjective rather than objective. That is, it is always about *to whom* something is "abominable." As Rabbi Geller *et al.* note, drawing upon some of the examples in the list of references, including the fact that Egyptians find shepherds to be "an abomination" (Genesis 46:34):

> The term is not used to describe the inherent or universal quality of an item or human action, it expresses its culturally or religiously determined value in a given society and identifies specific material objects or behaviors that are denied to its members.
>
> Scripture views some *to'evoth*, however, as abhorrent not only to a given society but to God. The falsifying of weights and measures is an inequity that places the vio-

whether such prostitution ever existed. Perhaps these were a class of clergy or dedicated worshipers, who served the idolatrous temple in the same way Levites served God's temple. Whatever these persons were about, *it was connected with idolatry and cult*—hence the insistence on their removal by the reformers. The real point is the connection—in the Jewish mind of biblical and post-biblical times—between male same-sexuality and idolatry, and whatever recent researches may have demonstrated about the actual significance of the *qadeshim*, they were long believed to be male and female cult prostitutes. This understanding may well lie behind Paul's thinking in Romans and his use of the term *arsenokoitai* in 1 Corinthians 6:9—where it appears to be a translation of the Hebrew term for what was going on in Leviticus 18:22, and labeled as *to'evah: mishkav zakur* = "male bedder." Moreover, when we look at the actual range of meaning applied to the word *to'evah* it is clearly located within that same mental geography.

So, is Leviticus condemning *all* male-same sex relations (as the tradition would have it to this day in a significant portion of Orthodox Judaism) or is this a reference to a practice that was condemned chiefly due to its connection with idolatry, and to which it no longer applies? If the latter is true, what relevance, if any, might that have for us today concerning same-sex relationships between Christians?

Don't be so shellfish

Finally, based on the reference in Deuteronomy 14:3ff ("Do not eat any *to'evah*," spelled out in some detail), I would like to address what Kendall Harmon has caricatured as, "The Shellfish Argument." According to him, this argument goes, "You have noted that Leviticus is against same sex practice, but Leviticus says we

lator in this category although other forms of commercial cheating do not. Most often the phrase is used to describe idols and idolatry as abhorrent to God (Deuteronomy 7:25, 18:9–12, 23:19, 27:15) but so is cross-dressing (Deuteronomy 22:5), while homosexual intercourse is not identified in this way. And even when an object or action is designated in the Torah as a *to'evah l'adonai*, there is the recognition that non-Israelite societies may not react with the abhorrence felt by Israelites or their God. (16)

It would also be good to remember the distinctions Jesus made concerning the source of moral right and wrong—from the inner dispositions of the heart rather than in external acts. As he said to the Pharisees who ridiculed him, "You are those who justify yourselves in the sight of others; but God knows your hearts; for what is prized by human beings is an *abomination* in the sight of God."

should not eat shellfish. So how could we possibly listen to Leviticus?" That is, of course, a straw man, similar in some respects to the "slippery slope" argument; but is not in fact the substance of the real argument. Which is: "The law on forbidden diet has changed, and we are now seeking to examine if the law on same-sexuality is closer, in its bases, to the dietary law or to laws concerning matters that we agree represent moral principles and are still binding upon us." So the real question is about the nature of the dietary law—how described or marked off in Scripture— and whether same-sexuality is more like the dietary law as Scripture describes it, or more like the things we all acknowledge to be wrong, like theft or murder.

This sobriquet does not really address the scriptural question before us, nor is it confined to Leviticus. It is true that Leviticus 11:10–12 prohibits the consumption of shellfish, in English translation referred to as an "abomination." The Hebrew here, however, is not *to'evah*, but *sheqetz*. To be fair, this word has a similar range of meaning, including its associations with idolatry, and appears in a doublet with the root of *to'evah* in Deuteronomy 7:26. However, in Deuteronomy, similar restrictions on shellfish receive the full-blown label *to'evah* (Deuteronomy 14:3ff). Note as well, that as Deuteronomy 14:21 makes abundantly clear, these laws are intended to mark Israel off *as a holy nation*; some foods are not *morally* wrong for anyone else, and Israelites are free to sell foods forbidden to *them* to resident aliens and foreigners, "for *you* are a people holy to the LORD your God." (Though compare Leviticus 17:15.)

So the argument is not, "Since we have tossed out one biblical law we can toss out any law," but rather, "Since we have discerned that we are no longer bound by a law clearly labeled as belonging to a particular category of offense by Scrip-

God's Shellfish Argument

The "Shellfish Argument" also appears in Acts 10, and God is the one making it. It is an instructive story, and should give one pause before dismissing the other "shellfish" argument entirely; since it appears that this is precisely the argument with which God confronted Peter, when he showed him all the unclean animals and told him to eat. Peter rightly understood that this wasn't about food, but about people, and how one ought to treat them: not as unclean, but as loved by God—and by accepting God's argument thereby opening the way of salvation for all of us Gentiles.

So it isn't about shellfish, it isn't about food and drink, about commandments regarding things that "perish with use" and which we are told we should not "taste, touch, or handle"—commandments that have an "appearance of piety" (Col. 2:21–23). Rather, it is about respecting the dignity of every human being as much as God does, and considering the possibility—as difficult as that may be—that the church has had it wrong for all these years, and missed the point God made and Peter understood.

ture itself, can we *consider* if we are also able to feel ourselves no longer to be bound by another commandment with *exactly the same label.*"

This is, in my opinion, a very different argument. More importantly, it is the actual argument we are having, not a straw man or slippery slope.

Law and Narrative

A second distinction can be made between matters specifically expressed as laws, as opposed to ideas derived from historical or prophetic passages. Hooker addressed this distinction in the debates of his time:

> I wish they did well observe, with whom nothing is more familiar than to plead in these causes, "the law of God," "the word of the Lord;" who notwithstanding when they come to allege what word and what law they mean, their common ordinary practice is to quote by-speeches in some historical narration or other, and to urge them as if they were written in most precise exact form of law . . . When that which the word of God doth but deliver historically, we construe without any warrant as if it were legally meant, and so urge it further than we can prove that it was intended; do we not add to the laws of God, and make them in number seem more than they are? (III.5)

Thus there is a clear distinction between, for example, the explicit and narrow legal restriction on male same-sexuality in Leviticus 18/20, as opposed to the narrative in Genesis 19. The former is expressed in an "exact form of law" including an explicit penalty; but the latter is a page out of history, recounting something no doubt to be condemned (whether rape or murder). No one, I dare say, would suggest that the "men of Sodom" were innocent.

However, we do not know the nature of their antecedent sin that "cried out to heaven" and led God to send angels to see if the citizens were as bad as they were said to be (Genesis 18:20). The rest of Scripture points to their selfishness, pride, and hostility to strangers (e.g., Ezekiel 16:49, and the symbolic comparison Jesus makes with towns that fail to welcome the disciples, Luke 10:12). Sodom came to be a synonym for a wicked city that mistreats those from outside, in its abuse of strangers. The rabbinic tradition adds harlotry, idolatry, and blasphemy (Tosefta 13:8, bSanhendrin 109A), and saw Sodom as completely self-satisfied and self-absorbed, interested only in seeing its own rights maintained (mPirke Aboth 5.10, bBaba Batra 12b). Its population knew right from wrong, but deliberately chose to do wrong. Whatever the earlier wrong that brought about the angelic embassy, they only *added* to it by their attempted assault upon the angels, whatever its nature, whether homosexual or homicidal.

It might be asked whether the entire population of the city, from "every quarter"(so the KJV translates accurately, while the NRSV has "to the last man") could reasonably have expected to have a go at the visiting angels. So it is reasonable to suggest that the "evil thing" they intended may well have been understood by Lot as mayhem, not rape, whatever they meant by, "Bring them out so we may know them."

In any case, while the prohibition in the law code remains a matter for legal discernment, the narrative of Sodom's sin and fall is irrelevant to our concerns, as no one is suggesting that rape or murder are being defended. What we can say about the men of Sodom is that they were not themselves gay (at least not all of them, or not exclusively—witness Lot's sons-in-law, Genesis 19:14); nor did they see gay sex (if that is what they threaten) as something good: when Lot begged them to turn aside from their intended "wickedness" they threatened to "do *worse* to him than to them" (7,9). It was the men in the house, Lot's visitors, God's angels, whom the men of Sodom regarded as strange, foreign, different, *queer*—and they meant them harm because of it.

The destruction of Sodom stands as a warning—not to gay and lesbian persons, but to those who revile them, demean them, or impose upon them a greater discipline than they themselves are willing to bear. The church has a choice to turn its back on or persecute "the others" in its midst, or to open its gates in welcome. It is in how we treat "the others" that we are judged.

Who is this that speaks?

Another factor in determining the relevance of a commandment lies in the *source* of the commandment: is it reported to come from the hand of God, from Moses, from Jesus, or from Paul? Hooker was also well aware of this distinction, and used it to contrast the Ten Commandments with the rest of the Law. (In this

---

A note on "Experience"

Sometimes "Experience" is added to the traditional triad of "Scripture, Tradition and Reason" that is (wrongly) attributed to Richard Hooker. (Not that Hooker would object to the concept, though for him these three did not serve as separate "authorities," but as interrelated sources, with Reason playing an essential part above all.) In that light, what we call "Experience" would be regarded as part of "Reason" as Hooker understood it—not simply as deductive reason, but as the human faculty of reasonableness. As such, Experience is not a source of authority, but rather a part of that Reason which is a "necessary instrument"—and without which the Scripture itself cannot be comprehended. All revelation is, after all, revelation *to*—God does not speak in a void, and the Word goes forth to bear fruit. The human being is the receiver of this Word, in whom spiritual fruit is borne, to bring forth abundantly.

passage Hooker also catalogues some other distinctions I will address below.)

> What I am suggesting is that we do as Jesus did and look at all of the various laws through the lens he provided, asking, In what way does any given law fulfill the command to love God and neighbor?

> The positive laws which Moses gave, they were given for the greatest part with restraint to the land of Jewry . . . Which laws he plainly distinguished afterward from the laws of the Two Tables which were moral . . . Of the Ten Commandments, it followeth immediately, "These words the Lord spake unto all your multitude in the mount . . ." (Deut 5.22) But concerning other laws, the people give their consent to receive them at the hands of Moses (Deut 5.27) . . . From this latter kind the former are distinguished in many things. They were not both at one time delivered, neither both of one sort, nor to one end. The former uttered by the voice of God . . ., written with the finger of God, . . . termed by the name of Covenant, . . . given to be kept without either mention of time how long, or place where. On the other side, the latter given after, and neither given by God himself, nor given unto the whole multitude immediately from God, but unto Moses . . .; the latter termed Ceremonies, Judgments, Ordinances, but nowhere Covenants; finally, the observation of the latter restrained unto the land where God would establish them to inhabit (III.11.6).

Jesus also made a distinction between commandments of God and those delivered by Moses, suggesting that the latter may not have been entirely in keeping with God's will, when he set aside the Mosaic allowance for divorce (Deuteronomy 24:1) in favor of what he regarded as the divine order towards indissoluble marriage.

For example, the church's decision to admit Gentiles to its fellowship rested initially not on Scripture, but on Peter's vision of the sheet let down from heaven and his experience with Cornelius' family when the Spirit descended upon them as it had on the disciples (Acts 10); Peter offers his explanation in Acts 11:1–18. Only *after these experiences* and in their light did the church come to recognize that Isaiah's prophecy was thus fulfilled (Acts 13:46–48). Similarly, it is only the experience of the Risen Christ (in person or in the preaching of the Good News) that allowed the disciples to understand the Scriptures that were there all along (John 20:9,20; Luke 24:25–29, 41–49; Acts 8:30–39, 13:46–49). Experience is the key that unlocks the Scripture.

This is a way of reading for which we have the living Word's word. When we look to the written word, we find that the legal code of Deuteronomy is book-ended with citations that indicate its contents derive from God, though given to and through Moses: "These are the statutes and ordinances that you must diligently observe in the land that the LORD, the God of your ancestors, has given you to occupy all the days that you live on the earth . . . Moses and the elders of Israel charged all the people as follows: Keep the entire commandment that I am commanding you today" (Deuteronomy 12:1; 27:1). The same sort of general description applies in Leviticus, which often takes up the refrain to keep all of the statutes and ordinances delivered by Moses (Leviticus 20:22, 25:18).

Yet Jesus clearly distinguished between these collections of Law and the commandments of the Decalogue, in much the same way as Hooker described. When the young man asked Jesus how he might inherit eternal life, Jesus cited only Decalogue commandments (Mark 10:19, Luke 18:20). He did, in Matthew's version at 19:19, add the law to love one's neighbor from Leviticus 19:18, obviously a crucial point in Jesus' moral system, though it is the only law he quotes from Leviticus.

By no means do I wish to suggest that because Jesus emphasized the Decalogue over the other laws, and set aside a number of the latter laws explicitly (more on this below), that *all* of these laws are no longer to be observed. I am merely noting here that this places these laws in a category in which, by Jesus' own authority committed to the church (Matthew 16:19, 18:18; John 20:23), we are able to review them for their applicability, in keeping with the general principle which Jesus affirmed as his own touchstone for moral action: loving one's neighbor as oneself. This is the explicit conclusion reached in Jesus' discussion with the lawyers concerning what is most important in the Law (Luke 10:27–28; Mark 12:33–34). As Keith Stanley noted in comparing the Pauline method to that of Jesus:

> Beyond Paul's case-by-case effort to resolve the conflicting demands of his own inherited conservatism and an impulse towards eschatological conclusion, Jesus' treatment of the law remains our model (Stanley, 84) .

In the matter at hand, we would examine the law from Leviticus 18:22 (clearly given by Moses and not part of the Decalogue) in connection with the possibility that one could "love one's neighbor as oneself" even if violating this law; I dare say further, even *by* violating this law. This is not a matter of seeking exceptions on the basis of a particular case; it is rather an effort to see that the law itself has lapsed, or been superceded, and that following it may no longer be in keeping with the higher principle enunciated in the commandment to "love one's neighbor as oneself." It seems evident that this is not only a possibility, but for many people a reality.

Questions for Discussion or Reflection

• *Are there any inconsistencies in Scripture that you find troubling?*

• *How do you feel about observance of the Sabbath? To what extent do you find that culture has had an influence on changes in observing it?*

• *Have you ever had a life-experience that gave you a new or better understanding of a scriptural passage?*

10

Entrusted with the Oracles of God

I TURN NOW TO EXAMINE SOME ADDITIONAL DISTINCTIONS CONCERNING SCRIPTURAL mandates: the recipients of the commandments, the scope of those commandments, and the changes made to the commandments—in some cases even by God.

To whom shall I send?

About twenty-five years ago, I was at an interfaith conversation of Christians and Jews. An Orthodox rabbi issued a rather blunt challenge, "Why do you Christians think that the Ten Commandments apply to you? And if so, why do you not keep the Sabbath?" These are good questions, both of them. The Scripture shows the Decalogue being delivered to the Chosen People, those whom God has brought "out of the land of Egypt, out of the house of slavery" (Exodus 20:1). And although few would argue with the universality of certain of these laws—such as those forbidding murder, adultery, theft, and perjury—and acknowledge the goodness of honoring one's parents and avoiding envious covetousness, the law against worshiping other gods clearly was not directed (at least at the time) against other peoples of the earth, each of whom "walks in the name of its own god" (Micah 4:5). Obviously, from the time of the prophets on, the folly of idolatry was a prime topic for Jewish criticism of Gentiles. That being said, even Saint Paul was willing to acknowledge that one could be a moral pagan, a seeker after God, even if idolatry itself was a mistaken way to go about it (Acts 17:22f).

However, when it comes to observing the Sabbath, it is only fair to agree with the Rabbi's observation that Christians do not observe it, and haven't for centuries. The Council of Laodicea, as noted above, adopted a canon against such a "Judaizing" observance, insisting Christians keep Sunday, not Saturday, as a day of rest. As I noted in the citation of Hooker in the previous chapter, in his time it was regarded as part of "the moral law" that all should rest one day in seven, though shifted to Sunday from Saturday in honor of the "new creation."

However, since the last century, anyway, most Christians do not observe even the Lord's Day, at least not with the kind of care that was common even a generation ago. As Blue Laws have fallen one by one, more and more institutions and businesses make observance of a Sunday of worship and rest nigh on to impossible.

So most Christians rather blithely ignore a "moral commandment" either in its literal application (to Saturday) or its adaptation (to Sunday). The irony is that, as the text itself makes clear, this is a commandment that was never intended for them in the first place, even though it was once fashionable to inscribe it on the *reredos* of many an Anglican altar, or the lawn of a courthouse. It is probably bad enough to disregard a set of laws to which such lip-service is given; but how many *other* of the laws of Moses, delivered to the Jewish people, are we in the habit of ignoring, in spite of the fact that they too are contained in Scripture even if not addressed to all the world? And how do we decide which, if any, of these laws we *are* to hold as binding upon ourselves, even though delivered solemnly to others? After all, even though, for example, the laws in Leviticus 18 and 20 are only addressed to Israel, the closing verses of each chapter indicate a deep repugnance

◖◖◗ Law, Natural and Otherwise

Natural law is not a native Jewish concept, and there is no Biblical Hebrew word for what we would now mean by "nature." There is no "natural" moral law; everything is according to God's will as revealed in positive commandment. Even the natural world itself comes into being and functions only as a result of God's express command, "Let there be . . ." Without God's command the sun would not shine, and the animals would not be fruitful and multiply.

Post-biblical Jewish thinkers continued this general trend against Hellenistic natural-law concepts. The principle was articulated with regard to ethics by Maimonides (*The Eight Chapters*, VI): there is no natural or "rational" moral law, though there may be generally accepted principles (cultural constructs). All so-called law is *given*, whether by God or human authority, and hence is positive. Note in Romans 1:32 and Acts 17:30–31 the *positive* nature of so-called natural moral law. It might be argued, on the basis of Romans 1:20, that Paul regarded the prohibition on idolatry as an exception, since nature teaches that there is a creator-God behind the visible world. However, *knowing* God as Creator (through nature) does not *necessarily* render illicit the *worship of lesser gods*, as even Paul appears to acknowledge when he alerts the Athenians that what they worship as unknown has been made known in these latter days.

for these acts which were committed by the prior inhabitants of the land and on account of which the land became defiled (Leviticus 18:24–29, 20:22–26).

The problem, of course, is that even among biblical laws we make distinctions concerning those to which we give attention. Christians explicitly disregard the commandments concerning clean and unclean animals (Leviticus 20:25) even though this is also explicitly related to the call to holiness; and very few Christians would place sexual relations with one's wife during her menstrual cycle in the same category as incest with one's sister, even though they entail an identical penalty (Leviticus 20:17–18). So some other mechanism must be at play in reaching an informed decision about what of the Jewish Law is, or should be, binding on Christians.

Post-Diluvian Legislation

One approach is to examine what are commonly called the Noahide Commandments. In Jewish thinking, some things were held to be immoral because God had delivered explicit commandments concerning them to all of humankind (to Adam and Eve, or Noah and his immediate descendants).

It might be good to note here that the Jewish tradition had little use for "natural law" as understood today. In the rabbinic perspective, things are wrong not on the basis of general principles, but because God has issued explicit command-

The prohibition on the worship of other gods, by the Jews, was established in the positive law given at Sinai. The Rabbis held that the prohibition on idols (not lesser gods but material objects "that are no gods") was also *not* natural, but to have been among those laws given to Noah (and hence binding on all of humanity), an event recorded in the Oral rather than the Written Torah. (Mekilta on Exodus 19:2; Sifre, Deuteronomy 40; Sanhedrin, 56a) The Decalogue, of course, repeats and reaffirms the prohibition on worship of idols *by Israel* (Exodus 20:4.).

The Rabbis are firm that there can be no crime unless a prohibition has been given in advance, i.e., a positive law: "The Lord does not punish unless he has previously declared such-and-such an action to be an offense" (Sanhedrin 56b).

This is one of the reasons for the rabbinic reluctance to see female same-sexuality as equivalent to male same-sexuality: "There is no specific negative commandment against it" (Maimonides, *Mishneh Torah*, 'Issurei Bi'ah 21:8). This does not mean the Rabbis approved of it, of course, as it was still considered a violation under the general opprobrium attached to "what the Egyptians do" (Leviticus 18:3), which in spite of lack of a specific reference in the text that follows was held to include: "a man marries a man, a woman a woman, a man marries a woman and her daughter, a woman marries two men" (*Sifra Aharei Mot* 8:9). Note, however, another example of the gender imbalance—Jewish law allows a man two wives, but a woman cannot have two husbands.

ments concerning them—which explains why, under this understanding, an observant Orthodox Jew will obey laws even if there is no evident rationale for keeping them. The Sabbath, for example, might be examined as a good principle to ensure workers are not overtaxed; but ultimately the commandment is to be kept because God ordained it to be kept. Paul reflects something of this rabbinic understanding as he wrestles with the law in Romans, acknowledging that the wrongness of sins is only marked out or revealed by law, when God pronounces judgment upon them: "Sin was indeed in the world before the law, but sin is not reckoned where there is no law" (Romans 5:13). That doesn't mean it is permissible to sin, as Paul goes on to say; but that the sin isn't *marked* as such without the law to mark it.

To take an explicit example that will lead us back to the discussion of the Noahide commandments: although God clearly condemns Cain's murder of his brother Abel, the act of murder itself had not been explicitly forbidden, and Cain does not, therefore, receive the penalty that would only later be enunciated in the commandment given to Noah: "Whoever sheds the blood of a human, by a human shall that person's blood be shed; for in his own image God made humankind" (Genesis 9:6). Even though the crime is described with intimate reference to the Creation itself, still the first criminal escapes this punishment on a technicality, and there will be no judgment *ex post facto*.

This commandment (and the repeat of the commandment to be fruitful and multiply given to the First Humans) is addressed to Noah in the scriptural account. The only other explicit commandment recorded as delivered to Noah is the commandment not to eat meat with its blood still in it (Genesis 9:4). This commandment is linked with the commandment against murder, and it was repeated and upheld throughout the Torah and in the Prophets, and in the Jerusalem Council of the Apostles (Acts 15:20), though widely ignored in Christian society since the close of the patristic era and almost completely ignored at present. Once again, we see that the criteria applied for whether we ought to follow a given law appear not to rest on its being scriptural, nor, in this case, according to the recipient of the law: many Christians casually disobey a commandment Scripture holds to have been given to all humanity, while enjoining obedience to laws given only to the Jewish people.

As to the Noahide laws themselves, the seven laws as commonly described (Sanhedrin 56) include prohibitions on idolatry, blasphemy, theft, murder, eating meat "with its life" (either with its blood or while the animal is still alive), sexual immorality, and a positive mandate to establish justice.

It will be noted that the Noahide list is not unlike the list of commandments the Apostolic Council (Acts 15) required of Gentiles: prohibiting fornication (*porneia*), idolatry and consumption of food offered to idols, and eating things strangled and with blood (related because a strangled animal would not have been properly bled).

Some have alleged the Noahide laws were *not* in the Apostles' mind because the list is incomplete. However, a ready explanation for this objection lies in the fact that the Apostles needed only to forbid things that were *legal* under Roman law. Roman civil law permitted prostitution (though it regulated it)—if we take the basic definition of *porneia*—and allowed idolatry as well as the consumption of meat with its blood, so the prohibition on these would have to be spelled out for Gentiles seeking to enter the Christian fellowship. Civil-law-abiding Gentiles need only avoid these specific things *in addition* to what the Roman law already forbade (murder, theft, slander, and so on) in order to be good Noahides—or Christians.

The question will arise, as it does with the Apostolic prohibition on *porneia*, as to whether the Noahide laws include homosexuality. This was a matter of debate in the Jewish tradition, which variously expanded or contracted the list, supplementing it or refining it to include other offenses in greater detail, including homosexuality in some cases—but there remained significant disagreement in the rabbinic community as to whether same-sexuality was covered. For example, Rabbi Ulla is recorded as adding the creation of male same-sex marriage contracts—not "homosexuality" as is commonly asserted—to the Noahide list (Hullin 92a), but the context indicates he was trying to find an allegorical way to reach the number 30. It is, incidently, very unlikely that God gave Noah a commandment not to write up a marriage deed (*ketubah*) for another man, since the institution of the *ketubah* dates from the time of the Law of Moses—it is the very prenuptial agreement to which Jesus refers in his critique of a law given for hardness of heart, which *conflicts with* the Divine intent for permanence in marriage (Matthew 5:31, 19:7).

It is doubtful if extended analysis of the Noahide commandment list, about which there is significant disagreement among the Rabbis once one gets beyond the original seven commandments listed at Sanhedrin 56a, will provide us any easy answer as to whether there is a positive law against same-sexuality *among Gentiles*. The least that can be said is that there is no such positive law *in the Torah*; the only explicit law is that forbidding one form of same-sex behavior to Jewish males—and that only in the Holy Land. Which brings us to the important matter of sacred geography.

The Where and the When

Rabbi Jacob Milgrom, in his massive three-volume commentary on Leviticus, points out the *geographical* nature of much of the law enshrined there, including the prohibition on one form of male same-sexuality. This answers the objection raised concerning the rationale for all of the other injunctions: these are things by means of which the former residents of the land, whom God is now casting out, *defiled* the land, a land meant to be set apart as holy for the holy people. This might at first appear to offer some promise to those who wish to use this language in an argument against the possible goodness of same-sexuality in *any* form. Unfortunately, we return to the same dilemma we have encountered before, when we see that this applies equally to *all* of the laws given in Leviticus, not just the ones some would like to single out for perpetual opprobrium.

Let me examine one particular law, that of the Sabbath and its relationship to the land, which is emphasized at length throughout Leviticus 25. This chapter outlines the law of Sabbath and Jubilee; and the failure to allow the Holy Land to have its Sabbath rest is punished with exile and dispersion—so that

> the land shall enjoy its sabbath years as long as it lies desolate, while you are in the land of your enemies; then the land shall rest, and enjoy its sabbath years. As long as it lies desolate, it shall have the rest it did not have on your sabbaths, when you were living on it (Leviticus 26:34–35).

These "festival" commandments, even though intimately linked to the Holy Land, are still carried out by pious Jews even in the dispersion and far from the Holy Land. Even though intimately linked with the cycles of harvest and seedtime, such festivals as Succoth and Shavuoth are still observed even in urban settings.

When we turn to the laws of Leviticus 18 and 20, however, we see a similar reference to the land. Clearly the Levitical Code is negative towards male samesexuality, as well as a number of other things; no one is denying that. The question is the *force* of the Law as given, in connection with the references to the Land and the Law itself. Note these things:

- The commandment is given only to the Jewish people (and resident aliens), in contrast to their following "the statutes of [Egypt and Canaan]" (Leviticus 18:2). So there is a distinction here between two law codes (or three), a *legal* distinction: Egyptian laws, Canaanite laws, and Jewish laws.

To turn the Scriptures themselves into an unchanging "thing" rather than approaching them as the story and song and case history of which they largely consist, is to come very close to a form of idolatry. The Scripture, like the Sabbath, exists for the good of the people of God, and they have the right and responsibility to engage it and understand it in each succeeding generation.

This principle is recognized in Jewish jurisprudence under the principle known as *gadol kavod habriyot.* (bBerakoth 19b). Long before the Episcopal Church added respect for "the dignity of every human being" to the Baptismal Covenant, the Rabbis had understood and elaborated on this basic truth. "So great is human dignity that it

- The antecedent problem is that the Law of the Canaanites was the wrong Law for the Land in which they lived—thus the land expelled them (Leviticus 18:25). This land has been destined by God for the Jewish people, from the time of Abraham, and God has given them their own proper Law for that Land. God punishes the land itself, as well as the people who had lived in it.

- Although the people of Egypt also had statutes along these lines, doing things that were forbidden to Jews (brother-sister marriage, for example, was a feature of the Pharaonic monarchy), the Egyptians were not similarly "vomited" out of *their* land. There is a tacit recognition that the Law of Egypt was suitable to the Land of Egypt—Egypt was not "defiled" by these things, only Canaan, trespassers in the holy land; so it is not, from the Law's perspective, a matter of *intrinsic* wrongness but of wrongness *in relation to the land and people.*

> For those interested in pursuing the finer points of the limits to the Levitical proscription on one form of male same-sexuality, I commend Jacob Milgrom's *Leviticus*. In it he takes a very narrow view of the text at hand, that the law in question is directed to the Holy Land. That is, of course, what the text says.

So the Jewish People are given a Jewish Law for a Jewish Land—and they are to keep it, so that the land will not repulse them. So important is the concept of the Law of the Land that even the resident alien is required to keep the law (Leviticus 18:26f). But there is no suggestion that this law applies to anyone other than these two groups. It is not presented as a universal law, but as the Law of the Land.

This raises the very questions concerning Leviticus we are at pains to examine. Are we to toss all of it out as inapplicable to all people, simply because it is not presented as a universal law—or because we do ignore large sections of it already, either on the basis of direct overturn by Jesus (the dietary regulations of Leviticus 11), the decisions of the Jerusalem Council (circumcision as required in Leviti-

can set aside a negative precept of Torah." Dorff *et al.* have argued that this principle, while only applicable to rabbinic rulings, is sufficient to allow for toleration of same-sex relationships within the Conservative Jewish community, with certain limitations. They stop short of the more radical principle of *takkanah*—an overturn of a Torah law on the grounds that it is no longer serving a positive purpose, as this is held to require a majority of a given population (17). Still, this demonstrates the degree to which Judaism remains open to dynamic engagement with its traditional sources of authority, weighed against standards of human worth and dignity.

The Law itself, though subsisting in fixed letters written on stone tablets, is imbued with a living spirit as the people of God engage in understanding it, as the law comes to be engraved upon their hearts. The Scriptures witness to this process. God appears (from a human perspective) to "change his mind" as circumstances change (2 Corinthians 3:3–11).

cus 12), or the passage of time and the reality of history (no one, Jew or Gentile, can avail him or herself of the Levitical priesthood to examine medical conditions as required by Leviticus 13)?

The answer is a clear No. There are still portions of the law that we, as Christians, do deem it appropriate to follow. The point is, we do not do so on the basis of the law being biblical—for we have already abandoned laws that can make that same claim. Some other criterion for judgment is at work. No one is questioning the permanence of laws against robbery or fraud (Leviticus 6) or the matters addressed in the Decalogue (summarized in Leviticus 19)—even while we disregard the commandment on blood (Leviticus 19:26, which was affirmed by the Jerusalem Council, but has fallen into disuse through the generations).

The point is not so much that Christians have cherry-picked Leviticus, but rather that we have taken to heart the one law in Leviticus that Jesus singled out as of prime importance, and as a means to determine the applicability of any other law whatever. Jesus gave us a key: when he quoted one (and only one) of the laws in Leviticus (19:18)—"You shall love your neighbor as yourself." This, for the Christian, is a test of which laws we keep.

The mutability of God's Law

> If the authority of the maker do prove unchangeableness in the laws which God hath made, then must all laws which he hath made be necessarily for ever permanent, though they be but of circumstance only and not of substance. I therefore conclude, that neither God's being author of laws for government of his Church, nor his committing them unto Scripture, is any reason sufficient wherefore all churches should for ever be bound to keep them without change (Hooker III.10.7).

One of the assertions that comes up from time to time is the suggestion that Divine Law doesn't change because God doesn't change. The problem with this assertion is that Scripture provides ample testimony to changes in Divine Law, changes made by God; and the church adds its voice and authority in making further changes. I will explore a few notable examples herse, and suggest that change is part of the reason the faith has survived, rather than being a threat to its nature or substance.

Change by God

I have already noted one change in God's direction, right at the beginning of creation. In Genesis 2, God first creates Adam as a solitary creature, and then perceives that this solitude is not good. We are so used to this story we easily miss the startling fact that something *God has just created* is, by circumstance, *judged by God not to be good*. Anyone who talks about "God's plan" fails to take adequate note of the interaction here between God and what God creates: it is dynamic, not fixed. In reaction to his judgment of *not-goodness*, God creates the animals as companions for Adam; but no suitable companion can be found—still not good. Only then does God create Eve from Adam's substance, and leaves it to Adam— to Adam's experience—to pronounce that this is the acceptable solution.

Food for thought

God also made another significant change recorded in Genesis, about which I will say more below. God's original intent for humanity was vegetarianism: Adam and Eve are given (Genesis 1:29) only the plants and vegetables and fruits to eat (with one notable exception, Genesis 2:16–17). This is a "creation ordinance"— God did not create the animals to be eaten, but as the first companions for Adam. It is only with the coming and passing of the flood that God first permits humans to consume meat, and then only when it has been thoroughly drained of its blood (Genesis 9:3–4). This marks a significant change in the human relationship with the rest of creation: it is only after the flood that God sets the fear of humanity upon all the other creatures, whom God delivers into human hands—and they had best fear. The gentle dominion of Eden is transformed into domination and literal consumption:

> God blessed Noah and his sons, and said to them, "Be fruitful and multiply, and fill the earth. The fear and dread of you shall rest on every animal of the earth, and on every bird of the air, on everything that creeps on the ground, and on all the fish of the sea; into your hand they are delivered. Every moving thing that lives shall be food for you; and just as I gave you the green plants, I give you every- thing. Only, you shall not eat flesh with its life, that is, its blood. For your own lifeblood I will surely require a reckoning: from every animal I will require it and from human beings, each one for the blood of another, I will require a reckoning for human life. Whoever sheds the blood of a human, by a human shall that per- son's blood be shed; for in his own image God made humankind (Genesis 9:1–6).

It can hardly be argued that this recapitulation of Creation, in a form of "re- Creation," does not mark a significant change in direction and attitude.

Inherited weakness

Another example of a change in the Law is a bit more prosaic, but as it concerns marriage law and custom, it is not out of place to make mention of it here. The Hebrews observed the principle of male inheritance rights, going back long before the Law to the time of the Patriarchs: sons took possession of a father's

property on his death. At the numbering of the descendants of those who came
out of Egypt, the apportionment of the promised land is to be settled by lot,
divided among the adult men ("from twenty years old . . . able to go to war")
from each tribe (Numbers 26). In Numbers 27, however, an apparently unforeseen eventuality arises: Zelophehad has died without sons, but with five daughters. They argue it is unfair that his name should perish. Moses brings the case to
God, who gives this instruction, dealing with this exceptional case and making a
new law:

> The LORD spoke to Moses, saying: The daughters of Zelophehad are right in
> what they are saying; you shall indeed let them possess an inheritance among
> their father's brothers and pass the inheritance of their father on to them. You
> shall also say to the Israelites, "If a man dies, and has no son, then you shall pass
> his inheritance on to his daughter. If he has no daughter, then you shall give his
> inheritance to his brothers. If he has no brothers, then you shall give his inheri-
> tance to his father's brothers. And if his father has no brothers, then you shall give
> his inheritance to the nearest kinsman of his clan, and he shall possess it. It shall
> be for the Israelites a statute and ordinance, as the LORD commanded Moses"
> (27:5–11).

That would appear to settle the matter, and cover all the eventualities. However, a further unforeseen problem arises. In Numbers 36, Zelophehad's surviving male relatives protest and point out a problem for their clan: if their nieces
marry outside of the tribe, the inheritance will then pass from the tribe with
them. And once again, God gives Moses both a specific response to this case, and
a new general commandment:

> Moses commanded the Israelites according to the word of the LORD, saying, "The
> descendants of the tribe of Joseph are right in what they are saying. This is what
> the LORD commands concerning the daughters of Zelophehad, 'Let them marry
> whom they think best; only it must be into a clan of their father's tribe that they
> are married, so that no inheritance of the Israelites shall be transferred from one
> tribe to another; for all Israelites shall retain the inheritance of their ancestral
> tribes. Every daughter who possesses an inheritance in any tribe of the Israelites
> shall marry one from the clan of her father's tribe, so that all Israelites may con-
> tinue to possess their ancestral inheritance. No inheritance shall be transferred
> from one tribe to another; for each of the tribes of the Israelites shall retain its
> own inheritance.'"

And so the five daughters marry their cousins (36:10). It is difficult, in reading
this history, not to wonder how much of the Law of Moses really came from God
and not from Moses the micro-manager. That is less shocking than it sounds, as

Jesus made this distinction in his teaching on divorce, countering God's intent for permanence with Moses' provision for the hard-hearted men who put their wives away for any cause.

Not to separate

I noted in an earlier chapter that Jesus produces a *midrash* of Genesis 1 and 2 to frame his response to those who questioned him on divorce and remarriage. Much ink has been spilled over that passage through the years, in an effort to broaden the scope of permission for both divorce and remarriage, including fervent searching of rabbinic debates concerning just what "any cause" might mean. A close look at the text (Matthew 19:3–9), however, seems to indicate that both Jesus and his interlocutors are thinking about Deuteronomy 24:1–3 — how, when a man finds "something objectionable" in his wife and is moved to divorce her, he is to give her a certificate of divorce. That Jesus also makes this linkage in the Sermon on the Mount (Matthew 5:31–32), apart from prompting from any questioners, makes it clear that this is a settled dominical teaching — no divorce except for harlotry.

My primary concern here is not the extent to which Jesus permitted divorce, but the distinction he appears to be making between God's law as established in creation (that a husband and wife should not separate) and the Law of Moses, that permitted divorce for *eruth davar* = a naked, that is shameful or unclean, thing or word. (The same phrase appears only in the preceding chapter, Deuteronomy 23:14, in reference to the holiness of the Israelite camp, that no "unclean thing" shall be seen there, causing God to turn aside from the people. This appears to call upon the analogy of the relationship between God and Israel and husband and wife, at least in the mind of the Deuteronomist.)

In the Sermon on the Mount, Jesus uses a similar turn of phrase as that in the Law: *logou porneias* = word or thing of harlotry, in this case as a cause for divorce. It is very likely in both cases that the reference is to *suspicion* or *rumor* of infidelity. Obviously real infidelity was cause not just for divorce but execution, since adultery was a capital offense, and no divorce would be necessary if it could be proven; nor if she were guilty of adultery would it make sense for Jesus to say that when a man divorces a woman he "causes her to commit adultery."

That being said, Jesus clearly "changes" the current law as it was understood — and this was a revolutionary change in a society in which divorce for "any cause" had become common for many causes. Moreover, dealing with Jesus' primary objection: since the days of Moses, marriages had been contracted with an "out-clause" in the form of the *ketubah* — the prenuptial contract assuring that the husband would give his wife all her rights — and a monetary settlement on divorcing her. From Jesus' perspective on the permanence of marriage, this essentially rendered all marriages contracted by *ketubah* defective in intent: for how could one simultaneously intend a life-long commitment while providing for a divorce settlement in advance? In any case, such is the extent of the disciples' amazement that they find the new teaching—or reaffirmation of an old one, that marriage is to be permanent—so difficult as to make marriage unadvisable (Matthew 19:10).

Jesus as agent of change

Of course, the most well-known change in the Law on Jesus' part concerns how he was understood to have set aside the dietary laws. Whether this was his intent, or is a reading back into the text on the part of the early church under the influence of the later movement towards wider Gentile inclusion, is not terribly important to this discussion. I have noted above how this teaching reflects, or is reflected, in Peter's understanding of the vision of the sheet let down from heaven (Acts 10). Peter seems not to have been aware of the teaching recorded by Mark in this regard, else there would be no need for the sheet. (Luke, as author of Acts, either omitted or did not have the phrase "what is outside a man cannot defile" at his disposal.)

Whatever its provenance, from the time of Peter and Mark on, the church understood Jesus to have made this decision, whether in his teaching or in his appearance to Peter: nothing from outside a person defiles a person. To which

That "Jesus taught us to hate the sin but love the sinner" appears as a truism from time to time. But Jesus didn't say anything about hating sin *or* sinners, did he? Luke alone preserves the saying about hating one's family (a strange twist on "family values") and one's life (14:26) and John the instruction to hate one's life in order to gain eternal life (12:25). But hating other people's sins? This floating quotation seems not to be an authentic *logion*.

But suppose one wants to argue that it is in keeping with what Jesus *would* have said? First of all we have to ask, what is sin? (If that's what we're supposed to hate.) Wrong actions? Would Jesus have said that? No, because defining *behavior* alone as sinful is not only non-Christian, but non-Jewish. The Tenth Commandment ("Thou shalt not covet") and the Sermon on the Mount (Matthew 5:20–48) reveal a higher moral law in which it is not enough just "not to kill, not to commit adultery . . ." but in which one must not indulge in hate (even of one's enemies) or anger, must not lust, must not *desire* (possessions or actions) wrongly. There may be victimless *crimes*, but there are no victimless *sins*.

Jesus recognized, in his critique of "the Pharisee" who looked down on the tax-collector, how by categorizing certain actions as sins it becomes very simple to justify *oneself*. When behavior alone is the criterion, it becomes painfully easy to stand in judgment: "I thank God I'm not one of *them*!" is a cry of self-justification through the judgment of others who do "what I don't do." "I may be bad, but at least I'm not . . ." You can fill in the blank.

Mark adds his gloss, "Thus he declared all foods clean" (Mark 7:19). Clearly, God, in Christ, has been understood to have overturned a significant portion of the Jewish law code—and one that is central, in Leviticus (11), to the concept of holiness.

It is only fair to note as well that Jesus also changes the scope of some laws in a *more* conservative direction. For example, under Mosaic law a man could only commit adultery with another man's wife or betrothed (Leviticus 20:10, Deuteronomy 22:22–27). Jesus expands the concept to a man violating his own marriage even by merely lusting after a woman in his heart (Matthew 5:28). He also expands the law on homicide to include anger and insult (Matthew 5:21–22). This tendency to locate morality in intent and disposition even more than in action is something we should well bear in mind in the course of our discussions and debates—in particular given the constant appeal to regulation of *behavior* as opposed to *orientation*.

The keys of the kingdom

[Laws] being instituted are not changeable without cause, neither can they have cause of change, when that which gave them their first institution remaineth for

So it would seem on the first count, the very nature of sin, that Jesus would not have said, "Hate the sin, not the sinner." But there is a further difficulty. How does one separate the two, if sin involves more than behavior, as both the Decalogue and Jesus maintain? Jesus does not deal with sin *apart* from sinners. Without a word about hatred, Christ on the contrary tells us that we should *love* the sinner and *forgive* the sin. Be hated—yes, you will be if you truly follow Jesus—but do not return that hatred with hatred.

It is ultimately impossible to "hate the sin" apart from the sinner, as if sin had some reality apart from the desires and actions of fallen human beings, as if you could somehow extract the sin from a person and vent your purifying fury upon it in the abstract. Such a notion is very far from the Gospel. What is worse, those who begin by "hating the sin" in this abstract way soon will come to hating the sinner in a concrete way, as indeed they must, since the one cannot exist apart from the other. And when those who legislate against what is sinful have sufficient power, we have seen what results: the *auto da fé* was intended to save the souls of those repentant heretics being burned alive.

There have been enough burnings. There have been enough crosses on the hillside. If we are to hate any sin, let it be only our own. Jesus said we could be as hard on ourselves as we like, even up to and including eyes and limbs (Matthew 5:29–30, 18:8–9; Mark 9:43–48).

ever one and the same. On the other side, laws that were made for men or societies or Churches, in regard of their being such as they do not always continue,
but may perhaps be clean otherwise a while after, and so may require to be otherwise ordered than before; the laws of God himself which are of this nature, no
man endued with common sense will ever deny to be of a different constitution
from the former, in respect of the one's constancy and the mutability of the other.
And this doth seem to have been the very cause why St. John doth so peculiarly
term the doctrine that teacheth salvation by Jesus Christ "an eternal Gospel";
because there can be no reason wherefore the publishing thereof should be taken
away, and any other instead of it proclaimed, as long as the world doth continue:
whereas the whole law of rites and ceremonies, although delivered with so great
solemnity, is notwithstanding clean abrogated, inasmuch as it had but temporary
cause of God's ordaining it (Hooker I.15.3).

Jesus committed authority to the church in questions of law, and the church has
exercised that authority with great passion down through the years. One need only
review the canons of the ancient church to see with what relish the various synods
and assemblies set to work enacting and amending legislation. Much of this
involved matters of "rites and ceremonies"—about which Anglicans have felt themselves to have a particular freedom of adaptation—unless the rites and ceremonies
concern same-sex blessings or the ordination of persons in same-sex relationships.

A doctrine on loan

But many of these changes down through history clearly touch on matters of
morality. I have alluded to the changes in church policy on divorce and remarriage; there have been similar changes on clearly biblical topics ranging from the
ownership of slaves to the charging of interest. Those who try to argue that these
are not relevant to discussions of any possible change in the teaching on the

---

Accommodating Culture

The movement eventually to tolerate and even participate in usury (lending money at
interest) was precisely the kind of "giving into the culture" that those conservative on
the issue of sexuality complain about. No one suggested, for example, that there was a
"loving" way to take interest; or that there was anything "mutual" about it; and it could
hardly be said that it would be fine as long as the usurious relationship was only
between two consenting adults for life. The argument actually took the form of ignoring
the clear prohibition on any interest, and transforming it to cover only excessive interest. That is, of course, an entirely subjective judgment, not unlike that by which slavery
was justified so long as slaves were well treated.

morality of faithful, monogamous same-sex relationships often find very ingenious ways for working around the *fact* of the changes. For example, usury is defined away as *excessive* interest, rather than any *interest* at all. (If credit card interest rates aren't usurious I don't know what is.) So modern day Christians have almost universally swallowed the camel of usury with very little difficulty. Yet, as C.S. Lewis noted,

> There is one bit of advice given us by the ancient Greeks, and by the Jews in the Old Testament, and by the great Christian teachers of the Middle Ages, which the modern economic system has completely disobeyed. All these people told us not to lend money at interest; and lending money at interest—what we call investment—is the basis of our whole system (*Mere Christianity*, 72–73).

Long forgotten (or at least neglected) are the biblical teachings that reckoned interest-taking among very serious crimes (Ezekiel 18:10-13, where interest-taking is classed with other crimes as *to'evoth* = abominations), or the ancient and patristic teachings that described taking interest on a loan as "unnatural" in much the same way as they viewed sodomy. There is a reason Dante put sinners in these two categories next to each other in his *Inferno*. Trying to make money "breed" was as bad, to the mind formed by Aristotle, as sex in which breeding was impossible.

Slaves to the past

When it comes to the change on the view of slavery, the arguments usually touch on such points as: (1) a mandate for slavery, unlike the prohibition on same-sexuality, wasn't part of Jewish law; (2) slavery, unlike heterosexual marriage, is not established in creation. Neither of these defenses will stand up to very close examination.

So complete was the accommodation that our modern economy depends upon usury—much as the ancient economy depended upon slavery; and there are certainly analogies between those suffering under massive debt from which they find it impossible to extricate themselves and the involuntary servitude of slavery. Although the acceptance of usury appears to have been necessary to establish what Adam Smith called "the wealth of nations," it is also fair to observe it is the source of many of our present economic problems. Here is a change in the church's moral teaching that appears to have no *moral* basis—and yet the church and the society have swallowed it more or less entirely, while straining at the gnat of truly loving, permanent, and life-long human relationships, on the basis of biblical texts far less clear in their condemnation.

First of all, the provision for slavery under the law has all the qualities of a mandate, in some cases explicitly so. It is surprising that we have so soon forgotten the arguments of the nineteenth century—perhaps the most notorious penned by none other than the Presiding Bishop of the Episcopal Church, John Henry Hopkins of Vermont. These were eloquent in pointing out the curse (Genesis 9:24–26) that said Canaan should be slave to the other sons of Noah, on account of his father Ham's sin. How this was used to justify the enslavement of non-Canaanite Africans just goes to show how flexible people can be when interpreting the Bible to their economic advantage. And the fact that this curse came not from God but from Noah (with a hangover, no less) seems not to have fazed those who cited it for authority. (We might as well bring up the fact that Ham's sin can be understood as homosexual rape—"seeing his father's nakedness" is a euphemism—so this text is not so far afield as it might at first appear.)

Another example of such a mandate—again, not from God but on human authority—is Joshua's instruction to enslave the Gibeonites (Joshua 9:22–26) who had saved their lives by pretending to come from a far country. Joshua takes his vow seriously, which forces him to contradict a divine command to wipe out all of the native peoples.

In the Law of Moses itself we get closer to the recognition and regulation of slavery in a number of laws, including the Decalogue's prohibition on coveting another's slaves, which ratifies the concept of ownership. The most explicit mandate for slavery (Leviticus 25:44–46) shows chattel slavery in its fulsome sense: slaves who are to be owned and treated as heritable property. Unfortunately, modern translations of this passage attempt to make it sound less of a mandate

    Here, therefore, lies the true aspect of the controversy, and it is evident that it can openly be settled by the Bible. For every Christian is bound to assent to the rule of the inspired Apostle, that "sin is the transgression of the law, namely the law laid down in the Scriptures by the authority of God—the supreme "lawgiver, who is able to save and to destroy." From his Word there can be no appeal. No rebellion can be so atrocious in his sight as that which dares to rise against his government. No blasphemy can be more unpardonable than that which imputes sin or moral evil to the decrees of the eternal Judge, who is alone perfect in wisdom, in knowledge, and in love. . . .

    With entire correctness, therefore, your letter refers the question to the only infallible criterion—the Word of God. If it were a matter to be determined by my personal sympathies, tastes, or feelings, I would be as ready as any man to condemn the institution of slavery; for all my prejudices of education, habit and social position stand entirely opposed to it. But as a Christian, I am solemnly warned not to be "wise in my own conceit," and not to "lean unto my own understanding." As a Christian, I am compelled to submit my weak and erring intellect to the authority of the Almighty. For

than it is, and insert spurious permissive or conditional language where the Hebrew is indicative. So here is the KJV of the relevant passage:

> Both thy bondmen, and thy bondmaids, which thou shalt have, shall be of the heathen that are round about you; of them shall ye buy bondmen and bondmaids. Moreover of the children of the strangers that do sojourn among you, of them shall ye buy, and of their families that are with you, which they begat in your land: and they shall be your possession. And ye shall take them as an inheritance for your children after you, to inherit them for a possession; they shall be your bondmen for ever: but over your brethren the children of Israel, ye shall not rule one over another with rigour.

A.J. Jacobs, in his *Year of Living Biblically: One Man's Humble Quest to Follow the Bible as Literally as Possible*, found, as he noted in an NPR radio interview, that the closest he could come to carrying out the mandate to hold slaves was to hire an intern.

The permanence of this mandate was such that the Rabbis held it to be a grave failing to set such a slave free (bGittin 38b). They could hardly incur guilt for freeing slaves if they didn't have them in the first place, so holding slaves is assumed—slavery was, after all, an inextricable part of Mediterranean culture and economy; not to exaggerate, but slaves were the household appliances of those times and places.

This is, of course, nothing to be flip about. In spite of Bishop Hopkins' devout wish that the opponents of slavery had followed Jesus' lead and remained silent, in order to preserve the precious peace of the United States, by the middle of the

then only can I be safe in my conclusion, when I know that they are in accordance with the will of Him, before whose tribunal I must render a strict account to the last great day. . . .

First, then, we ask what the divine Redeemer said in reference to slavery. And the answer is perfectly undeniable: He did not allude to it at all. Not one word of censure upon the subject is recorded by the Evangelists who gave His life and doctrines to the world. Yet, slavery was in full existence at the time, throughout Judea; and the Roman Empire, according to the historian Gibbon, contained sixty millions of slaves on the lowest probable computation! How prosperous and united would our glorious republic be at this hour, if the eloquent and pertinacious declaimers against slavery had been willing to follow their Savior's example!

—The Rt. Rev. John Henry Hopkins, Bishop of Vermont and Presiding Bishop of the Episcopal Church, writing in 1861 in *A Scriptural, Ecclesiastical, and Historical View of Slavery, from the Days of the Patriarch Abraham to the Nineteenth Century*, pages 5–12 *passim*

Hopkins' appeal for preserving
peace in the United States by
not advocating for the repeal of
slavery resounds with the calls
to maintain peace in the Anglican Communion by not pressing
for change in the understanding
of sexuality. Is peace and unity
more important than doing what
is right and just?

nineteenth century enough Christians had come to realize that just because the Scripture commended slavery
was no reason to consider it good. The Episcopal
Church, sadly, was not a leader in this effort.

The second argument is that slavery is not part of the
"creation order" of God. In one sense, I can agree: but for
that I have to go beyond the biblical account of creation,
into a modern sense of the dignity of each human being.
After all, Genesis shows that God created Adam to be
God's *eved*—the ambiguous Hebrew word for servant or
slave. And God's liberation of the Israelites from Egypt
was not absolute—it was reclamation of *God's rightful
property, bought* or *purchased*—as Christ did the church!

This relationship between God and the people *of* God—and doesn't that have
a different resonance when you think of it in terms of *ownership?*—is reflected in
the portrayal of idolatry as "*serving* other gods." The true God is addressed as
"Lord"—the same word a slave would use for a master.

The language of slavery—which as noted was an inextricable institution in the
societies in which the Scriptures were recorded—is also intimately bound up
with biblical language for the mystery of salvation itself. For example, the prophet
Isaiah uses the inversion of slavery as a symbol for the redemption of people
Israel. Justice will be embodied, Isaiah says, in a great reversal of fortune: Israel
will have the mandate to enslave those who held her captive. (Isa. 14:1–2) This
kind of language, of course, is familiar in the Psalms and the Deuteronomic History, where the overthrow of enemies, and their subjugation, is seen as proof of
the righteousness of the people—and their failure to do so, or their own enslavement, a sign of their imperfection.

Even if by the time of Paul we find a less enthusiastic endorsement of slavery,
we must note that Paul analogizes slavery with the relationship of believer and
Christ, in parallel to his analogy of the relationship between husband and wife
(Ephesians 5:25–33, 6:5–9). Paul describes both relationships in terms of people
taking their natural roles in the hierarchy and keeping their place. So to say that
the models for "appropriate" slavery and sexuality are *not* related is an exercise in
strained reading of the text.

The fact is that nowhere in Scripture is slavery condemned as immoral in
itself, and it is the mandated norm in certain narrow circumstances. There are, of
course, hints that something was trying to break through, and that slavery was
going to be subverted by a more righteous understanding. A suggestion of the
restoration of a greater mutuality in human relationships is hinted at in Hosea
2:16, where the wife is no longer to call her husband, "My master" but "My man
(= husband)"—and this is, of course, a hopeful allegory for a better relationship
between God and the people of God. The same can be said for the famous pas-

sage in Galatians 3:25—it is a hint that the old order of who is in power will be changed utterly, not simply inverted, so that human relationships, in Christ, will be based on mutuality and love rather than possession and control. There is a recognition, however imperfect, that for one human being to own another, and to have the power of life and death over them, is to usurp a sovereignty that belongs to God alone.

The most eloquent example of and pressure towards overturning of the old institution, of course, is in Jesus himself—the Son of God and servant of God, who stoops not only to become one of us, but as one of the lowest; who takes the position of a slave in washing his disciples' feet. We will return to this powerful image in the next chapter, when we focus on the work and mission of Christ, but it is worth noting here that in this action, Jesus takes the role of a slave and servant, a task that was performed for him *by women*; and in this he subverts notions of authority and power. This is "acted out" in John's version of the Supper, but is implicit as well in the Lukan setting: "The kings of the Gentiles lord it over them . . . but not so with you; rather the greatest among you must become like the youngest, and the leader like one who serves" (Luke 22:25–26).

However, even with these clear hints to a better way, with a very few exceptions it was not until the nineteenth century that ecclesiastical challenges to the institution of slavery rose to the level of condemnation, denying the right of any person to take possession of another.

Lest there be any misunderstanding, I'm not bringing all of this up in order to defend the institution of slavery! What I am attempting to show is that there was a process of moral evolution at work—and that something that could be defended as licit and upright in biblical and even relatively modern times is now clearly seen to be a serious moral failing. The fact is that this condemnation goes beyond the explicit positive texts that would support slavery to find an underlying subtext that renders slavery impossible and unacceptable, for slavery goes against the moral principle upon which Jesus established his teaching: Do unto others as you would be done by.

There will be blood

In both Genesis creation accounts God restricted human beings to a vegetarian diet (Genesis 1:29, 2:16–17). After the flood, God through Noah granted humanity all birds, fish, and animals that move as food, putting the fear of humankind into them, with the proviso that eating their blood was forbidden (Genesis 9:2–4). This prohibition was repeated in the Leviticus 3:17 as something to be observed not only in the holy land, but "a perpetual statute throughout your generations, in all your settlements: you must not eat any fat or any blood." The importance of the command is repeated at Leviticus 17:10–14, where eating blood is forbidden to Jews and sojourners alike. In the New Testament, the Jerusalem Council upheld this law as binding upon Gentile converts (Acts 15). So it is clear that there is consistent opposition to the practice throughout the Scripture—and it is rooted in the Creation narrative, in which no animal food is allowed, and the "re-Creation" narrative in Genesis 9, when humans are given quasi-divine authority over life and death in the animal realm.

It is important to note that the blood prohibition is not like the rest of the dietary law, neither in the antiquity of the commandment to Noah, in the way the commandment is presented in the Law itself, nor in its reaffirmation by the first Council of the Apostles. There is no evidence that any figure in the apostolic church would have regarded the eating of blood in the same category as, for example, eating pork.

Moreover, the early church continued the ban: "If any bishop, or presbyter, or deacon, or indeed any one of the sacerdotal catalogue, eats flesh with the blood of its life . . . let him be deprived; for this the law itself has forbidden. But if he be one of the laity, let him be suspended" (*Apostolic Canons* 63). "If anyone henceforth venture to eat in any way the blood of an animal, if he be a clergymen, let him be deposed; if a layman, let him be cut off" (Quinisext Council of Turllo canon 67). Eusebius records Biblias' defense of Christians against accusations of infanticide: "'How,' she said, 'could those eat children who do not think it lawful to taste the blood even of irrational animals?'" (*Ecclesiastical History* 5.1)

The Orthodox East continues to hold these regulations "on the books" to this day in the *Pedalion*—though it is doubtful if many observe them except in avoiding the most extreme forms of blood-eating: black sausage and similar items, which are common on many Western menus and in many cultures. (Say goodbye to the traditional Irish breakfast, with its blood sausage, and to Louisiana Cajun *boudin*, if you want to follow the biblical rule!)

The West, from a fairly early period, set aside the biblical, apostolic, and canonical injunctions. This was done primarily by noting the *purpose* for the apostolic regulation, which, some held, was to allow for fellowship between Gentile converts and Jewish Christians who would have been scandalized by seeing anyone doing such a horrible thing as eating meat with its blood.

Augustine of Hippo (*Contra Faustum* 32.13) is among the first to argue that since the church has become overwhelmingly Gentile in constitution by his time, the regulation of the Apostles has lapsed. Calvin much later made the same argument and held that the law could lapse as circumstances changed (*Institutes* IV.10.20)—that the purpose of the Jerusalem edict was charity rather than cultic regulation. The Lutherans (*Conf. Aug.* II.7. (29)) had taken a similar approach, emphasizing that the ordinance was for charity and quietness' sake, and no longer binding: "The Apostles commanded to abstain from blood. Who observeth that nowadays? And yet they do not sin that observe it not." Anglicans went further and simply held the Church of Jerusalem to have erred (Articles of Religion XIX).

But the matter still engendered debate long after the Reformation. Witness this citation from Wesley's *Journals*:

A young gentleman called upon me, whose father is an eminent Minister in Scotland, and was in union with Mr. Glass, till Mr. Glass renounced him, because they did not agree as to the eating of blood. (Although I wonder any should disagree about this, who have read the fifteenth chapter of the Acts, and considered, that no Christian in the universe did eat it till the Pope repealed the law which had remained at least ever since Noah's flood.) Are not these things in Scotland also for our instruction? How often are we warned, not to fall out by the way? O that we may never make any thing, more or less, the term of union with us, but the having the mind which was in Christ, and the walking as he walked! (October 29, 1745)

This raises an important question: even if the Apostolic Council was believed to have erred, or its regulations to have lapsed by virtue of a change in circumstances, how does one address the clear prohibition given to Noah? Though the Mosaic law *included* the prohibition, the Jerusalem Council did not hold it to be on the same level as the dietary regulations which they believed to have been set aside by Jesus. Even Paul, while he disagreed with the Council on the matter of food offered to idols (witness the Corinthian correspondence) is not recorded as having contested the matter of meat with blood in it. Ironically, Augustine uses Noah's ark as a type for the apostolic church, including both Gentiles and Jews, in the very passage in which he discounts the relevance of the commandment given to Noah concerning blood, and ultimately only argued for setting aside this commandment under Christ's general rubric—"that which is outside does not defile"—as an afterthought.

However, to this day some particular churches and communions still forbid the consumption of blood or red meat (or even blood transfusion—understood among Jehovah's Witnesses as a form of "eating blood") on the basis of the commandment to Noah, or holding fast to the decision of the Jerusalem Council.

Chapter 32 of Augustine's *Contra Faustum* presents an interesting mirror for our own debates. Faustus criticizes Christians for simultaneously embracing the Old Testament as divinely inspired while ignoring some of its mandates and prohibitions (not because Manicheans wanted to follow it themselves, but because they wanted to do the same with the New Testament). Augustine responded that the church is able both to embrace the Old Testament as divinely inspired and reject certain of its provisions as temporary mandates for the "old dispensation" and as "being symbolical to us of truths in which they still have a spiritual use, though the outward observance is abolished." Thus the church's application of interpretative principles to the letter of the text is productive of meaningful governance for the Christian life—even if it means changing or disregarding a divine law.

This has not prevented the vast majority of western churches from setting this commandment aside through the application of the authority to decide which of the biblical commandments are still held to be binding.

This will answer to some extent those who argue that only "the whole church" has the power to make such changes, but not a particular church. Here is a point of discipline on which the West broke with the East, and about which there is still at least a technical difference of opinion, even if it does not make the headlines.

A General Principle: What is the Point of the Law?

We have, in this chapter, seen how much law can change both within Scripture itself and under the church's care. The church makes changes in the emphasis it gives and the extent to which it is bound by the commandments recorded in Scripture. In addition, we recognize that the legal principle of *desuetude* is well established: that is, laws can pass out of use due to circumstances that alter their applicability, or simply by not being enforced.

More importantly, we believe that law is to a purpose, and the Scripture all the more so. Its purpose is to save: and it is sufficient unto that end. If the law itself becomes an obstacle to salvation—or if insistence on the following of a law should be found to keep people away from hearing the gospel, and from salvation itself, there is no doubt but that it can be mitigated if not set aside completely.

I noted above the rabbinic principles of *gadol kavod habriyot* and *takkanah*—both of which provided mechanisms to set aside laws when either their purpose or utility had ceased, and all the more so if they were found to stand in the way of human dignity and salvation. Similar principles were articulated by Richard Hooker in the midst of the Elizabethan Settlement of Anglicanism, itself torn with controversies of various sorts. Note the following, to which I have added some emphasis:

> If the reason why things were instituted may be known, and being known do appear manifestly to be of perpetual necessity; then are those things also perpetual, *unless they cease to be effectual unto that purpose for which they were at the first instituted.* Because when a thing doth cease to be available unto the end which gave it being, the continuance of it must then of necessity appear superfluous. And of this we cannot be ignorant, how sometimes that hath done great good, which afterwards, when time hath changed the ancient course of things, doth grow to be either very hurtful, or not so greatly profitable and necessary (III.10.1).
>
> Even that law which the Apostles assembled at the council of Jerusalem did from thence deliver unto the Church of Christ, the preface whereof to authorize it was, "to the Holy Ghost and to us it hath seemed good;" (Acts 15.28) . . . This law therefore to have proceeded from God as the author thereof no faithful man will deny. It was of God, not only because God gave them the power whereby

they might make laws, but for that it proceeded even from the holy motion and suggestion of that secret divine Spirit, whose sentence they did but pronounce. *Notwithstanding, as the law of ceremonies delivered unto the Jews, so this very law which the Gentiles received from the mouth of the Holy Ghost, is in like respect abrogated by the decease of the end for which it was given* (III.10.2).

With the introduction of contraception (and its acceptance *de jure* in Anglicanism and *de facto* even among many Roman Catholics, in spite of official opposition) and the growing awareness of significant numbers of faithful gay and lesbian members of the church seeking to frame their lives in accordance—not with legislation from the desert wanderings of Israel, or the concerns of Jews engaged in their first contacts with Hellenism—but with the same moral principles of love, honor, respect, permanence, dignity, and fidelity that are expected of mixed-sex couples: might it not be that the time has come to reexamine those laws, and set them aside as no longer serving the purposes of God? Even more importantly, to what extent does the maintenance of this double standard eviscerate evangelism to unchurched gay and lesbian persons, who may be kept from ever considering the church because of what they see either as impossible or hypocritical demands?

Jesus said to his disciples, "Occasions for stumbling are bound to come, but woe to anyone by whom they come! It would be better for you if a millstone were hung around your neck and you were thrown into the sea than for you to cause one of these little ones to stumble" (Luke 17:1–2). "But woe to you, scribes and Pharisees, hypocrites! For you lock people out of the kingdom of heaven. For you do not go in yourselves, and when others are going in, you stop them" (Matthew 13:13).

And so, in the next chapter, with these questions (and accusations) in mind, we will turn to examine even more closely the teaching of Jesus.

Questions for Discussion or Reflection

- *Can you think of any changes in church teaching or practice that have happened in your lifetime? What was it like to live through that time of change?*

- *Do you see any connection between changes in policy on contraception, remarriage after divorce, and a move towards normalizing same-sexuality?*

- *Regardless of which of the many sides of this issue you find yourself, how do you apply Scripture to it?*

11.
WWJD

*L*ong ago God spoke to our ancestors in many and various ways by the prophets, but in these last days he has spoken to us by a Son, whom he appointed heir of all things, through whom he also created the worlds (Hebrews 1:1–2).

The final and crucial distinction to be made between and among texts of Scripture falls under the heading, "the scandal of the particular." I refer, of course, to the teaching of Jesus Christ, as recorded in the gospels, and to a lesser extent, referred to in a number of the epistles.

One of the dilemmas we face in trying to understand Jesus lies in this limitation: we have only so much evidence from which to deduce answers to unanswered or debated questions. How can we imagine or understand WWJD (What Would Jesus Do . . . in such and such a situation?) when all we have to go on is WJD&S (What Jesus Did and Said in other situations).

This is, of course, not limited to our understanding of Jesus—ultimately all we know about what anyone thinks is based on what they say (or write). We cannot "read" people's minds, but only their words and expressions—what they say and do. When we come to Jesus, we deal primarily with what is recorded of his word and actions in Scripture, but also the "body language" of his church—his Body. Thus there is a sense in which the doctrine of the Incarnation, and the presence of Christ in and with the church, allows Christ to speak, and be understood, even as time passes.

That places a heavy responsibility upon the church to be very sure it understands its Lord's intent, and does not misrepresent him—and the history of the church indicates that such misunderstandings happen from time to time. As a preventative to wandering too far astray, the words of Jesus as recorded in Scripture must have primacy of place, serving as the core of our evidence for any understanding of what he might think about a contemporary issue. For he is the Living Word, to which all of the rest of Scripture bears witness as Written Word. Citations from Jesus himself along these lines are familiar enough:

> You search the scriptures because you think that in them you have eternal life; and it is they that testify on my behalf (John 5:39).
>
> Then he said to them, "These are my words that I spoke to you while I was still with you—that everything written about me in the law of Moses, the prophets, and the psalms must be fulfilled." Then he opened their minds to understand the scriptures . . . (Luke 24:44–45).
>
> Then he said to them, "Oh, how foolish you are, and how slow of heart to believe all that the prophets have declared!" . . . Then beginning with Moses and all the prophets, he interpreted to them the things about himself in all the scriptures (Luke 24:25,27).

What is not as often noted is the tension between some of Jesus' particular teaching, as recorded in the gospels, and the teaching of Paul (and his followers) in the Epistles. This represents an initial tension between what Jesus said and what the church understood. There are two explanations for this, and they are related.

J & P in the NT

Just as the textual critics of the nineteenth century perceived different sources in the composition and redaction of the Pentateuch (commonly called by helpful letters such as J, P, E, and D), so too there are various sources in the New Testament, with two primary voices who dominate the discourse: Jesus and Paul. (As I noted in the introduction, I am less interested in the historical authenticity of linking any particular text to the historical Jesus or the historical Paul; I recognize that in both cases redaction has taken place, and words placed in others' mouths by disciples and editors. The distinctions I make concern the text as the church received it, and I forgo any attempt to color-code it in an effort to a surmised historical accuracy. Ultimately, it is what the church has received as Jesus' or Paul's word that is significant for the church.) Now, to some distinctions.

First, as Paul testifies, he had no direct personal experience of Jesus apart from the blinding impact of his own guilt on the road to Damascus. Jesus appeared to Paul as to one "untimely born"—a stillborn or aborted child. (Interesting, isn't it, how comfortable phrases like "untimely born" can soften the power of such a testimony about oneself.) Whatever else of Jesus' teaching Paul handed on was given to him first by others. He also relied on his own inner inspiration. First Corinthians 7 offers a good illustration of the contrast:

To the married I give this command—not I but the Lord—that the wife should not separate from her husband . . . (10) To the rest I say—I and not the Lord—that if any believer has a wife who is an unbeliever, and she consents to live with him, he should not divorce her (12) . . . Now concerning virgins, I have no command of the Lord, but I give my opinion as one who by the Lord's mercy is trustworthy. (25) . . . A wife is bound as long as her husband lives. But if the husband dies, she is free to marry anyone she wishes, only in the Lord. But in my judgment she is more blessed if she remains as she is. And I think that I too have the Spirit of God. (39–40)

Paul's honesty in making these distinctions is commendable; but it is surely interesting to note that in the one extended discussion on marriage in the whole of Scripture, a good bit of the policy Paul commended is explicitly given as his own thinking, *and not that of the Lord.*

Second, and more importantly, although we have the gospels at the beginning of our New Testament, and although in terms of their content they antedate the apostolic period and the epistles, the texts themselves were set down after many of the epistles were already in circulation, in the case of Luke/Acts with the explicit purpose of setting the record straight. The closing of John's Gospel also attests to a concern for such an accurate report. As such, those who recorded the gospels had the opportunity to react to Paul, and the activity of the apostolic church, in what they chose to record from the life of Christ.

To give one example: Luke has an overall intent in writing Luke/Acts—to show a grand arc of history moving from Palestine to Rome, the gradual broadening of salvation from the people of Israel to the Gentiles. Thus he may have chosen to omit the story of the Canaanite woman (Matthew 15:22) as introducing a character not in keeping with the broad sweep of his narrative. Similarly, Matthew is interested in linking the life of Jesus to the fulfillment of prophetic texts, so he structures his version of the infancy narrative to include details not found elsewhere.

It is reaction to the teaching of Paul that I am most interested in noting, however. Paul always was, to some extent, an outsider, and there are hints in Acts that although hands of fellowship were shaken, the circle of the original apostles, especially around Peter, does not seem to have entirely trusted him—and Paul's writings also testify to his feelings of rivalry with Peter and others of the apostolic group. There were factions in the early church, and the Pauline letters attest to these differences of opinion, though we have little from the other side, beyond Peter's acknowledgment that Paul's letters are sometimes confusing (2 Peter 3:16). And it is certainly possible that whoever authored Revelation was making a veiled reference to Paul or his followers, concerning the teaching of "Balaam" and "Jezebel" (2:14, 20), who allowed eating food offered to idols; something about which Paul himself seemed much less concerned than was the Jerusalem Council (1 Corinthians 10:25–33, with more nuance than might have been understood by his opponents—or his followers). The cynical might even read into Acts 21:17–29 a covert attempt by James of Jerusalem and his circle to have Paul put out of everyone else's misery. (Recall as well the discrepancies between Paul's developing doctrine concerning grace and James' emphasis on righteous works.) But let us not be cynical.

Rather, let us face the fact that whatever the source of the discrepancy, we are left with an apparent disagreement between Jesus and Paul on the role of judgment in the life of the church. There is clearly a tension between Jesus' admonition, "Do not judge, and you will not be judged; do not condemn, and you will not be condemned" (Luke 6:37, cp. Matthew 7:1), and Paul's "Do you not know that the saints will judge the world? And if the world is to be judged by you, are you incompetent to try trivial cases? Do you not know that we are to judge angels . . ." (1 Corinthians 6:2–3). This latter text has been relied upon by the church to do, in some cases with horrific results, the very thing Jesus warned against. (And in spite of the fact that Paul appears to be talking about lawsuits, rather than moral judgment.)

It is also important to note that this same struggle is mirrored in the career and ministry of Paul himself, and there is a clear evolution in his thinking—which shows part of the difficulty with taking such texts as "Do you not know we are to judge angels?" out of the larger context of his own developing thought revealed in other epistles. It simply does no good to take the Scripture as a unitary source, plucking verses not only from their immediate context, but from the larger context either of salvation history or personal journey, when there are such clear notes of development evident within it.

Paul, proud of his tradition as a Pharisee, wrestled throughout his later life as a Christian with the issues dear to the heart of the Pharisee movement, a movement which unfortunately gets rather uneven treatment in the later tradition. Close attention to the Scripture reveals that the Pharisees were not for the most part hypocrites or villains. On the contrary, some of them were moved towards joining (Acts 15:5), protecting (Luke 13:31), or at least not openly opposing (Acts 5:34–39) the early Christian movement—Paul himself being a prime example. Still, as Paul realized, it was the Pharisees' preoccupation with personal holiness and righteousness which itself became a tangle of self-reference, and at its worst edged over to become the very caricature that would later become a commonplace of the church's anti-Judaism. This is tragic, for it misses the greater dimension of Paul's own struggle that is laid out most eloquently in the Letter to the Romans and in Galatians—by which time he has come fully to realize that righteousness cannot come from punctilious following of the law, but only from the grace of God. This, in fact, comes to be the heart of his "gospel"—and it is here that his teaching is fully congruent with the teaching of Christ himself.

The idea that one can find the way to salvation by resisting certain inclinations or actions has a venerable history in the various religions of the world. Jesus appears to have intended himself as the substitute for this "way" of salvation. It is in him and by him that we are saved, not by patting ourselves on the back for having avoided certain behaviors. Jesus addressed the danger of this approach in that it tends to lead to self-satisfaction and the critique of others, primarily in identifying behaviors one has either not been tempted to or which one has overcome, as a way of separating oneself from those who have "failed" in this respect. The root of the name "Pharisee" means, *one who is separate*. Jesus opposes not so much the individual Pharisee, as the Pharisee *method*.

I cannot help but think that Saint Paul might be uncomfortable to find that anyone would assert that his every written word was the Word of God. I think he might rather react as Peter did when Cornelius fell to worship him: "Stand up, I am only a mortal" (Acts 10:26). When Paul sat down to write (or stood up to dictate) any of his letters to the churches, did he for a moment think that some day people would claim that whatever he wrote was to be given equal weight with things like the Ten Commandments, or the teaching of Christ? He himself makes the distinction from time to time, as when he says he is passing along something "from the Lord" and at others is emphatic that he is expressing his own opinion. Surely Paul would be horrified to find that every word he wrote was being treated as if it came from the mouth of God. Paul avoided that claim—so why should we make it? It is when Paul is congruent with the teaching of Christ that we can assuredly take him at his word.

The Silence of the Lamb

In seeking moral guidance, it is natural that we should look to Jesus, the "pioneer and perfecter" (Hebrews 12:2) to see what, if anything, he might show us about the rightness or wrongness of our actions. If we are looking for explicit direction, however, we are with very few exceptions not going to find a list of *dos* and *don'ts* in the teaching of Jesus. For example, when the rich young man asked what he must do to inherit eternal life, Jesus cited some of the commandments from the Decalogue, and ended with the only commandment from Leviticus which he is recorded anywhere to have cited: "You shall love your neighbor as yourself." (Matthew 19:16–22). Jesus seems to favor the general principle over the exhaustive list, when it comes to moral guidance.

When we come to the specific issue of same-sexuality, even the most ardent opponent of change in the policy concerning it will, I hope, admit that there is no *explicit* statement on Jesus' part concerning this traditional prohibition. Some who argue for the status quo suggest that Jesus' silence results from the obvious fact that he didn't need to say anything about a matter which the law so clearly condemned, any more than he had to say anything about incest or bestiality. They argue that since he explicitly overturned any number of other laws, he might as well have overturned this too, if that was his intent. This is true as far as it goes, but it doesn't actually offer a decisive answer any more than the contrary argument that "silence implies consent" advanced by Hopkins in his defense of slavery.

The fact does remain that Jesus overturned—or at least reinterpreted—a number of other laws. We will return to some of these overturnings shortly, but first I want to turn to some of the other arguments advanced to suggest that Jesus offered either implicit or nearly explicit guidance on the subject.

First, it is common to hear that Jesus' teaching on marriage and celibacy brooked no other possibility; that his reference to the creation account in response to the question on divorce offers a clear indication of his thinking on same-sexuality. As I noted in earlier chapters, this is a stretch, especially when advanced apart from, or even in virtual denial of, the explicit concern Jesus was addressing: the permanence of marriage and the sinful status of remarriage after divorce. It is the permanence of marriage that is at issue, and Jesus locates his teaching on this permanence in the context of Genesis.

An argument advanced by Robert Gagnon is that when Jesus included *porneiai* ("harlotries") in the list of "things that defile a man" (Matthew 15:19–20) he must have intended to include male same-sex intercourse. "No first century Jew could have spoken of *porneiai* (plural) without having in mind the list of forbidden sexual offences in Leviticus 18 and 20 (incest, adultery, same-sex intercourse, bestiality)" (Gagnon 2001, 191). The same goes for the inclusion of *porneia* in Paul's vice lists (1 Corinthians 6:9, 1 Timothy 1:10), as well as the injunction of the Jerusalem Council (Acts 15:20). The argument goes that *porneia* is a relatively generic term that includes *any form of sexual behavior judged irregular*, with specific reference to Leviticus 18. In some lexicons it is explicitly claimed that this includes same-sexuality between men and women.

In fact, in biblical usage, *porneia* (or its Hebrew equivalent *z'nut*) has two primary meanings for the great majority of instances, and it is usually clear from the context which is intended:

> 1) actual prostitution, in relation to the root word *zonah* / *pornē* = whore, harlot, and
> 2) figuratively as a metaphor for idolatry, neatly summarized in Wisdom of Solomon 14:12, "The idea of making idols was the beginning of fornication."

In the biblical text the figurative use is very common, and there are a few instances where it can be confusing as to which meaning is intended, even on the basis of the context. There is some question as to whether and when adultery is intended to be included, but it would be fair to say it sometimes is, under the broader heading of "infidelity"—which is how it is used in the passages in which

Israel is portrayed as an errant and unfaithful spouse. This imagery, linking idol worship with harlotry, is highly developed in Ezekiel and Hosea, and characterizes the people corporately as the unfaithful wife who has forsaken her true Lord and master, and become a harlot to "serve" (or "service") other gods.

However, when it comes to same-sexuality, of all of the uses of *porneia* and its related words in the Septuagint and the Greek text of the New Testament, there is only one in which reference might possibly be made to male same-sexuality, and that is a remote possibility that depends on a number of other factors. It is in Deuteronomy 23:18, where the LXX translates the Hebrew *qadesh* with the paraphrastic "one who is fornicating (*estai porneuōn*) of the sons of Israel." As noted above in relation to this text, it is not entirely clear what the *qadeshim* were, but whether literally engaged in prostitution or not—perhaps even with women rather than men—they were involved in *the idolatrous cult*. Thus, as some readings of the Greek have it, this is a reference, in the case of both men and women not to prostitutes literally but to initiates or votaries ("ones made holy"—the Hebrew root of *qdsh*) of the idolatrous cult. So under this reading the emphasis is not on the literal sex or sexuality of the participants, but as with many of the uses of the *porn*- root, with figurative idolatry. On the other hand, if it refers to male prostitutes, the language of *porneia* attaches to the fact of *prostitution*, not the gender of the prostitute or his clients. The idea that this is somehow specific to male-male sex simply doesn't carry through.

Further against the position that *porneia* includes same-sexuality there are several persuasive bits of evidence. The first requires a return to Gagnon's argument that the plural, *porneiai*, in Jesus' list of the things that defile (Matthew 15:19, Mark 7:21–22) is significant. He has claimed that this is an indication that the "harlotries" referred to represent any and all of the various forms of sexual misconduct listed in Leviticus 18. He offers a similar reading for *pornoi* in the list in 1 Corinthians 6:9 and *pornois* in 1 Timothy 1:10 as similarly covering all of the sexual offenses in Leviticus 18. (Via, 77–87 *passim*) There are a number of problems with this analysis.

First, while the NRSV translates them in the singular, *all* of the sins in Jesus' list are in the plural, and no special significance should be drawn from the use of the plural form *porneiai*. The *only* time the plural form is used in the Greek version of the Hebrew Scriptures, it refers metaphorically to the "harlotries of Jezebel," an almost certain reference to the idolatrous cult practices she had introduced (2 Kings 9:22). So no special significance should be given to the use of the plural in this case.

Moreover, the assertion of a link between male-male same-sexuality and the *porn*- root words cannot be based on the text of Leviticus itself, which does not use the terms *zonah / z'nut* (or in the Greek version, *porne / porneia*) to refer to any of the sexual behaviors in the relevant chapters of Leviticus. The only uses of these words in Leviticus are clearly with the figurative meaning of the idolatrous cult (17:7, concerning Molech worship; 20:5–6, concerning divination) or the simple meaning of "prostitute" (19:29; 21:9), including the type of woman a priest may not marry (21:7,14).

This latter is important as it offers additional rationale for not seeing same-sexuality under the heading of *porneia*, in terms of how the Rabbis later applied this term. It soon becomes evident in their debates that the meaning of *zonah* = harlot is intimately connected with a class of "women not allowed to marry a priest." In bYebamoth 61b, it is clear that this applies to "a prostitute" and to an "unfaithful wife" (based on the etymological relation to the word for "straying"). In fact, much of the rabbinic debate on this topic follows a kind of circular reference: A priest may not marry a harlot. What is a harlot? A woman disqualified from marrying a priest. This included, interestingly enough, "a woman incapable of procreation"—such is the emphasis on following the commandment to be fruitful and multiply (mYebamoth 6.5, bYebamoth 61b).

Rabbi Eliezer maintained that if a man had carnal relations with a woman without the intent to marry her, he rendered her a *zonah* (bSanhedrin 51a). This is about the closest thing to the traditional meaning of "fornication" (= sex before marriage or between unmarried people) one finds in the literature, and may relate to the provisions of Deuteronomy 22:28–29, concerning a man who seizes a woman not engaged to another and has sex with her. He is *required* to marry her (after payment of a bride-penalty to her father) and can never divorce her. Of course, there being no marriage liturgy in biblical times, a man who slept with a woman with the intent to

◠◡ Not the Same

The claim that *pornoi* includes male-male sex in 1 Corinthians 6:9 fails on grammatical grounds, if we are to take it that *arsenokoitai* and *malakoi* do refer to male-male sex. (Notice again there is no mention of female same-sexuality in the 1 Corinthians "vice list.") There is some argument about the later term, which used to be widely understood to refer to masturbation. More recently the terms taken together have been held to refer to the "active" and "passive" partner in male-male intercourse. Thanks to the work of Robin Scroggs, the former term is now usually seen as a Greek relative of the Hebrew rabbinic term for male-male sex: *mishkav zakur*. Both the Hebrew and Greek essentially mean "bedder of a male" and reflect the terminology of Leviticus 18:22, which refers to a male performing *mishk'vei ishah*—the beddings of a woman—with a male. (As noted elsewhere, the Leviticus proscription may relate more to idolatrous practices than sexuality per se.) The presence of *malakoi* is of little significance, except to those who wish to follow the older teaching of the church that this was a condemnation of masturbation. As the Rabbis said, *mishkav zakur* required two men, and both were culpable—so there was no need for a second term to describe the "passive" partner.

keep her, and presumably with her father's permission—that is, a man who *takes* a woman *given* by her father ("take" and "give" being the operative words still used in marriage to this day) has essentially married her.

It is, at the same time, not unlikely that the term *z'nut* applied to the violations of the incest laws spelled out in Leviticus 18:6–18, even though this cannot be demonstrated from Scripture itself, and we must depend on much later texts such as the Testament of Reuben (1:6) for this linkage. More importantly for the matter at hand—a purported linkage of *all* of the sexual offenses in Leviticus 18: it is rather the case that the incest restrictions of the "forbidden degrees" were seen as a unity within the chapter, apart from the rest of the laws, and the Rabbis gave them a special sanctity. These regulations were classed along with property laws, laws concerning the Temple, and the laws of what is clean and unclean as among "the essentials of the Law" (mHagigah 1:8).

It is also determined that a child born of intimacy within the forbidden degrees is a bastard. (mHagigah 1:7; mYebamoth 4:13, adding any issue from intimacy punishable by *karet*) We might remember in this light the accusations noised concerning Jesus himself, rhetorically suggesting his illegitimacy (by asserting their own legitimacy) : "We are not born of *porneias*" (John 8:41). So there is a clear linkage between illegitimacy and *porneia*—but not with male-male sex.

When we move to the more recently available evidence in the form of the Dead Sea Scrolls, we find a similar range of meaning for *z'nut*. The Damascus

Our concern here is with the conjunctions that link the list of sinners, and which renders impossible the notion that the meaning of *pornoi* is inclusive of the other items in the list, rather than exclusive. For, as once again the NRSV fails to make clear, the list begins and is separated with *oute*, the Greek construction for "neither" and "nor." So, in this case, *pornoi* can include neither *arsenokoitai* nor *malakoi*. So the meaning of *pornoi* here is narrow, and refers to those who resort to or provide prostitutes, and perhaps to (male) prostitutes themselves.

The passage in 1 Timothy lacks conjunctions, and also reference to *malakoi*, but again it seems clear that this is a list, the individual items in which stand separately: as is the nature of lists. One might well say that if, as Gagnon claims, no first century Jew would hear this word without including male-male sexuality, then the use of *arsenokoitai* is unneccesary, and its use calls his thesis into question. Of course, his ultimate goal is to link this back to Jesus, in order to refute the claims of Jesus' silence on the subject. By overreaching for additional evidence he has, in fact, overshot his mark.

Thus the notion that *pornoi* necessarily includes male-male intercourse has no foundation, unless it includes male *prostitutes* who service men, rather than or in addition to women.

Document, for example, warns of not following "a guilty inclination and *'ayni z'nut* = whoring eyes" (2:16) and proceeds to follow up with an account similar to that in Jude and Enoch concerning the fall of the Watchers, who lusted after the daughters of mankind, and committed trans-species sex by going after "different" flesh. (2:18). The three snares of Belial are described as "fornication, wealth, and defilement of the Temple" (4:16) which neatly echo the Mishnaic categorization of these as essentials of the law, demonstrating an early parallel with rabbinic thinking (mHag. 1:8). Then follows immediately a condemnation of taking two wives in a lifetime as *z'nut*, since "the principle of creation is 'a male and a female he created them'" (CD 4:20–21) Clearly this is an early, and unusual, condemnation of polygamy, or even a second marriage (similar to the injunction in the Pastoral Epistles concerning clergy, and what the later church forbade under the term *digamy*) to be a species of *porneia*.

In column 5, matters from Leviticus 18—sexual congress with a menstruating woman, and a number of the incest prohibitions—come up, but no explicit reference to *z'nut* appears in this column, which is quite a distance from the last reference in column 4, and the next in column 7:1–2. There we find a call "for each to seek the peace of his brother and not commit sin against his own flesh, and to refrain from *z'nut* in accord with the ordinance"—which, if we take "sin against his own flesh" as a reference to incest, does give us some vague connection, unless the two clauses are dealing with different things. The "sin against one's own flesh" might well be an echo of Paul's injunction that brother ought not to

Porneia Unheard of Among the Gentiles

Does Paul's challenge to the church in Corinth (1 Corinthians 5:1–2) concerning the man who "has his father's woman" and is thus engaging in a kind of "*porneia* unheard of even among the Gentiles" constitute evidence of *porneia* applied to the forbidden degrees? This is possible, as is the reference in Sirach 23:16–17, which refers to a "a man a fornicator (*anthrōpos pornos*) to the body of his own flesh." These would then be the only biblical references connecting that distinct portion of Leviticus 18 with words of the *porn-* range.

However, even here it is possible that a more literal meaning of *porneia* makes equal sense of Paul's language. There are several reasons for this. First of all, it is clear that the woman is not the man's mother—if that were the case, not only would it not be "unknown among the Gentiles" (the story of Oedipus being well-known) but it would be incest of the sort that even the Corinthians would recognize as beyond the pale. After all, the letter goes on to suggest the Corinthians are "puffed up" about the matter rather than ashamed. So is this woman the father's second wife? This is also a possibility, and would be a case of incest by affinity and of a sort dealt with

cheat brother—there is not necessarily a sexual implication in "sin" here (1 Corinthians 6:6; though there may be at 1 Thessalonians 4:6). Meanwhile, back in Qumran, Column 8:5 and 19:17 return to the general language of "paths of harlotry." Other uses of *z'nut* in the Dead Sea sectarian corpus reflect a similar range of concerns: general avoidance of "harlotry" (1qPHab 5:7) or references to an actual or figurative harlot, in the style of Revelation (4QNahumPesher 4.ii.7).

So while there is an occasional connection between *porneia* and incest within the forbidden degrees, it is clear that all cases of harlotry (other than the figurative) thus far discussed involve, well, *harlots*. They all involve prostitution in one form or another. Just as under Jewish law a man commits adultery only with another man's wife, so under the same law he commits harlotry with a harlot—or is (perhaps) a prostitute himself.

An additional objection to including the prohibition of male-male intercourse along with all of the other offenses listed in Leviticus 18 under a general heading of *porneia* lies in the fact that the Rabbis *explicitly exclude* two of the offenses in Leviticus 18 from the category of *z'nut*: congress with a menstruant (bTemurah 29b) and bestiality (*ibid.* 30b). It will be noted that these offenses fall in the same separate section of chapter 18 of Leviticus, apart from the neat package of incest regulations identified with various forms of "nakedness." So if *porneia* does apply to the incest regulations, there is no indication it necessarily applies to the offenses outside this separate section, and we have rabbinical authority that *it does not apply* to at least two of them.

---

explicitly in Leviticus 18:8. This view, of course, assumes the father has died: that is, a son has taken his step-mother.

But what if the father is still living, and the woman is not his wife? What if she is a prostitute being visited by a father and son? Clearly visiting prostitutes was still a problem for the church in Corinth, and Paul will return to this in the following chapter (1 Corinthians 6:9–20). It would seem that not only "such were some of them," but some of them are still trying to defend prostitution, and may even be proud of it. This would explain Paul's fervent appeal to shun this behavior, and also the Corinthians' apparent lack of concern about it.

Add to that the fact that a man and his son visiting the same harlot would definitely rile a rabbi like Paul as a vision of a depraved world in which "father and son go in to the same girl, so that my holy name is profaned" (Amos 2:7). Given this, it is quite enough to take *porneia* at its most literal—and as Paul most often uses it—as a reference to prostitution, rather than bringing in tendentious references to Leviticus' incest code.

The final blow, though a glancing one, comes with another rabbinical judgment concerning the never-biblically-mentioned phenomenon of female-female sex. This, the Rabbis affirm, is not *z'nut*. Rabbi Huna had argued that women who are *mesolelot* (= lewdly sporting) with each other are thereby rendered harlots and may not marry a priest. This was disputed on the basis of a decision by Rabbi Eleazar, and it was held that such women were guilty of *prizut*, not *z'nut*; that is, *lewd conduct* but not *harlotry* (bYebamoth 76a).

This may seem like a long journey to address the single assertion that Jesus was referring to male-male intercourse when he used the word *porneia*. The point is that if he was, almost no one would have understood his intent—as, contrary to Gagnon's assertion, the literature does not support this as a common understanding.

But what about Sodom?

Ultimately, there is no clear and convincing evidence that *porneia* would have included male same-sex relationships, apart from the circular reasoning that scattered references in some of the apocryphal writings of the era to the "*porneia* of Sodom" must be understood in this light. It is much more likely that the *porneia* of Sodom referred to in documents such as the Testament of Benjamin was simply understood to be *porneia* in the primary uses of the word: harlotry and idolatry and "going beyond the bounds." For example, the *Testament of Benjamin* 9:1 says, "I believe that there will be also evil-doings among you, from the words of Enoch the righteous: that ye shall commit fornication with the fornication of Sodom, and shall perish, all save a few, and shall renew wanton deeds with women; and the kingdom of the Lord shall not be among you, for straightway he shall take it away." Clearly "wanton deeds with women" should offset any suggestion that this is about same-sexuality!

This is very likely the meaning in Jude 7 (and the parallel sections of 2 Peter 2), in which the excesses of the contemporaries are analogized to Sodom chiefly in relation to their bombastic slander of the heavenly beings. The rabbinic literature refers to the *z'nut* of Sodom (Tosefta 13) and parallels Jude in including some of the same cast of villains—Korah (v. 11) and the unfaithful of the wilderness (5). Mishnah Sanhedrin 10, in a similar context, adds Balaam (11) and the generation of the Flood, relating to the parallel condemnations of 2 Peter 2:5. The general theme is not sexuality, but overweening pride and the disorder attendant on rejection of authority, typified in idolatry, which replaces God with a creature.

A similar catalogue of villainy with similar themes and examples come up in another late Jewish document, 3 Maccabees. This book is so late that it is not included in the Western Bible at all, although the Eastern Orthodox tradition includes it. In 3 Maccabees 2:1–5, insolence and arrogance, and more importantly, denying the faith—which is the theme of the Maccabean story (as it is for Jude)—form a catalogue of divine retribution, including the generation of giants killed in the flood, and this time adding Pharaoh and his chariots and troops. Verse 5 on the fate of Sodom is substantially parallel to Jude 7.

There are a few early writers who saw Sodom in terms of same-sexuality, but even more as a caricature of effeminacy—such as Philo of Alexandria (see *De Abrahamo* 135–137). Philo does not, in any case, connect Sodom with *porneia*. He also maintains a clear distinction between his "feminizing" view of male same-sexuality and harlotry in *De Spec. Leg.* 1:325–326. This passage is a summary of those excluded from the worship of the assembly, and Philo is repeating the injunctions of Deuteronomy 23:1–2, adding his own twist on rejecting men who "act like women" along with the eunuchs specified in the legal code.

Philo's concerns reflect those of later figures in the early church regarding effeminacy. This may be due to the role and prevalence of same-sexuality in a more Hellenistic setting, which Philo and others read back into the biblical texts. This concern with effeminacy in particular seems to be characteristic of the Alexandrian environment, and similar passages appear in the work of Clement. None of this seems to relate clearly to the biblical account of Sodom, and how it was understood in a Palestinian setting, even in the post-apostolic period.

For the rabbinic tradition, when it comes to spelling out the sins of the wicked city, follows Ezekiel, and in consonance with the figurative use Jesus makes of the wicked city, portrays it as an example of harsh hostility to outsiders, of selfishness, self-absorption, and greed. There is no suggestion of any connection with same-sexuality. Throughout the Talmud, the phrase "to act in the manner of Sodom" has nothing to do with sex or sexuality at all, but refers to the kind of spiteful selfishness typical of one who says, "What is mine is mine and what is thine is thine" (mPirke Aboth 5.10). This is the kind of person who, for instance, if he saw his and your property about to be consumed by fire, would save his own and leave yours to be destroyed. The people of Sodom knew what was right, but chose to do wrong.

Gagnon, on the contrary, tends to read any reference to Sodom (or "abomination" or *porneia*) as *including* a reference to male same-sex intercourse. For example, he cites Ezekiel 16:50 as an example of a reference to same-sexuality, and 18:12, a text explicitly "connected with man-male intercourse" simply because it uses the word *to'evah* (Gagnon 2003, n46).

This approach precisely begs the question concerning what to read into any particular reference to Sodom, and ignores two essential facts:

- As I have shown, the ancient sources, including the biblical ones, apart from those few steeped in the atmosphere of Hellenism, do not read the Sodom account as involving male-male sex, and Ezekiel above all doesn't do this as he actually enumerates the sins of Sodom, in the verse just prior to the one Gagnon cites as a purported reference to same-sex intercourse: "This was the guilt of your sister Sodom: she and her daughters had pride, excess of food, and prosperous ease, but did not aid the poor and needy."

- The language of abomination and harlotry throughout these chapters refers explicitly to idolatry—the most common focus for the term to'evah. That male same-sex intercourse was one of the behaviors included under the heading of to'evah in Leviticus, thus linking it to idolatry in much the same fashion as Paul does in Romans, does not mean that every time to'evah is mentioned it must be a reference to male same-sex intercourse. Sometimes, in fact most times, as Freud observed, a cigar is just a cigar.

Gagnon tends, with all of these terms, to a employ a peculiar kind of "dictionary fallacy"—that when a word has several meanings and uses, all of them must be intended whenever the word is used. This is far from true even when we come to everyday language. Moreover, in the present case, it should be clear from the evidence I have adduced that the assertion that *porneia* was understood to include male-male sexual intercourse, or that any references to Sodom or *abomination* or *dogs* must similarly be understood—or was so understood by Jesus and the apostolic church—does not stand up to close scrutiny. Words with multiple meanings have to be understood in the context in which they are used.

We can therefore return in confidence to the assumption that Jesus said nothing explicit on the subject of same-sexuality.

The Sin of Sodom

The Rabbis taught that Sodom was a land that produced bread and jewels and gold, all of itself. The people there grew haughty, and said, "Since our land produces such of itself, why should we allow travelers to come our way, and rob us of what is ours. Let us forbid travel in our land . . . When a wealthy man came to their city, they would seat him next to a toppling wall, and when it fell on him take all his goods; as it is written, "like a leaning fence or toppling wall" (Psalm 62:3). Or they would give him balsam to keep, and when he stored it with his precious goods, they would come out by night and sniff it out like dogs, find it, break in, and steal his goods; as it is written, "in the day they hide themselves; they do not know the light; in the dark they dig through houses (Job 24:16); and by night they snarl like dogs and prowl around the city (Psalm 59:6)." They strip people of their clothing, so they have no protection from the cold; they take the donkey of the fatherless, and the ox of the widow in pledge; they remove landmarks and steal flocks and raise them as their own (Job 24 passim) . . . They required a man with one ox to tend all of the town oxen for one day; but a man who has no oxen had to tend for two days. They established a rule that if you took the ferry across the river you had to pay the toll, but if you waded across you had to pay double. If you set out bricks to dry, they would all come and take one, but say, each of them, "Oh, I've only taken one." They would do the same if you set out garlic or onions to dry, "Oh, I've only taken one . . ." Soon you had none!

He had nothing good to say

Of course, as King Lear said, "Nothing will come of nothing"—and the fact that Jesus said nothing negative about same-sexuality must be balanced by noting he said nothing positive either. We are left with several possibilities:

- in common with most Palestinian Jews, this was a matter so far from his concern and consideration that it never even came to mind, or was not brought to his attention
- given the prevailing negative view towards at least male same-sex intercourse, he would have disapproved if it had come up, or
- had it come up he would have applied the same kind of moral principle to this as he did to other moral questions, which is to say, not simply following a legal code, but looking for marks of consonance with an overriding concern for human dignity and fellowship, generosity and self-giving.

It is only the latter possibility that gives us anything further to say on the subject. There are, after all, any number of problems in morality that were not expressly addressed by Jesus, yet we do trust he gave us guidance in how to address them.

They had four judges, named Liar, Double-Liar, Forger, and Mix-Up-Justice. This is how they ruled: If a man attacked and injured another man's wife, they would say to the husband, "Give her to him so he can finish the task and make her pregnant." If a man cut off his neighbor's donkey's ear, they would rule, "Give him the donkey until it grows a new one." If a man wounded his neighbor and drew blood, they would tell the wounded man to pay him the standard fee for bloodletting. Once, Abraham's servant Eliezer was attacked in Sodom, and when he came before the court, the judge said to him, in accord with this rule, "Pay your attacker the bloodletting fee." Wily Eliezer took a stone and hit the judge, who said, "What is this!" and Eliezer said, "Since you now owe me, you can pay him what I owe." They also had beds for travelers, but if they were too tall to fit they cut off their feet, or if too short they stretched them. They tried to make Eliezer sleep in one, but the wily servant said, "Oh, I have vowed never to sleep in any bed!" . . . They also had a rule that if anyone invited a stranger to the town to a feast, the one who invited would forfeit his clothing. Eliezer came once when a banquet was in progress, and sat down at the end of a row. The man beside him said, "Who invited you?" and the wily servant said, "You did." Whereupon, the man, fearing they would hear and strip him of his clothing, fled away. And so Eliezer did to the next, and then the next; and when they were all gone he had the banquet to himself—and feasted! Such was the sin of Sodom.

—based on bSanhedrin 109a–b, as retold by this author

So, since Jesus never apparently had to deal with the issue of same-sexuality directly, let us turn to look at how he dealt with other moral questions.

Throughout his ministry, Jesus was confronted by a number of religious questions concerning right and wrong. Some were presented in ways designed to trip him up, others by people who seemed genuinely interested in finding the right way. So how did Jesus apply Scripture to these questions? How did he respond to these challenges? Jesus offers us two keys with which to unlock the moral treasury of his thinking.

Inside out

When Jesus was understood to have set aside the dietary laws he did more than simply change the menu. The dietary laws symbolized for him a whole approach to discerning morality that was based on "the outside." (It should be noted that although Mark understood Jesus as "declaring all foods clean," the

---

⌒⌣ The Centurion's Dear Servant

It is sometimes suggested that the incident of Christ healing a centurion's servant (Matthew 8:5–13, Luke 7:1–10; cp. John 4:46–54) is to be seen as an endorsement of same-sexuality or at least of a refusal to condemn it.

I think it goes too far to suggest a *necessary* sexual relationship between the centurion and "his boy / slave / servant." It is certainly *possible*; and it is also true that the Jewish opinion of Gentiles was to suspect all of them of same-sexuality. Jesus appears not to have been of the suspicious type, however, and the Jewish elders speak well of the centurion, and likely not just because he financed the synagogue. (Though, again, there is a long tradition of constituents being blind to the "faults" of their benefactors so long as they bring home the figurative bacon.)

Moreover, there is good cause to think that the relationship between the centurion and his servant is more significant than mere slave / owner (besides the centurion's obvious concern and affection and going well out of his way to seek Jesus' help). This is on account of the use of the ambiguous word *pais*. In Matthew's version (8:9) the centurion uses the less ambiguous word for slave (*doulos*) when referring to his normal daily life of giving orders; so he clearly has the various words at his disposal and appears to make a distinction. At the end of the story the *pais* is healed (in some manuscripts with an added "his" emphasizing the personal connection).

In Luke's version of the story, when other people talk about the servant they use *doulos* but the centurion refers to him as *"ho pais mou* = my boy / servant"—and as in Matthew uses *doulos* in his description of giving orders; so he appears to make a distinction between this servant and servants in general. Of course, this may indicate nothing more than the affection a master might have for a particularly good and faithful servant.

question that was presented to him actually had to do with hand-washing, not food.) In any case, Jesus used this incident as an opportunity to reflect upon the locus of morality. Morality, he says, is not about what goes into one from the outside, but about what comes out of one, from the heart. In this, Jesus is advocating an ethic of disposition or intent, as opposed to an ethic based primarily upon a list of externally exercised *dos* and *don'ts*, which finds its most primitive form in moralities based on taboo and purity. As he said, "Do not judge by appearances, but judge with right judgment" (John 7:24). And as he noted further, concerning hypocrisy:

> Woe to you, scribes and Pharisees, hypocrites! For you are like whitewashed tombs, which on the outside look beautiful, but inside they are full of the bones of the dead and of all kinds of filth. So you also on the outside look righteous to others, but inside you are full of hypocrisy and lawlessness (Matthew 23:27–28).

To dispose of another possibility, it is unlikely the servant is his son (another meaning of *pais*), as there are other far more precise words for that, and surely he would have made that clear if it were so. However, we note that the word for son (*huios*) *is* used in John's account, as well as *paidion* and *pais*. (Note as well that we are also no longer dealing with a centurion, nor in all likelihood with a Gentile. This may, in fact, be an entirely different incident merely parallel in form and some of its content.)

The age of the servant is also up for grabs. *Pais* was sometimes used in Graeco-Roman literature to refer to older servants as well as younger ones, including, perhaps most significantly in the case of a soldier, an armor-bearer or groom. Note, for instance, we still refer to the *infantry*—just as the Septuagint has David call his troop of soldiers *paidaria* (1 Samuel 21:5). So this is not necessarily a pederastic relationship, *if* it is a sexual or affectional one at all. The relationship between an officer and his aide de camp may be exactly what is being described, and while it goes too far to read a sexual relationship here with any certainty, it can also not be entirely ruled out. Such relationships were not unknown in the Roman world though Roman law had no way to formalize them.

However, and most importantly, it does hardly seem to be the point of the story, and whatever the relationship between the master and servant it appears irrelevant to Jesus. He doesn't ask, and the centurion doesn't tell. In this sense, it may serve as an example of how we can move away from "sexual behavior" to the more important question of human relationships. This is the story of someone who cared deeply about another person, who in the normal course of events would have been regarded as you or I might regard our refrigerator. He cares enough to seek the help of Jesus, and Jesus praises his faith, and grants his request. That would appear to be the lesson for us.

Jesus took a tolerant view on questions of food and ritual purity. He was more concerned with the laws of charity and fidelity—more concerned with the "inside" than the "outside"—more desirous of a pure heart than clean hands.

As I noted above, this contrast between inside and outside was addressed in Peter's miraculous vision of the sheet let down from heaven; and he rightly understood that this was not about a change in the dietary law, but about *how people are to be treated*—not as unclean because of practice or nation, outward action or appearance, but as inwardly capable of receiving and manifesting the love of God from within. It is abundantly clear that Jesus had little patience with the focus on purity as a means to please God; and Paul continued this teaching—see Colossians 2:21–23 and 1 Timothy 4:3–5—although, given his Pharisee training even he occasionally slipped from confidence in grace into reliance on law.

The other *locus classicus* for Jesus' teaching on morality resides in the summary of the law and the "Golden Rule." Jesus refines the specifics of the Decalogue down to the pure gold of the love of God and neighbor, with the subjective touchstone of doing as one would be done by. Even his critics recognized the wisdom in this approach.

So, bearing these two keys in mind, when I return to the actual text and look at the passages that are traditionally advanced against the allowance for same-sex sexuality, I have to ask: are these moral prohibitions, based upon the disposition of the heart, or are they rather ritual or cultic matters related to external acts? Do these prohibitions take account either of the love of God and neighbor, or the subjective judgment of mutuality and responsive care, or are they simply absolute and categorical?

To take another example from Jesus' confrontation with the Law: How did Jesus relate to the question of the Sabbath? The text of the law is abundantly clear; it is explicitly categorical in listing all the categories! Yet Jesus recognized circumstances in which this clarity was forced to bend to charity—the rigorous interpretation that one could do no work of any kind is bent to allow for works of love and care. The Sabbath exists not as an end in itself, but as a means to the rest and refreshment and betterment of human beings.

Some of the current angst over the fate and future of the Anglican Communion, and the extent to which novel developments are held to cause tensions or outright tears in its fabric, remind me of the question of the Sabbath. The institutional church—for that is where the tensions and tears exist, in the structures of polity and governance, not in the unbreakable net of baptism which hoists us all aboard the one and indivisible church of God in Christ—that institutional church is made for its members, and not they for the institution. When the institution asks us to forgo charity and generosity and morality in favor of exclusion and judgment and moralism, it has ceased to serve that for which God intends it.

This is where I have been trying to pitch the discussion concerning sexuality. People do not exist for marriage, but marriage exists for people—stemming from the deep human need for an instituted and regularized companionship, in recognition of the final work of Creation in response to the fact that it is not good for one to be alone.

The various arguments from a surmised "complementarity" of the sexes are still too much concerned with the "outside" of sex—the sexual dimorphism that we share with most of the animals and some of the vegetables, the level of anatomy and the "flesh"—rather than with the "inside," the spirit that makes us truly human, and wherein resides our similarity to God: in the capacity to choose, to reason and to love. The dismissal of all same-sex relationships, without regard to anything other than the gender (or anatomy) of the parties, the explicit declaration that all this talk of love and commitment is irrelevant to the question, does not strike me as being in keeping with the ethical world of Jesus Christ. Marriage, as we are assured by Christ himself, will one day pass away, when we rejoice in the endless Sabbath of the Lamb's wedding feast.

Although I am loath to add to Scripture, the following application of what I've said above occurs to me, purely as an imaginative exercise:

Some lawyers came to Jesus and said to him, Teacher, we found two men who have set up household and live together after the manner of a man and woman. Shall we do unto them as it is written in the law of Moses? And he said unto them, For your hardness of heart Moses gave you this law. But it was not so at the beginning, when God made companions for Adam and allowed him to choose the one suitable to him, the one who was most like him. And they said to him, But was not that Eve, the mother of all living? And he said to them, Do not be deceived, 'the Lord does not see as mortals see'—you lawyers look only to the outside, and do not look to the heart. But God knows what is inside a man, and it is from inside that true love flows. And do you not know that when Jonathan looked upon David his soul was bound to him, and he loved him as his own self, and gave up his life for his friend? David spoke rightly when he said there is no greater love than this. If these two should set up their lives together, what is that to you? Love the Lord your God, and do not judge.

As I say, this is purely imaginative. But it does strike me as in keeping with the gospel.

The Pharisee and the Harlot

I leave to one side the well-worn story of the woman taken in adultery (John 8:1–11). It is familiar enough not to require further comment beyond noting Jesus' interesting suggestion that the law, which required the eyewitnesses to cast the first stone (Deuteronomy 17:7)—and we know there were eyewitnesses, since the woman was caught in the act—should be understood in terms of their own internal state of sinfulness, concerning sins to which they were witnesses because they had committed them. Certainly this is in keeping with his general advice not to judge one's neighbor, and not to condemn others, or pretend to take motes from others' eyes while beams are protruding from one's own. Jesus calls all people to rigorous self-examination, rather than turning judgment against others. However, though this episode is cited by "liberals" for its notes of tolerance and suspension of judgment, "conservatives" are quick to point out the call for reformation of life. As with much of Scripture its one-size message fits all. However one wants to apply it, the lesson seems plain: the church's task is not to punish, but to forgive; to urge people not to sin, but not to condemn them.

The more interesting pericope is "The Anointing of Jesus." John (12:1–8) places the scene in the hospitable and somewhat irregular household of Martha, Mary and Lazarus, while Matthew (26:6–13) and Mark (14:3–9) place it in the home of Simon the leper. All three evangelists highlight the extravagant offering of perfume, the diversion of resources that might have served the poor, and Jesus' response that serving him takes precedence.

Luke (7:36–50), however, with his characteristic urge to highlight issues of salvation and redemption, places the scene in the home of Simon the Pharisee, who, no doubt intrigued by what he has heard of Jesus, invites him into his home to dine with him. A woman from the city, a sinner—and it takes no imagination to tell what kind of sinner she is—comes in and makes an incredible display of herself at Jesus's feet.

It also takes no imagination to picture the look of indignation on Simon the Pharisee's face. His concern is not with perfume or the poor, but with the woman, or rather, with the *sort* of woman he knows her to be—and about which he is surprised that Jesus seems *not* to know or care. Simon sees her not as an individual *person* so much as a member of a despised *class* of people. The Pharisee no doubt thinks that he has escaped the snares of sin by his careful observance of the rules. There is no hint that it ever occurs to him to think, "If this man were a prophet he would not accept my invitation to dinner, for he would know what sort of man I am." No, the Pharisee is prudent; he is temperate. As I noted earlier, the Pharisees (as portrayed in the somewhat unkindly light of the Gospels) were very concerned about careful observation of the law—not touching anything unclean, washing hands before eating, and making sure all the vessels are ritually pure. They are represented as the Hyacinth Buckets—"It's Bouquet!"—of first-century Judaism.

To be more balanced and fair to this movement, as Bonhoeffer points out in his eloquent description of the Pharisees in the opening chapter of *Ethics*, they are among the best-intentioned people in the world. But they are attempting the very thing in which Paul told Peter no one could succeed (Galatians 2:14f): to gain salvation by following the law in all its details down to the last jot and tittle, including how to fold your napkin after you've wiped your hands. Like his con-frère who compared himself favorably to the tax collector, the great gulf between Simon the Pharisee's upright life and this fallen woman's lifestyle is obvious to him. "Yes," he might say, "We are all sinners; but some are clearly more sinful than others."

And Jesus appears at first to ratify this assessment: he offers the analogy of debt forgiveness, forgiveness to one who owed much and to one who owed little. But Jesus doesn't stop there, with what the Pharisee could well take as a flattering assessment of his success in sin-avoidance, a pat on the head for his correct answer to the moral drama unfolding at his dinner table.

Instead Jesus presses home the significance of the answer: the Pharisee has judged himself, correctly this time, and Jesus goes on to compare and contrast Simon's parsimonious welcome with the woman's lavish and costly offering and service.

The Pharisee welcomes Jesus to the table, but keeps him at arm's length and sits in judgment—and in error. For Jesus not only knows what sort of woman it is who is ministering to him, but knows it better than the Pharisee possibly can, better than the Pharisee knows himself. The Pharisee cannot fathom why Jesus would allow a sinner to be a minister to him, or at least *such* a sinner. Of his own trifling sins he cares but little, for he is sure of his own righteousness. But this *woman*! That is another matter altogether. And so he sits in double judgment, of the woman and her Lord.

She, on the other hand, isn't worried about her sins, which indeed are many. Nor is there a mention of repentance concerning her tears—unusual for Luke, who mentions repentance so often. Rather her tears reveal faith, hope, and love, flowing from the knowledge of forgiveness. We see in this incident the essence of the virtues incarnate in a woman thought by the Pharisee to be incapable of goodness, a woman who enacts the sacrament of baptism: with her voiceless con-fession of faith, the washing of her tears, anointing her Lord with fragrant oint-ment, sealed with the kiss of peace—she is then sent out in that peace to love and serve her Lord in the world. (And, unlike the woman taken in adultery, without that final finger-wag of "sin no more.")

This incident presents us two models for our encounter with Christ, and for Christian ministry, two models for service to the body of Christ which is the church—the household of God. All who serve the Lord are sinners, yet all who serve the Lord are forgiven. Some will prefer to spend their time worrying about other people's sins and whether the church can tolerate them. They will seek to obstruct their service, thinking all the while that they protect God's body from the touch of unclean hands, from those who, if only the truth were known, would not be allowed to serve. They are simply being good housekeepers of the household of God—like Hyacinth Bucket making people take off their shoes before entering her spotless house.

Others will get on with the hopeful works of faith and love, of justice and compassion—the kind of good housekeeping that accepts the fact that there will be some cleaning up to do from time to time, because so many people have been made welcome in the house. Is there any question at all which of these Christ would rather have us do?

Faith, hope and love

We have been assured that the three theological virtues are what really count, above all love. Love is the means by which we are called to act and the standard by which we are to judge our actions, and when we fail, the remedy and forgiveness for those failures. Love covers a multitude of sins (1 Peter 4:8), for love is of God (1 John 4:7), for God is love (1 John 4:16). One cannot love without God being the cause—so every loving act is not due to ourselves, but to God at work in us (Philippians 2:13). In one sense, the only works-righteousness to be found is in the works of love, against which there is no law (Galatians 5:22–23).

As we know, love is not really about sex—sex may be the medium but it is not the message. This is perhaps the heart of the problem we face—the concern with the flesh rather than the spirit, the form rather than the content. In this case it is the literal flesh, the anatomical flesh, that serves as an obstacle to our understanding. Perhaps it is not so strange that, just as circumcision involved a physical mark on a sexual organ, we still find our concerns drawn to such physical signs—*as if God really cared*. But as Paul boldly said, "circumcision is nothing"—thereby declaring indifferent the object of centuries of tradition and divine commandment, even while arguing the importance of keeping the commandments (1 Corinthians 7:19)!

This is not to say the body is indifferent. It is not. What we do in and with our bodies matters, for we are embodied beings. But the body that matters most at this point is the body of Christ, the church, of which and in which we are individual

♋ The question of justice

Sometimes the recognition of or support for same-sex relationships is cast as a matter of justice. In response, people suggest that justice isn't the issue—in the face of all of our failings we need mercy, not justice. It is better to think in terms of equity rather than justice—the principle of fairness in the application of justice. We can recognize inequity in the unequal application of laws, and of laws that in their application effectively become "unjust laws." That is in part what lies behind the biblical concern with equal weights and measures. In applying the law, then, Jesus appears to be most critical of those who let themselves off the hook while laying heavy burdens on others (Matthew 23:4).

members—and in that edifice we build with what we have and what we are. Do our actions build it up, or tear it down? Do we edify as building blocks and living stones, or serve as stumbling blocks and stones of scandal about which the builders are bewildered, as indeed Jesus said of himself? As organs in the body, do we contribute to its overall well-being, or spend our energy in attempts at ecclesiastical self-mutilation in removing portions deemed cancerous or malignant, but which may be vital to the health of the whole? Do we overly concern ourselves with outward appearances and forms, or seek the content and the values that lie within? Do we concern ourselves with what goes into the church, or what comes out of it? Do we love much, or little?

Jesus expressed his love most completely in his choice to give himself up for our sins. He said that this was the greatest love anyone could express—the perfect sacrifice of himself once offered, freely given, a life freely laid down, to save a fallen world. He said that to give one's life for one's friends was the greatest love of all (John 15:13).

In this he was echoing the greatest love story in the Hebrew Scriptures: the story of Jonathan's love for David, the love which David said "surpassed the love of women" (2 Samuel 1:26). Jonathan risked his life to save David's life—such was his love. As the Rabbis said,

> All love which depends on something—if the thing ceases, the love ceases. If it does not depend on something it lasts for ever. What love is that which depends on something? This is the love of Amnon and Tamar. And that which does not depend on something? This is the love of David and Jonathan (mPirke Aboth 5:19).

The love of Jonathan for David did not *depend* on anything: Jonathan loved David "as his own soul" and their souls were "knit together" and joined in "a

Thus, the gospels offer significant support both for what is called "the social gospel" and for equity in the application of laws. Search as I might, I find nothing at all, one way or the other, about faithful, life-long, same-sex relationships, those who live in them, and whether they should be ordained or not or blessed or not.

But when we look to Jesus, he appears, in the case of the Samaritan woman at Jacob's well, to have been quite capable of making use of one living in an out-of-wedlock relationship (John 4:18) to spread the gospel—the saving and sufficient gospel that points to Messiah. Even broken vessels can still hold their share of living water, and spread it to other thirsty people. Only the disciples appear to have been at all concerned with why he should be speaking with a Samaritan woman.

covenant of love" (1 Samuel 18:1–3). They were not just "good friends." Friendship is, as C.S. Lewis pointed out long ago, based on a common interest—it "depends on something." The Hebrew word for "friend" appears nowhere in the story, except in the idiom that means "each other"—reminding us that even if the word *re'ah* were used, in Hebrew it has exactly the range of meaning as the word *mate* does in English.

No, the Scripture is quite clear: Jonathan and David were lovers. However much one wants to wiggle away from it, that is what the text of 1 Samuel 18:1–6 says, and the rest of the story attests to this devotion. The word used to describe their devoted and sacrificial love, *ahava*, is the same used to describe the entirely lustful love that Amnon had for Tamar (2 Samuel 13:15)—which may be why the Rabbis drew the contrast between the two. In fact, the Hebrew text is so clear that we are dealing with a love story that the more completely Hellenist (or Hellenized) translators of the Septuagint, perhaps with concern about how it might be understood, did not include that touching scene from 1 Samuel 18 in their version of the Scripture; much as Jerome, in his Latin version, amended the text of 2 Samuel 1:26 to add "for their children" after "beyond the love of women."

Now, of course, all of the usual objections will be raised. *Surely this would have been a serious crime under Jewish law.* True: but the law did not seem to be observed with great care in this period. David has household idols—Michal uses them to deceive the angry Saul (1 Samuel 19:13)—and idols were as much, if not more, against the law than same-sex intercourse. Indeed, as we've seen, the only commandment against same-sexuality is labeled in reference to idolatry.

Jonathan and David were both married to women, and we know David's inclinations based on later incidents with Bathsheba. True: but married men often live "on the down-low"—perhaps we should recall the affairs of the fictional shepherds of *Brokeback Mountain* as not inapplicable to those of the Judean hill country. And while David was certainly a womanizer, there is a strong suggestion that power was as much at play in his relationships with women as sex. When one includes Saul in the picture—someone similarly smitten with the beautiful David (one of the very few characters in the Hebrew Scriptures whose appearance is described, and whose name, after all, means "Beloved")—there is all the more reason to see the tale as having an undeniable triangular shape, geared towards tragedy. I would suggest this explains Saul's fits of jealousy, and references to incest on Jonathan's part (1 Samuel 20:30—surely an odd curse otherwise), and those disturbing passages in which Saul attempts to pin the young men *with his spear* (1 Samuel 18:10, 19:10, 20:33).

Finally, it will be said that *the text does not give an explicit account of sexual intercourse between David and Jonathan.* Also true: but then, there are very few explicit descriptions of sexual acts in Scripture at all, nor is there a distinct vocabulary for sex, sexual organs, or most other matters sexual: the Hebrew world is one in which "bed" and "knowing" and "feet" and "flesh" have sexual meanings as well as their ordinary significance. People's sex lives are generally private in Scripture, and are shrouded in euphemisms.

The story of David and Jonathan was recorded and told for centuries with few perceiving any erotic overtones. These only became evident with the coming of the Hellenists. We are dealing, in the Hebrew culture, with a prudishness about sex; a world of don't ask, don't tell; a well-closeted world in which "Israel is not suspected" of same-sexuality (bKiddushin 82a). The greatest love story in Scripture is hidden in plain sight.

However, for those with an interest in something more specific, there are two more open hints. First, in the touching scene during which David and Jonathan plan David's escape, we find this: "Said Jonathan to David, Come let us go out into the field." (1 Samuel 20:11). This same expression, "[I] said to my beloved, Come, let us go into the field," appears in the Song of Songs 7:12. Recalling that "beloved" and "David" share the same consonants, the texts are virtually identical. Marvin Pope reminds us that the phrase in Song of Songs, "could be as innocent or as suggestive as one may wish to make it." (Pope 1977, 645). As in the present case there is no real reason for the two young men to go out into the field, this phrase suggests that there is more going on than plans for escape. The same goes for the touching final scene between them, also set in the field, and also to no apparent end—since the whole elaborate scheme with bows and arrows and the boy to pick them up is quickly abandoned so that the two can share their final tearful embrace, "until David *higdyl*." (1 Samuel 20:41)

This troublesome causative verb ("made greater," "magnified," "enlarged") without a stated object has been variously understood, usually along the lines of David's weeping exceeding Jonathan's weeping. That may well be an appropriate understanding, and mark a transition in the relationship—which has up until this point emphasized Jonathan's great love for David. However, the sexual connotation has not escaped careful readers, with the other possible suggestions that the text is missing something, or that this is a different root entirely—*gdl* can also mean "to intertwine" or "to braid." This may be a sexual innuendo, not unlike the Greek words *syndesmos* and *symplokōn* (bind and intertwine) which in the LXX serve as euphemisms for the male cult prostitutes in 1 Kings 14:24 and 22:46. There is, finally, no easy solution to this: the Hebrew text becomes "corrupt" precisely at the point where a romantic incident seems to have occurred. "Every time the reader seems to get too close to understanding the more intimate details of David and Jonathan's relationship, or the contents of their mysterious 'Lord's covenant,' the text becomes suddenly unintelligible." (Culbertson, 86)

We are left, then, with a story of sacrificial love—a love greater than any other recorded in Scripture until Jesus' own self-offering, and to which he made a telling reference. So, to ask, "Did David and Jonathan 'do it'?" is to reduce their love precisely to the level of gross anatomy that gets us into the problem in the first place. Does it matter? Is it any of our business? Do we need to "make windows into people's souls"—or bedrooms? And should the fact that the "love that dare not speak its name" has found its voice at long last really create so many problems for a church that has embraced so much change, and which, more importantly, worships a God whose very nature and being consists of Love?

The lovers in the Song of Songs find their ends and reasons to exist in each other ("my beloved is mine and I am his," 2:16, 6:3)—and this mutual self-giving is not dependent on their sexual dimorphism. Only one other couple in Hebrew Scripture, in addition to the bride and bridegroom of the Song of Songs, are described as having loved with such complete selflessness and self-giving: Jonathan loved David "as his very self" (1 Samuel 18:1–4), his *nephesh*—another word with a wide range of meanings, translated as *soul*, *self*, or *body*, the latter in its complete range of meanings from physical body (= corpse) to *person* as in "some*body*."

The soul (*nephesh*) is used elsewhere in connection with erotic attraction (Genesis 34:3,8), and that passage also echoes the role of the spouse's father in "taking" or "getting" the partner (Genesis 34:4 ≈ 1 Samuel 18:2, cp. Gen 2:24). For our purposes the most significant parallel is the Pauline language in Ephesians describing the intimate self-giving and self-sacrifice of Christ and the church, and husband and wife, echoing Leviticus 19:18 ("You shall love your *re'ah* (= mate) as yourself")—which the Rabbis later also applied to marriage (bKiddushin 41a):

> In the same way, husbands should love their wives as they do their own bodies. He who loves his wife loves himself. For no one ever hates his own body, but he nourishes and tenderly cares for it, just as Christ does for the church (Ephesians 5:28–29).

It is this partnership of a self with another to such a degree that transcends selfhood and otherness for which marriage is a sacrament and sign. And the sex of the partners is irrelevant to its achievement.

Crusts from the table

Finally, I would like to take a look at Jesus in a moment of what appears to be uncharacteristic harshness (Matthew 15:22–28). A Canaanite woman cries out to Jesus asking him to save her daughter. Jesus gives her the cold shoulder—not saying a word. The disciples complain, and Jesus says, essentially, "Not my people; not my problem." She kneels before him, refusing to give up, and begs for his help. And he then says something so shocking it is hard to believe it comes from the lips of our loving Savior: "It isn't fair to give the children's food to dogs."

Now, I could at this point note that, as Robert Gagnon insists in other contexts (e.g., Gagnon 2005, 54, 58), mention of "dogs" indicates reference to male-male intercourse; and that this was also one of the things that Leviticus tells us got the

Canaanites kicked out of the Holy Land. But I do not insist on these intertextual echoes—and instead want to focus on the turn in the story, the point that Jesus makes, and what the church today might do with it.

For the woman persists, this unrelenting woman with the sick child: she will be driven away neither by silence, nor by complaints, nor by insults: she reminds Jesus that even dogs get the crumbs that fall from the table. And finally, after ignoring her, shrugging her off, and even insulting her, Jesus relents, and acknowledges her persistence—and her great faith; and her daughter is instantly healed.

It may well be that in all of this Jesus was simply testing the disciples, renowned for their "little faith" as opposed to this woman's *great* faith. He may have been waiting to see what they would do—if they would continue their approach of getting rid of troublesome people, appealing to Jesus to send them away: whether hungry crowds seeking spiritual and earthly food (Mark 6:36), innocent children seeking a blessing (Mark 10:13), even those exercising ministry in Jesus' name though not part of his inner circle (Mark 9:38). It gives one pause for thought.

And one thought is to ask, To what extent do the heirs of the apostles continue their efforts at exclusion and dismissal? Or will they finally get the message of Jesus' wish to fulfill the prophecy of Isaiah that all will be drawn into his kingdom, even the formerly hopeless eunuchs and unclean foreigners (Isaiah 56:4–6)? All, all, belong to the Bridegroom, and his Bride is not fully clothed until every soul God loves is included in her.

We who appeal to the church for understanding and compassion, do not do so in vain, I am sure. Even if we must keep knocking long into the night, we trust that the door will eventually be opened. For I am reminded of another saying of our Lord (Luke 11:11–12, in the Authorized Version):

> If a son shall ask bread of any of you that is a father, will he give him a stone? or if he ask a fish, will he for a fish give him a serpent? Or if he shall ask an egg, will he offer him a scorpion?

You know how the rest goes. I do not believe the church to be so hard-hearted, nor are those of us who are pressing the church to reexamine its past positions on sexuality asking the impossible. The church has shown itself to be remarkably flexible in its interpretation and application of any number of biblical injunctions and restrictions down through the years, some of them even involving sex and marriage. It is not an earth-shaking abandonment of the gospel—the claims of some notwithstanding—to consider the possibility of recognizing and blessing the relationships of faithful partners *in* life, who wish to commit themselves to each other under that blessing and in that bond *for* life. This present volume is a part of that effort to a new understanding and a better way forward.

I know it will not be the last. Those of us engaged in this patient and earnest appeal, though we be ignored, rebuffed, and labeled as less than worthy, less than human even, will not cease from mental toil, nor from prayer, nor from giving thanks for the scraps thus far cast in our general direction, nor from pleading our case, nor from claiming our blessing, though we must wrestle until dawn, and be put out of joint on its account.

Questions for Discussion or Reflection

- *Can you think of other incidents in which Jesus confronted the rules and regulations of his society and culture?*

- *What, to your mind, is the essential teaching of Jesus? How does this relate to the present discussion?*

- *If you are a parent, how would you / did you react if / when a child told you he or she was attracted to a person of the same sex? Is / was your reaction in keeping with the teaching of Jesus as you understand it?*

12.
Heirs of the Promise

*T*HIS FINAL CHAPTER IS A VIRTUAL DIALOGUE REVIEWING SOME OF THE MOST common objections to a change in policy on same-sexuality. Some of these have come up already, but a few are new to this chapter. I will begin with some of the secular objections, and as I go on proceed more and more to the theological concerns.

Isn't homosexuality contrary to nature?

It depends in part on what you mean by *nature*. Same-sex behavior occurs in almost every human culture, even though many cultures either refuse to acknowledge it, or condemn it as an aberration or a moral failing. In the animal world same-sexuality has been documented among hundreds of species, so it is "natural" in that respect. The work of Bruce Bagemihl (*Biological Exuberance: Animal Homosexuality and Natural Diversity*) has catalogued this evidence extensively. The problem with this, and with the assertion that same-sexuality is *unnatural*, is that both seem to assume that what is *natural* is *good*, and what it *unnatural* is bad.

Isn't it?

No, nature (in the sense of "what is") is morally neutral—the "it was good" of Genesis doesn't refer to *moral* goodness, but existential goodness. The fact that forms of same-sex erotic behavior exist in nature is simply a fact. What you think about its morality is secondary. It is a little odd to be talking about animals being *moral* or not, isn't it?

Awareness of same-sex behavior among animals is nothing new, although better documented now, and how this reality was treated reveals the dilemma of trying to derive a moral principle from nature. For example, Clement of Alexandria inconsistently holds up the monogamy of pigeons and turtledoves as a paradigm to shame unfaithful human spouses, while he portrays the equally natural "lewdness" of hares and hyenas as a warning against pederasty—in part because hares and hyenas are forbidden for food under the Mosaic dietary prohibitions (*Strom.* II.23.139; *Paedog.* II.10). Clement, and others who follow this course, are not arguing *from* nature in order to determine what is moral, but are imposing a moral view they already hold upon it, in what might be described as proof-texting nature's book. It should also be noted in passing that the concepts of clean and unclean animals return us once again to the realm of the dietary laws—so those who claim this is irrelevant to the discussion of sexuality have Clement against them, even if they agree with his conclusions.

The presence or absence of a given behavior in animals is irrelevant to moral discourse concerning human beings. As Jeffrey John observed: "We do not regulate our behavior or derive our moral precepts simply from observation of what nature does or does not do" (John 1993, 11). When we look to "nature" for moral guidance we will most often simply find our own prejudices reflected back to us, rather than learning anything new.

But when we say that homosexuality is unnatural, don't we mean that it is not suited to the natural ends for which sex exists?

That is the view of those who argue from the position of natural law. They hold that actions have appropriate ends, or goals. For example, the natural law argument as articulated by Aquinas is that the primary end of marriage—procreation—derives from our animal nature; the secondary end—the shared life of the couple—from our human nature; and the third end—sacrament—from the nature of the couple as believers. The problem with this argument is that it places undue emphasis on the surmised behavior of "animals"—that is, it begs the same question of animals that it does of humans: that sex is for procreation.

But isn't it?

In a wide array of animal creatures and in many plants sex is the necessary means by which procreation takes place. It is a means to that end. But it clearly also serves other purposes—has other ends—and who is to say which is the most important? Is the beginning of life more important than the life that is actually lived? Current research into human sexual behavior suggests that the human capacity to have sex during infertile periods (including pregnancy) is significant in the development and maintenance of monogamous bonding—so sex serves a social as well as a biological purpose, even if you see the value in such bonding to be the help it provides for raising children.

This contemporary finding echoes some early patristic speculation. Lactantius observed that human women, unlike the females of other species, can have sex during pregnancy, so that their husbands won't stray (*Divine Institutes* 6.23). Similarly, recent studies show that sexual activity (including homosexual activity) plays a role in maintaining harmony in colonies of bonobo chimpanzees, and among adolescent male dolphins.

Now we're back to the animals, it seems.

Well, it is hard to get away from them if one wants to talk about what is *natural*, or what a natural function is *for*—that is, its *end*. The assumption is that the sexual organs are obviously designed for sex, and that sex is obviously meant for procreation. My point is that the sexual organs are not designed *solely* for procreation—both the organs and sex serve other functions. Let's take another organ of the body as an example: the nose. This organ serves multiple functions, and the fact that one of them—breathing—is essential to life doesn't obviate or overrule the other functions, such as providing for the sense of smell. Smell too is important in terms of survival (including finding food and in sexual attraction), but it is also important in enjoyment, and no one would suggest that our use of the sense of smell for "mere enjoyment" was a perversion or morally flawed. And one can, after all, breathe through one's mouth as well as through one's nose, and there are times when that is necessary. No one would give moral weight to one way of breathing over another.

More importantly, it is hard to see why a rich human relationship or a life of faith should be subordinated to any biological function, in a kind of biological determinism. The limits of the human body should not be given moral status, as if anatomy was the determining factor in what it means to be a human being.

Aren't you slipping into some kind of Gnosticism there?

To espouse the idea that the physical world is an illusion, or has no importance at all, would indeed be to wander off into a kind of Gnosticism. But the opposite end is to take the physical world as the necessary delimiter of all that is good and holy—and that is idolatry. The proper position should be somewhere in between: we observe nature, and we learn from it; but ultimately the fact of something's existence will not tell us if it is good or bad or indifferent. To do so is to fall into a logic similar to that which says, "If God had wanted us to fly he would have given us wings." In fact, human beings have the skill and wisdom to do things that are contrary to nature—including postponing death through medical science. Human beings are both physical and spiritual, or as Paul would say, flesh and spirit. To over-emphasize one or the other is to fundamentally misunderstand what it means to be a human person.

We are often in danger of ignoring the experience of gay and lesbian *persons*—and more importantly, gay and lesbian *Christians*. This oversight was recognized even in the midst of the debates at Lambeth 1998.

Isn't it dangerous to introduce experience as a source of authority?

Experience is a part of Reason, as Hooker understood it, a part of *what is*—the reality of the natural and human world. As such it has a limiting function even over the fundamental authority of Scripture. When we learn some new reality—for instance, that the earth revolves around the sun—we can choose to ignore that experience and the new knowledge that it brings us, and turn back to Scripture and say, "No, the sun goes around the earth, as it says in the Psalms" (19:5–6). Or we can accept that the Scripture is limited in its description of the real world—in part because the Scripture itself is limited by the experience of those who recorded it—and from time to time we have to readjust our appreciation of Scripture and realize its limitations when describing the natural world. This is also true even in some areas of *morality*.

Our experience leads us to see that some things Scripture approved in the cultures and worlds of its composition can be found to be morally wrong at a later time and in a different world—like slavery or polygamy. We can also find that things condemned in Scripture might come to be accepted as morally neutral or even as good—like lending money at interest, which Ezekiel (18:13) said was an abomination, but which Adam Smith argued was essential to the wealth of nations.

Much as you might downplay it, you can't deny the form of the human body—male and female; they seem to fit, and moreover, to fit when employed in the process of bringing other human beings into the world. Isn't that significant?

I have to raise the issue of experience once again: the fit of any one man and one woman may or may not match the fit of an abstract ideal. And those who do fit well (anatomically) will fit whether they can bring about a new human life or not—or whether they want to or not. Procreation does not always result from sex even between fertile men and women, even when that is what they want; and procreation never results from sex between an infertile man and woman—by definition.

But wasn't everyone who is born the result of heterosexual sex?

No one argues otherwise, except those defending a literal interpretation of the Virgin Birth. The issue is, What are we to make of this obvious fact? For we are confronted with two statements, both plainly true: (1) every person comes to be through sex, but

(2) not all sex results in persons coming to be; that includes non-procreative sex between men and women as well as sex between same-sex couples. If one is going to say that (a) because sex is for procreation, therefore (b) any sex that doesn't lead to or cannot lead to procreation is morally wrong, wouldn't a deliberate effort to thwart procreation by a couple capable of it be morally *more* wrong than sex between a same-sex couple, for whom procreation isn't possible at all?

I don't think anyone challenges the understanding of where people come from—except when it is somehow transmuted into an argument against same-sex relationships. One might just as well say, "All of Rembrandt's paintings were painted by Rembrandt as part of his unique contribution to the creation in co-operation with God's inspiration." That may well be true, but it does not rule out either other artists, or other paintings. There are other "goods" to sexuality than the production of children—as even the church and society acknowledge. Both still allow marriage when infertility is a permanent condition. If the church or state were to hold that procreation was the *only* permitted use of sexuality, or that sexual activity is only permitted when procreation is possible, that would be a different matter. But they don't.

When I was sketching out some of these ideas on my blog, commenter "Tom" reminded me of what he called "the Diet Coke argument." If sex is only for procreation, why allow it at all when procreation is either impossible or deliberately avoided? He asked, "How is sex without procreation different than food without nourishment?" Is it only because we think sex is more important than food and drink—or is there really some moral correlation between doing things which do not achieve the end towards which (some think) they are ordered?

But isn't sex between persons of the same sex never reproductive, while sex between persons of mixed sex is sometimes reproductive?

This is a fallacy by category. You group persons by sex, as if their sex, rather than their actual capacity to reproduce, were the issue. Obviously same-sex couples cannot reproduce; but neither can infertile mixed-sex couples—to exactly the same extent. That is, such a mixed-sex couple is no more "sometimes" going to engage in reproductive sex than a same-sex couple. The individual man who has had a prostatectomy or the individual woman who has had a hysterectomy is no more capable of reproducing than the individual member of a same-sex couple. They all belong to the class "people for whom sex is *never* reproductive." And who suggests that a mixed-sex couple who are definitively incapable of reproduction can't be married and have sexual relations? Neither the church nor the state—for both recognize that there is more to marriage than procreation.

One of the things same-sex couples can, I hope, teach the world is that biological reality need not determine one's personal or interpersonal reality. This is probably, in fact, why so many are uncomfortable with or disapprove of same-sexuality: it challenges the neat hierarchies and categories that give them security.

But doesn't homosexuality deny the obvious fact that men and women are different?

No one I know of denies the reality of the existence of the sexes or of biological reproduction, or of the fact that there are some differences between men and women. These differences may, however, be more related to culture and society than to any biological reality, anatomical difference, or psychological difference to which biology and culture (nature and nurture) may give rise. Culture and social structures can amplify any natural difference that may exist, and give it undue prominence. More importantly, as far as the church is concerned, there is no spiritual difference between men and women.

What I am challenging is the degree to which that reality is amplified into a defining or normative expectation for those to whom it does *not* apply, particularly one that marginalizes other forms of human interpersonal sexual relationship that do not fit that model. The real issue is: what *significance* is being read into the sexual difference between men and women?

All right, that's a good question: what is the significance?

The traditional significance is, sad to say, more about unequal status for women in society than it is about sexuality. The church, and through it Western society, embraced beliefs concerning the sexes, particularly of women as "defective males" originating with Aristotle but codified by Aquinas (based in large part on his application of Genesis). This way of seeing things had detrimental impact both on women as a group and on individual women—to this day, and even in this country, on practical matters as plain as equal pay for equal work. The fact that these arguments are still advanced in some places (I am thinking primarily of churches) against leadership by women is just one example. Positive teachings in the tradition (such as Aelred of Rievaulx' observation that Eve was taken from Adam's side to show she was his equal) are sidelined (or, as Aquinas would say, represent the antelapsarian ideal, which is not realized in this world, in which woman is "naturally" placed under man as a result of the Fall—and so women must maintain a subservient position, in spite of the fact that we are supposedly living in a world that has been redeemed)—and women are told they cannot serve as ministers.

The church and western society took a surmised quality of a group and applied it to individuals, employing their understanding of biology to shape social structures that led to a determined role in society based on sex. This is, in short, sexism. For instance, that some women bear children and breast-feed them is a rational statement. But to go from that to a belief that "women are naturally nurturing" and then further to apply this generalization to *individual* women is a rational error and a logical fallacy. It is true that *some* women are nurturing—many are—but to say, on the basis of biology, that all women *should* work in nurturing roles is clearly wrong—for biology does not tell us what ought to be, nor if the individual has this specific quality of the larger group. Fixed ideas about the roles of the sexes (ideas which have little rational basis but are the result of generalized cultural attitudes) continue to play a large part in both the status of women and the negativity towards gay and lesbian people.

I am not saying that men and women are "the same"—I am saying that the differences between men and women as groups, or between individual men and women, are not complementary, by any meaningful definition of that word. And I am not sure that any significance should be read into the differences that do exist. All people are different from each other.

To return to the notion of the proper "fit"—gay and lesbian persons precisely do not feel this "fit" with a person of the other sex. Many, perhaps most, attempt to live a heterosexual life at least for a part of their lives. Some are able to maintain a sexual relationship with a person of the other sex, and sometimes it is a deeply meaningful relationship. But they know that something is missing, and that what they *do* doesn't adequately reflect who they *are*.

Isn't it going too far to talk in essentialist terms like that? What you do isn't the same as who you are, is it?

That is largely a philosophical question. Certainly doing and being are related—for instance, to get back to your comment about coming to be: it takes a sexual *action* to bring about a *being*. And life is maintained and continues solely because of the constant actions of breathing, eating, and so on. We could get back to the old categories of mineral, vegetable and animal if you like—but surely for human beings our "being" is defined in terms of our capacity to *do* certain things: to reason and to love—and even our so-called animal nature is, well, *animate*: it is about *doing* things as opposed to simply existing.

You mention gays or lesbians who enter into heterosexual marriage. Doesn't that show that homosexuality is a lifestyle choice?

Whatever the origin of sexual orientation, including heterosexual orientation—and whether biological, psychological, or sociological (it is probably a mix of all three)—it appears to be largely part of the person's makeup, at a very deep level of identity. This is why most people tend to think of themselves in one category or another, and to feel that it is a given, not something that they have arbitrarily chosen from a menu of possible choices. It doesn't feel like a choice, but an awareness of an identity. I doubt that many heterosexual persons feel that they *chose* to be heterosexual; it is simply how they think of themselves, how they *are*. To that extent, one's sexuality is much less a "choice" than one's religion.

Deep down, sexual desire is a largely incomprehensible urge. In the film *Trembling Before G-d*, rabbi and psychiatrist David Ashkinazy confronts an older rabbi with the illogical nature of sex. "'Of course, of course.' He said it's a *taivah* . . . There is no reason for a *taivah*. A *taivah* is an urge. It's an illogical urge. That all of sex is a *taivah*, it doesn't have rhyme or reason to it. What a gay person does or what a straight person does, or wants to do, it isn't logical, it's something brought down from above."

But even if there is no choice about your orientation, isn't there a choice about what you do with it?

Yes, but the question assumes that a gay or lesbian person doing anything other than remaining celibate or entering a marriage that is likely to be less than fulfilling for both parties is making a moral error. I am interested in morality, that is, in how a person lives authentically in keeping with the virtues of faith, hope, and love, and the teaching of Christ. Is it, then, morally sound, for example, for a gay man to marry a woman if he is capable of having sexual relations with her only by fantasizing about sex with men? Isn't that a form of mental infidelity? This, it seems, reduces the other person to the level of mere external behavior—to "doing" in the crassest sense; I would even say *using*. From a moral standpoint, such a man is using a woman not even as a sexual object, but as a physical object, dehumanized and divorced from the mental image that is providing the real erotic focus for the experience. To argue that this is "virtuous" stands the concept of virtue on its head, and utterly reduces morality to the outward appearance instead of the inner disposition and action.

This ethical flaw has been recognized at least since Kant: it is inappropriate to treat a person as a means to an end, even a lofty end—as in the case of procreation at its best. How much worse in a case where a person is treated simply as an object for one's own sexual satisfaction, and worst of all if the satisfaction isn't even related to the actual person.

Well, speaking of Kant, wouldn't homosexuality be wrong under his understanding of the "categorical imperative"? As with Kant's example of suicide, isn't it something that we wouldn't want to be a universal mandate, since that would mean the end of humanity?

The idea that same-sexuality, if universally practiced, would lead to the end of humanity is actually less true than it would be of celibacy, unless one assumes all the same-sex couples might not also have a partner of the other sex as well. As I noted, many gay and lesbian people do marry and have children—it is not a complete incapacity to have a sexual relationship that is at issue. In many cultures people are free to engage in same-sex relationships without much social negativity so long as they do not make it public and *also* have a spouse and produce children.

But more to the point, few would say celibacy is a moral failure on the basis of the fact that if everyone practiced it there would be no more people.

What about a homosexual's choice to remain celibate? Isn't that a moral option?

Certainly that is a choice for any person, gay or lesbian or straight; and if it is a freely accepted choice, and a person has the gift for it, well and good. But not all people will be capable of maintaining a celibate life as an external requirement— just as few are able to maintain a faithful and monogamous marriage, in spite of religious and social expectations. We don't, for example, any longer insist that even the "innocent party" in a divorce remain celibate as long as the straying partner is alive—but that was the rule until just a few decades ago.

Celibacy and fidelity are both charisms, talents, or virtues—and not all possess them. Remember that Paul specifically allowed marriage as a remedy for those who were not gifted with the capacity to remain celibate. Effectively to *demand* celibacy of all gay and lesbian persons—or offer them only the option of heterosexual marriage which will in all likelihood be less than successful—seems an unreasonable expectation, when few heterosexuals are able to attain a level of ideal performance. And the fact that heterosexuals are essentially let off the hook for their failures, while gays and lesbians are held to a strict observance, is a form of double standard that is itself immoral.

Well, don't most gay and lesbian people not even want to be monogamous—or mean something else by "monogamy" than I do?

Certainly there are many gay and lesbian persons who don't want to commit to a single partner for life, especially among the young and restless. But it is probably true that in many societies, especially those with strong social standards against same-sex affection, the rate of promiscuity may be higher among young heterosexuals—for their gay and lesbian counterparts may find it more difficult to meet a partner, and risk more in doing so. When a homosexual relationship can lead to a death sentence or imprisonment, it is very likely that young gay and lesbian persons may be more chaste than their heterosexual counterparts.

After all, gays and lesbians didn't invent "free love" or "open marriage"—and many heterosexuals choose a promiscuous lifestyle. The fact remains that the majority of heterosexuals fail in their relationships at one point or another. Slightly over forty percent of all American first marriages end in divorce; and if we assume there is at least some sexual indiscretion even in marriages that don't end in divorce—well, you do the math.

Finally, to the present concern—finding a way to support same-sex couples who *do* want to profess a life-long commitment to each other—it is irrelevant that there may be many gay or lesbian persons who *don't* want to marry. There are many heterosexuals who choose to live together and have relationships without a formal commitment, either in the church or civil setting, but that doesn't stop the church or state from performing marriages for those who do wish to marry, who are prepared to take up those rights and responsibilities. Those gay and lesbian persons who seek the church's blessing or the state's support are seeking to live by exactly the same standard applied to and expected of heterosexual couples: life-long, monogamous, and faithful.

You seem to be appealing to the idea that recognizing gay and lesbian marriage is just one more step: we allow birth control and remarriage after divorce, so why not same-sex marriage. But if we begin to do that, what's to prevent a further step to polygamy, incest, or other forms of sexual expression that people might claim is their orientation, or that they need to be fulfilled?

The argument isn't simply, "Well you've permitted X, so why not Y?" extended ad infinitum—that is the "slippery slope" argument. It is rather, "You have permitted X, which is of the same type as Y, so why not Y?" There may, in fact be reasons not to permit Y—but those reasons need to be laid out, and it is not an "argument" to bring in Z, or to assume that the reasons which permit Y also permit Z. Z may be of an entirely different order—as I would say polygamy and incest are. We are talking here about same-sex marriage under exactly the same terms as mixed sex marriage.

The reason birth control is relevant is that it addresses the argument: (a) Sex is for procreation; (b) sex that doesn't lead to procreation is wrong; (c) same-sexuality doesn't lead to procreation; therefore (d) same-sexuality is wrong. Yet contraception is permitted, and in some cases even encouraged, so it could take the place of (c), yet does not lead to conclusion (d)—except for Roman Catholics, and as we know many Roman Catholics simply ignore this aspect of church teaching.

The issue of divorce is a bit more complicated, as it involves some biblical and theological questions; but there is as strong a biblical (and social) case against divorce and remarriage as there is against same-sexuality; and I would argue that fidelity in a same-sex relationship is morally superior to infidelity in a mixed-sex relationship.

Exactly; so what's to prevent moving on to incest or polygamy?

Let's take an example that is far from the present one, but no less important: The state permits the use of alcohol and tobacco (and firearms) but criminalizes the use of marijuana. To argue for the legalization of marijuana, on the basis that it is demonstrably less harmful than alcohol and tobacco (and firearms) is not to suggest or argue for the legalization of heroin—because heroin is as harmful as alcohol or tobacco. Or: to defend ownership of hunting rifles is not to automatically defend the ownership of AK-47s or tactical nuclear weapons.

To take another example: To support lowering the voting age to 18 does not assume one is going to seek to lower the voting age to 12. Even if you argue this is a logical direction, there is no reason to "slip" so far, and good reasons against it.

So the parallel social argument for allowing divorce and remarriage is: We recognize that marriages, like all living things, can die. (This is one of the common rationales advanced for allowing second marriages.) We no longer expect divorcees to remain celibate, but feel a second marriage after a failed first marriage is better than promiscuity or "living in sin." So gay marriage would be better for society and the couple than promiscuity, and would advance notions of stability and personal unity that are recognizably moral. So why not have same-sex marriage on the same basis as mixed-sex marriage?

The other items on the slippery slope (polygamy, incest, etc.) are more different from mixed-sex marriage than same-sex marriage is. Picture a Venn diagram: same-sex and mixed-sex marriage overlap in the area of "monogamy"—which polygamy, for instance, doesn't, although it overlaps in the area "heterosexual." I dare say it never occurs to opponents of same-sex marriage to ask, "If you allow *two* people of mixed sex to get married, why not *three?*" It doesn't follow logically to move from a couple to a trio, because there is a fundamental difference between two and three. Adding one more into the equation introduces the virtual impossibility of a truly mutual and balanced relationship—something which Scripture recognized even when it allowed polygamy (Deuteronomy 21:15–17).

Incest raises some interesting questions, but I'm not sure they are germane to the issue of same-sex relationships, nor is there any necessary or logical step from same-sex marriage to incestuous marriage. The incest prohibition is a limit on who is a possible partner or not. Different societies have different boundaries within which a relationship is considered incestuous, and therefore forbidden. First cousins, for example, cannot marry in many places, though this is not forbidden by biblical law. Ironically, the state of Utah only allows first cousins to marry if over the age of 65 (or 55 and demonstrably sterile)—explicitly *excluding* procreation as a rationale for marriage. On the other hand, biblical law allowed uncle-niece marriage. The primary contemporary concern appears to be biological rather than moral—the observation that incestuous marriages can lead to the amplification of some genetically transmitted diseases or conditions.

At the other extreme, some Christian traditions expand the notion of incest to include second or third cousins, or extend incest by affinity to include godparents. And, of course, there is the conflict of biblical passages that caused trouble to Henry VIII: Leviticus 18:16 forbids marrying a brother's widow, and Deuteronomy 25:5 mandates it in the situation in which Henry found himself after Arthur died childless.

Needless to say, the church and the world have found incest to have a poorly defined border once one gets beyond immediate blood relatives, yet that has not caused them to "slip" into allowing incest *within* those close degrees—in fact the slip has gone the other way to forbid marriages allowed in Scripture. So there is no reason to think that allowing same-sex marriage with the same limits would *cause* any further slippage.

The basic response to the "slippery slope" is to say, "Argue each case on its own merits."

You raise the biological concern with incest—what about the health issues related to homosexuality? Many same-sex practices are unhealthy; shouldn't we be responsible to warn people about the dangers—and in light of the dangers, is this something we should call good?

There are a couple of issues here. First, society does place limits on behaviors considered dangerous, most often behaviors dangerous to others. For example, drinking to excess is unhealthy, but society doesn't prohibit it, even if it frowns on it. Society does, on the other hand, prohibit driving while intoxicated—because the drinker is a hazard to others. If the state were concerned with controlling dangerous behavior, it would outlaw tobacco and alcohol—and probably firearms. But the state recognizes that individuals have the right to choose to make use of such potentially destructive things within limits. Whatever the alleged physical harm caused by same-sex relationships, they cannot possibly match the destructive power of tobacco or alcohol. But society has learned that prohibition is usually counterproductive.

Second, and more importantly, although some same-sex activities can be unhealthy, or cause disease or physical damage, those same activities are also practiced by heterosexuals. Almost all sexual activity of whatever sort, including missionary position heterosex, produces some micro-trauma (Norvell *et al.*, 1984). Moreover, many forms of same-sex sexuality are actually *less* risky and damaging, in terms of disease or injury. Sexually transmitted diseases are sexuality-neutral, and preventable by similar means regardless of one's sexual orientation. There is no reason to consider same-sex relationships as more damaging than mixed-sex, and in some cases (lesbian couples) perhaps even safer.

After all, until advances in medical science and antiseptic procedures in the late nineteenth century, one of the most life-threatening experiences a woman could experience was pregnancy and childbirth—a result of heterosexual activity.

What about the study that showed the average life expectancy for gay males was only in the mid-40s?

Paul Cameron's studies of the life expectancy of gay men have been exposed as at best misleading, yet they continue to be cited as if they were sound science. One of the problems with many such studies is the sample base. Cameron's study used obituaries in gay newspapers as its data source. Since many gay and lesbian persons do not show up in such listings (for any number of reasons, including not being public about their sexuality), it is clearly inaccurate to extrapolate such a finding to the general population. It would be just as misleading if you were only to include the names of gay and lesbian persons on church burial records. Bell and Weinberg's study on sexual habits of gay and lesbian persons took its sample for gay men from gay bars, clubs, bathhouses and referrals, but chose its straight sample based on random selection in neighborhoods, on the unwarranted basis that singles bars do not serve the same function in the straight community as gay bars do in the homosexual community. (29–38) This guaranteed unreliable results when applied beyond the relevant sample group even when it was published, and yet this study continues to be widely cited thirty years later.

What if homosexuality is bad for a society even if not for an individual?

That rather assumes that it is bad to start with. Although promiscuity (of any kind) can be detrimental to society, there is no indication that a proliferation of faithful, monogamous, same-sex couples will be anything but a positive influence on their societies. The notion that acceptance will cause a greater incidence of same-sexuality is probably ill-founded, and itself rests on the idea that same-sexuality is bad.

On the positive side, the support that couples would find in their civil life—gaining the benefits of hospital visitation, and responsibility of joint ownership of property, inheritance, and other benefits and requirements, should serve to strengthen the social fabric rather than weaken it. Such faithful couples would also serve as a resource for the adoption of unwanted children.

Don't children need a parent of each sex for their upbringing?

Sociological studies have shown that it is the *quality of parenting*, rather than the *sex of the parents*, that is most significant in healthy child development. Children (either biological or adopted) raised by same-sex couples are just as well adjusted and healthy as children raised by mixed-sex couples. While same-sex *marriage* has only been recognized in a few places for a few years, early indications based on studies of committed same-sex couples raising children suggest that the quality of parenting, and the fact that the parents are dealing with wanted rather than possibly unwanted children, is as important to their mental and social health. For example, Dr. Ellen Perrin testified before the Joint Committee on the Judiciary (October 23, 2003),

> The American Academy of Pediatrics (AAP) published a report last year that summarized three decades of research on the well-being of children raised by gay or lesbian parents. I was its primary author. As a result the AAP adopted a formal policy which stated that children who grow up with "gay or lesbian parents fare as well in emotional, cognitive, social and sexual functioning as do children whose parents are heterosexual. Children's optimal development appears to be influenced more by the nature of the relationships and interactions within the family unit than by the particular structural form it takes."

The Academy has noted that the main problem faced by same-sex parents—leading to difficult challenges for their children—comes from the lack of legal rights and civil privileges that come with marriage. People who are concerned about the welfare of children should encourage the legalization of same-sex marriage, as this would provide the hundreds of thousands of children being raised by same-sex parents with an additional degree of security.

But isn't same-sex marriage wrong because it goes against the basic principle that marriage is between one man and one woman?

That is a definitional argument: that is, if you accept the definition you have to agree to the conclusion. The problem is that the definition assumes the very thing we need to examine, which in logic is called "begging the question." In spite of the fact that marriage between one man and one woman has been the dominant model for marriage in western societies and the Christian tradition, there have been many other models for marriage, both within the biblical tradition and in western societies, to say nothing of the many forms of marriage in other cultures through history, and even today.

Even the "one man and one woman" model isn't as simple as that. From a legal perspective, within the western tradition, one would have to add qualifiers including

- neither party married to anyone else still living (not including divorce or annulment)
- not related to each other by blood or affinity (differently defined depending on the local law)

- of sufficient age of consent (which also varies depending on the sex of the person and the local law)
- freely consenting and not under duress, and actually intending what is said
- public (witnesses are required)

The Hebrew biblical tradition added the requirement that both parties be Jewish (Deuteronomy 7:3–4). The Christian tradition adds the requirement that both parties be baptized (based on 1 Corinthians 7:39 and 2 Corinthians 6:14–16), although this requirement has been abandoned in the Episcopal Church and many other churches.

O.K., but it's still one man and one woman, right?

Not universally either in time or place. Whether you like it or not, same-sex marriage or civil unions or partnerships are legally recognized in several places both in the US and abroad. Some Christian churches already formally recognize and perform same-sex marriages or blessings of same-sex couples. The blessing of same-sex couples is permitted in most strands of modern Judaism. So change has already come. We are dealing with a reality, not a possibility.

Even in the broader tradition, however, it should be acknowledged that allowing divorce and remarriage has created a kind of serial monogamy, so it would be better to say that the norm is "one man and one woman *at a time*." But when we look outside of Christianity to Jewish antecedents, and even further to other cultures and religious traditions, we see considerable variation in how marriage was and is understood. The most obvious is polygamy, to which the Hebrew Scripture attests, and for which it provides, and even urges at least in the case of a childless widow, who is expected to be married to her brother-in-law (Deuteronomy 25:5).

But, more importantly for this discussion, there are many human cultures that have recognized same-sex marriage, or some form of stable, life-long, committed same-sex relationship, alongside and sometimes in addition to forms of mixed-sex marriage.

Didn't all of those cultures collapse and die?

All cultures eventually collapse and die, or are superceded, regardless of their marriage customs. Most people are thinking of Greece and Rome when they bring this up. The Athenian Greeks, in general, did not look favorably on adult same-sex relationships, though a few in the Hellenistic era romanticized them; the model of pederasty existed alongside heterosexual marriage, and men of a certain class were expected to participate in both institutions. The Romans allowed male citizens essentially to do as they pleased in terms of how they made use of slaves—though free women had rights as well, they did not enjoy sexual freedom to the same extent as men; but again, adult males were not expected to form permanent relationships with each other. As to cultures dying, it should be noted that Rome declined and fell *after* it became Christian.

So where else were there examples of same-sex "marriages" or other "unions"?

A full list of cultures and societies in which some formal or informal recognition of same-sex relationships, unions, or marriages have existed or do exist is beyond the scope of this discussion. If we include societies in which such relationships exist but are underground or on the "down low" it is probably fair to say that almost every human culture has some experience of this phenomenon. David Greenberg's *The Construction of Homosexuality* and Martin Duberman's *Hidden from History* are both good general introductions listing the many forms in which same-sex relationships have existed and functioned in, with, and under the radar of various societies and cultures around the world, present and past. As Murray and Roscoe's study of African *Boy-Wives and Female Husbands* indicates, such relationships exist even in places and societies where they are most strenuously denied.

To highlight just a few: in the Americas prior to European invasion, and in some places for a good while thereafter, many cultures had a form of recognizing and regulating what we would now think of as "sexual orientation." Among Native Americans there are terms for such "two spirit" people in over one hundred languages. (Note that the European term *berdache* is considered offensive, as it derives from a Middle Eastern word for male prostitute.) People such as the Navajo *nadleeh* and the Cheyenne *heemaneh*, to name only two, were also often considered to be visionaries and healers. Such people often formed stable relationships with persons of the same sex.

Long-lasting same-sex relationships were recorded among aristocrats in China from before the Qin dynasty for nearly two thousand years on up into the modern era—and male same-sexuality was only criminalized in 1740. Same-sexuality between men was also common in Japan from at least the 13th century, and although it often took a form not unlike the Athenian model of man/youth, the terms were elastic and often involved men of approximately the same age.

Finally, it has to be acknowledged that even the Christian church tolerated same-sexuality in certain circumstances, even if it did not celebrate it.

Are you referring to the "brother-making rites" that John Boswell wrote about? Hasn't that claim been fairly well debunked?

Boswell's work remains controversial, in part because his (admittedly) ill-advised pre-publication talks led many to assume he was making broader claims than he actually did. His primary thesis was that, whatever the church may have intended, the "brother-making" rites were from time to time used as "same-sex union" ceremonies. Boswell was not the first to make this observation. Martin Smith noted in an Advent 1982 sermon a dozen years before Boswell's publication:

> In the Orthodox Church there is a rich sacramental rite of blessing friends called *bratotvornenie*. An expert tells me it is admitted ruefully that devout homosexual partners have used this service to covenant their relationship (12).

Boswell documented as well how the church suppressed these rites, precisely because they were being "misunderstood." Whatever the *intent* of the framers, or the precise nature of the misunderstandings surrounding them, same-sex couples who took part in them, and the congregations of friends who witnessed them, sometimes saw them as the equivalent of marriage, and there is no doubt that a sexual component "was a dimension of the relationship in many cases" (Stuhlman, 89).

It is important to remember the power of liturgy. Whatever the authors of any rite *intend*, the *meaning* of the rite will take form in the minds of the assembly, *and only there.* This basic rule of communication theory has long been overlooked in the church, in spite of its experience and knowledge that the law of worship constitutes and establishes the law of belief.

Boswell's strongest point along these lines involves the *visual* symbolism of the rites, where the greatest similarity with marriage rites lies, rather than their texts:

> The sight of a couple standing hand-in-hand at the altar, being joined and blessed by the priest, would last longer in imagination and memory than the precise wording of any ceremony, heard every now and then by congregants but not available in premodern societies with much lower rates of literacy and no printed books. The principal structural similarities between the ceremony of same-sex union and heterosexual nuptial offices were binding with a stole or veil, the imposition of crowns, the holding of a feast after the ceremony for family and friends, the making of circles around the altar, the use of a cross, occasionally the use of swords, and—virtually always—the joining of right hands (Boswell 1994, 206).

If the liturgists who crafted these rites did not want them to be seen as marriages, they were not counting either on the devices and desires of loving human hearts, or on the power of the symbols at their disposal.

But the church didn't intend them to be or call them marriages, right?

As far as we can tell, that was not the intent of the authors, although intent is sometimes very difficult to determine when all you have to go on is what was written. The "church" however includes those who used the rites as well as those who wrote them, and some of them used the rites to bless their unions—and the same rites or adaptations of them are being so used today in many places. A number of religious bodies, churches and governments have now adopted forms for blessing or regularizing same-sex relationships under the names of marriage, union, covenant, or partnership.

Why do they have to call it "marriage"; what's wrong with using those other words and keeping marriage just for one man and one woman?

The terms *bond*, *union*, and *covenant* are all synonyms with *marriage*, and are used within the marriage liturgy itself. As the BCP says, "Into this holy *union* so-and-so now come to be joined." As euphemisms they are unlikely to satisfy those opposed to same-sex marriage on the grounds of opposition to sex; and as with the older rites, if it looks like marriage people will think it is, regardless of what it is called, or what the church intends.

Civil and church understandings of marriage have been intertwined for so long (for mixed-sex couples) that there is little reason for the church to try to build a wall of separation *only* for same-sex couples. There has even been some movement toward the church relinquishing authority to formalize civil marriage (an authority it lacks in many places where separation of church and state is more rigidly observed, for example, under the Napoleonic Code). To that extent, as *all* marriages come to be seen in terms of "householding" they highlight non-sexual aspects of marriage. It is helpful to remember that the bedroom is only one room in the house—and has more than one use.

I can acknowledge that the civil society might have reason to provide a way to allow same-sex couples these kinds of civil rights, but why does the church have to get involved?

The church was not originally involved in mixed-sex marriage either: marriage was a civil phenomenon in the apostolic era and for long thereafter. After all, marriage existed in many human cultures long before the church came into existence, and exists today in many cultures in which the church plays a very small role. Christians slowly developed liturgical forms—prayers and liturgies—for blessing the bride (with prayers for a safe pregnancy), the marriage bed, the couple (in their home) and then finally in the church itself—but it was a long process that took centuries, and only came into its recognizable present form about the time of the Reformation. Much of the transition was due to the institutional role that the church came to play in society itself, as the chief recorder of births and deaths and marriages—so it was as much a *civil* function then as sacred.

For the present, faithful same-sex couples are seeking the church's blessing, for the same reasons a devout mixed-sex couple would. Not to "make" the marriage—the couple themselves do that, as the church has long taught—but to celebrate it and proclaim it in the midst of the wider community, asking for their prayers and support. The church is involved because the people involved in these relationships are members of the church—the church *is* involved. The question is the extent to which the larger institutional church wishes to be supportive of its members.

But how can the church bless something that is sinful? Doesn't the Bible condemn homosexuality?

It is precisely *by* blessing something that the church removes sin—a child is baptized to wash away the stain of original sin and a couple marry rather than "living in sin." Moreover, the Bible never mentions "homosexuality" although a number of translations make it seem that it does. Rather, there are a handful of verses that refer to specific forms of male same-sex behavior, and one that may in addition refer to female same-sexuality. Some of these are from narrative or historical passages; only two are from the legal code. Let's review them briefly.

Genesis 19 contains the famous story of the wicked city Sodom and its destruction. Although from the patristic era through to relatively modern times many saw this historical tale to be "about homosexuality," almost no one (in Judaism or Christianity) saw it that way in the biblical period. Even if the "men of Sodom" were intent on raping the angels in Lot's house (which they clearly recognized as something bad since they threatened to do "worse" to Lot)—whatever they were doing is not relevant to the question of same-sex marriage. Rape and mayhem are crimes, whoever perpetrates them, and against whomever they do so. More importantly, Scripture does not specify what brought Sodom to God's attention in the first place—what the outcry was against it. The biblical tradition is unanimous in describing the faults of Sodom as connected to idolatry, harlotry, bloodshed, pride, and selfishness.

What about Jude 7?

Jude 7 and the parallels in 2 Peter refer to pride, slander and malice, not homosexuality. "Going after [someone's] flesh" is a metaphor for slander. This idiom was common in Akkadian, Aramaic and Arabic contexts, in addition to the Hebrew tradition (Pope 1965, 143). For example, in Daniel 3:8 and 6:24/25 the idiom is simply accepted as such by the translators, and the colorful image of the Chaldeans "chewing on the Jews' parts" becomes simply, "they denounced them" and those "who chewed on Daniel's parts" becomes "who accused him.")

Another example of this turn of phrase is in Job 19:22, where Job calls out to his well-meaning friends who have been trying to convince him he must be a wicked sinner (or else God would not be punishing him), "Why do you, like God pursue me, never satisfied with my flesh." (Remember, Job feels that God has unjustly punished him, and his whole appeal to God is for proper judgment and acquittal.) In short, Job believes he has been slandered and wronged, unjustly accused and punished by God and blamed and slandered by his friends. The slander of "the glorious ones," whether angels or the rightful leaders of the congregation, is the focus of Jude's rhetoric.

It is likely Jude is drawing a parallel between the Sons of God (here as "Watchers") who mingled with the daughters of men (Genesis 6:4) and the men of Sodom who moved to assault the "different flesh" of angels—reading the text as a kind of human/angelic anti-miscegenation tract. This appears to be how the text is understood in the apocryphal literature with which Jude was familiar, such as Enoch and the Testaments of the Patriarchs (Testament of Naphtali 3:4–5), and the connection is also made with intermarriage outside of Israel (Testament of Levi 14:6, Testament of Benjamin 9:1).

So the story of Sodom, as understood by Jude, whether about slander or miscegenation, would have no relevance to the question of same-sex marriage, except perhaps as a warning to those who stoop to use slander or adopt malicious strategies—or perhaps even to those who, like Job's friends, thought they were right to try to get him to repent of sins he had never committed.

But there is another similar story in Judges, isn't there?

Judges 19 recounts a similar story, though this time without angels, and ending with the rape and dismemberment of the Levite's concubine, whom he turns over to the crowd of Benjaminites who demand to "know" him. Many see this as a threat of rape, as with Sodom, but the Levite himself, in the next chapter, clarifies: "The Lords of Gibeah rose up against me, and surrounded the house at night. They intended to kill me, and they raped my concubine until she died" (Judges 20:5). So let us take his word for it, and assume that this incident is also irrelevant to any discussion of same-sex marriage, recalling that in neither this incident nor that of Sodom does any same-sex activity actually take place.

In other historical passages there is passing reference to people who may possibly be male cult prostitutes (1 Kings 14:24, 15:12)—but clearly the difficulty with them does not lie in the fact that the men may have had sexual contact with other men, but that they are connected with the pagan cult. Again, neither prostitution nor paganism have anything to do with committed same-sex partnerships between Christians.

All right, but what about Leviticus?

Here indeed we have the only clearly legal prohibition of one form of male same-sexuality. "You shall not bed a male with the beddings of a woman; it is an abomination." (Leviticus 18:22) There are several things to note about this verse, and the parallel verse in 20:13 ("A man who beds a male with the beddings of a woman: they have done abomination, the two of them; they shall surely die, their blood upon them").

First of all, as the context of the chapters make clear, these laws are directed to the people of Israel in contrast to, and to set them apart from, the Egyptians and the Canaanites (18:1). Second, in reference to the Canaanites, these laws are directly related to the holy land—which has ejected the Canaanites because of what they had done (18:24–28). Third, the word *to'evah* (translated "abomination") is applied to a number of different offenses whose common element for the most part to relates to matters of cultic, ritual, or ethical purity. Fourth, the law specifically forbids only a man treating another man as a woman; this has traditionally been understood in Orthodox Judaism as a reference to anal intercourse, since that is one of the two possible "beddings of a woman"—the "unusual" one. Finally, it is very important to note that there is no reference whatsoever to female same-sexual activity of any kind in this or any other portion of the Law of Moses.

So what does this law have to say to a contemporary Christian? The majority of contemporary Jews, from Conservative through Reform and Reconstructionist, have come to some accommodation with this law, and do not see all male homosexual practice as a bar to service as a rabbi, and many of these congregations approve the blessing of same-sex relationships.

Clearly Christians are not bound by laws directed only to the people of Israel. Nor do we as Christians in fact follow most of the Jewish law—including much of the law laid out in Leviticus. We do not do this on the basis of Leviticus itself, which is quite adamant that all of the commandments must be followed by the children of Israel. The Christian church has applied a number of criteria to determine which of the laws it considers to be binding, but it has made use of its freedom with the laws in this chapter both to expand the list of prohibitions (for example, the incest laws in Leviticus 18 do not forbid a man marrying his niece) and to ignore others of them (for example, the requirement for abstention from sex during a woman's menstrual period, 18:19). Moreover, although it is clear from the closing verses of chapter 18 that these laws would apply to an alien visiting the holy land, there is no suggestion that they have any application to aliens *outside* of the holy land.

Even given all of this, the law is also limited to the context of ritual impurity or cultic violation, indicated by the use of the word *to'evah*; concerns only one specific sexual act; and does not apply to women. So it would appear that the law in Leviticus has no application to Christians, except possibly those visiting the holy land.

But you could use any of these arguments to defend other things forbidden in Leviticus 18, such as incest or bestiality, couldn't you?

I suppose one could, but I certainly have no interest in doing so. And I would argue that bestiality and incest are wrong not on the basis of the prohibitions in the book of Leviticus but on rational grounds, apart from any biblical reference at all. Incest entails an imbalance brought about by the *multiplication* and confusion of mutual relationships (for example, the couple are both brother/sister and lover/beloved). And bestiality makes use of another creature in a way that is beneath both human dignity and the dignity of the creature, as there is an *absence* of mutual relationship. Neither of these rational arguments apply to the case of same-sexuality, any more than they do to the case of the man who has sex with his wife during or shortly after her monthly period. In both of these cases the relationship can be mutual and loving and binary—in spite of the fact that Leviticus forbids them within its limited scope of application.

But surely Saint Paul ratifies this law when he holds it up in Romans, 1 Corinthians, and 1 Timothy?

Romans 1 represents Paul's only well-explained discussion of same-sexuality. In 1 Corinthians 6:9 and 1 Timothy 1:10 he includes *arsenokoitai* on his list of offenders. Robin Scroggs noted that this unusual Greek word is very likely based on the language the Septuagint uses to translate the Levitical prohibition, and it is fair to translate it as "male-bedder." There is no reason to think that Paul meant anything more by it than Leviticus did: that is, it is in reference to same-sexuality in conjunction with pagan worship or practice—and it occurs in letters addressed to a primarily Gentile readership.

This is consistent with his description in Romans, which describes male same-sexual acts among Gentiles in a kind of orgiastic setting, and a total collapse of all good order and decency as a result of people having turned to worship idols.

What about the women who "exchanged the natural use for that which is against nature?"

This is a difficult phrase, and people have understood it differently in different times. John Chrysostom thought Paul was referring to lesbians, but Clement of Alexandria and Augustine of Hippo thought he was referring to women who allowed their husbands to use them for non-procreative anal sex. In more recent times the tendency has been to follow Chrysostom rather than Augustine. The question for us would be, what was Paul trying to say? If he was referring to lesbians, why did he use this peculiar turn of phrase? Why not just say "females with females" as he says "males with males" in the next verse?

Didn't Plato use the phrase "against nature" (para phusin) to describe female same-sexuality, and wouldn't Paul have known about that?

Plato did use the phrase in this sense (*Laws* I.636c). However, he uses the phrase dozens of times in other contexts—both positive and negative—as do many other writers of the Hellenistic and Apostolic era, for things having nothing to do with sex. The sexual use is rare, compared with the more general use, even in Paul, who also uses this language later in Romans (11:24) in a non-sexual, and positive, context.

There is no reason to believe that Paul necessarily was familiar with this particular work by Plato—or any of his other works, for that matter. In general, Paul shows familiarity with philosophers other than Plato, and his use of "nature" is in keeping with what the Stoics said about it.

In any case, even in the passage from Plato, the Athenian speaker goes on to clarify in part that what is "natural" is "intercourse that leads to procreation." This is familiar philosophical ground for anyone used to Stoic thinking, as was Paul— "sex is for procreation" and any sex that is non-procreative is contrary to "nature." So it is no great stretch to accept that Paul would also have thought of non-procreative sex as being "against nature"—and while this would apply to lesbians, it would also fit male same-sexuality and men making use of women in a non-procreative way. The imprecise term "sodomy" is, even in our modern law codes, used in precisely this sense: more concerned with where a man puts his member than it is with the gender of the person into whom it is put. So it seems likely that Paul is referring to men who use "their females" in this way, and then having already given up "the *natural* use of their females" turn to make use of each other "in the same way."

Furthermore, when we come to Paul's unusual phrasing, in Jewish thinking, common in rabbinical texts, but also occurring in the Pauline writing, women are "vessels" (1 Thessalonians 4:4). There is no delicate way to describe the prevailing Jewish view: women are not sexual "users" but are the objects of use. So the "use" that is "exchanged" in this passage appears to be the exchange of one of the two available "vessels" a woman provides for the other; that is, men making use of women in non-procreative sex. Such use was technically permitted under rabbinic law, as the Torah said nothing about it; but it was not looked upon favorably. Paul, as a Jew influenced by Stoic thinking, would doubtless have looked askance at all of these things: nonprocreative sex between men and women, lesbianism, and male homosexuality.

Here, however, he seems to be offering an explanation for how or why men would end up doing something so "unnatural"—remember his larger purpose in this chapter is to portray the collapse of good order. He charts this by stages: failing to recognize and accept God through revelation in the natural world (Romans 1:19–20); *exchanging* the glory of God for idols of animals (1:23); being handed over by God for bodily degradation, because they worshiped the creature instead of the Creator (1:24–25); *their women* exchanging their natural use for what is unnatural (1:26); and the men then turning on each other and making use of each other *in the same way* they had used the women—get their punishment *in* themselves (1:27).

Well, that hardly commends it, does it?

There is no doubt that Paul, as a rabbinic Jew, would think of same-sex behavior among men—particularly in the kind of lustful orgy he describes in Romans—as characteristic of Gentile idolaters, and regard it with distaste or disgust. He would likely have thought poorly of lesbianism, although I do not think that is what he is referring to in Romans; and under the influence of Stoicism, he would have regarded non-procreative sex of any form as not in keeping with the purposes for which sex was created.

Our task, in dealing with this reality, and with our different philosophical view that sex is not only about procreation but about building up human relationships, is to attempt to discern what relevance Paul's views might have for us today, in a situation in which we are not dealing either with orgiastic behavior nor with idolatry, but with faithful, monogamous, same-sex partnerships between Christians.

But isn't the issue Paul addresses in Romans more fundamental, and based on an understanding of Genesis?

If you want an antecedent for this section of Romans, you won't find it in Genesis, but rather in the Wisdom of Solomon (12–16), which depicts the folly of the Gentile world, and in particular the origin and consequences of idolatry. This kind of argument formed a standard part of Jewish anti-Gentile polemic, and Paul makes use of all the rhetoric at his disposal in order to work up his largely Jewish audience so that he can turn the tables on them at the beginning of chapter 2. Paul's ultimate purpose in Romans is to assure all his hearers that salvation is to be found in Christ, and not in following a legal code. If all we carry away from Paul's Letter to the Romans is some notion about same-sexuality being wrong we will have very seriously misunderstood Paul's overall message.

What about the teaching of Jesus? Didn't he intend to condemn homosexuality when he included porneia *in his list of things that come from the corrupted human heart (Matthew 15:19)?*

Porneia is a word with a broad range of meaning but not so broad as to include same-sexuality. The basic meaning of the word derives from the Greek word for whore, harlot or prostitute. So *porneia* generally means "harlotry" of one sort or another. Most of the times the words of this group are used in Scripture they refer either to a literal prostitute or figuratively to the practice of idolatry, understood as infidelity to God. In a few cases both meanings seem to be intended. There is also some slight evidence from the Dead Sea Scrolls and the rabbinic tradition that the incest violations of Leviticus 18:6-18 were occasionally referred to as harlotry, though this clearly is a result of the general opprobrium and not intended as a kind of technical term—since the word is most commonly used in its normal context to refer to a harlot. This may be reflected in Paul's use of the word in 1 Corinthians 5; though he reverts to the common use for a prostitute in the following chapter—and if he is talking about the same person then this may not be a case of incest at all, but rather of a man and his father both having a relationship with the same prostitute.

More importantly, even if the Rabbis did use the term harlotry to describe incest, they thought of the incest code as a discrete portion of the law, and in other contexts explicitly excluded both bestiality and intercourse with a menstruating woman (also listed in Leviticus 18) from that category. So the idea that they—or Jesus—would naturally include male same-sex behavior under this heading is unlikely, although they recognized that a man could be a prostitute.

As with all words that have broad as well as narrow meanings it is important to look at the context to determine which of those meanings a person using the word intends—and it is not always possible to make a definitive interpretation. However, as there appears to be no evidence that harlotry was commonly understood to include male same-sexuality, and the rabbinic tradition specifically excludes female same-sexuality from this category, there is no reason to think that this was what was in Jesus' mind.

Rather, what Jesus is getting at in this passage is the distinction between the inner moral disposition and the outer form—a major concern in his overall teaching. This present passage comes up in the context of the discussion about handwashing and ritual purity, and the Pharisees' desire to appear to be doing the right thing but actually not having the proper inner disposition.

That same skewed preoccupation with "the outside"—with gender and sex— seem to be at the base of many of our problems concerning sexuality. Jesus said nothing about same-sexuality, but he did offer us basic principles to apply to discern moral values. The values he supports are those of love and care, and above all self-sacrifice. It is possible that his statement, "Greater love hath no man than this, that a man lay down his life for his friends" (John 15:13), refers to the greatest love story in Scripture, that of the love of Jonathan for his ancestor David.

Are you implying David and Jonathan were gay; weren't they both married men?

The Jewish culture really did not occupy itself all that much with same-sexuality. I seriously doubt that Jesus thought about the sexuality of David and Jonathan, any more than the Rabbis did when they contrasted Jonathan's pure love of David with Amnon's lustful love of Tamar. Yes, Jonathan and David were both married—in their culture this was expected as the norm, and the Jewish tradition regarded the requirement to have children to be a fundamental creation ordinance. Surely it is obvious that there are many gay and lesbian persons even today who still marry persons of the other sex out of social pressure, even in a culture where awareness of same-sexuality is much more open than the time of Jonathan and David.

It is probable that given the culture of their time, Saul and Jonathan did not understand the urges that came upon them both when they first set sight on the beautiful David, whose name means "Beloved." Doubtless it took some time for David to come to terms with this attraction—which in the case of Saul he appears never to have reciprocated, perhaps symbolically expressed in the transition from 1 Samuel 17:38–39, where David rejects Saul's armor, and 1 Samuel 18:4, where he accepts Jonathan's. But the biblical record is quite clear: Jonathan loved David with his whole being, with his very self, and his life was tied up with his; and he eventually turned against his own father, and lost his life, because he chose David. David appears eventually to have reciprocated— and after Jonathan's death recognized that this was the "most wonderful love" he had ever known. They were not "just good friends"—Scripture says, quite literally, that they were lovers, and we must make of that what we will.

For love goes beyond sex, after all. Isn't that the point? Isn't that what we're talking about here? I'm not trying to defend "homosexuality" any more than I think one can defend "heterosexuality." What I am suggesting is that it is time, as Jesus suggested, to look past the outside and into the inside of human relationships, into the heart, and realize that there is a blessedness there, and the signs of the Holy Spirit are manifest in the faithful relationships of same-sex couples, and that the church should celebrate and honor this reality.

Does the church have the authority to make such a change in its traditional practice?

The church has the authority to declare whether a given act or relationship is sinful or not. It has exercised this authority in a number of ways through history. The early church overturned the Jewish law that a man should marry his childless brother's widow, and forbade anyone keeping the Jewish Sabbath. The church ignored and allowed to fall into disuse the decision of the Apostolic Council against the consumption of meat containing blood. The church came to tolerate—and participate in—lending money at interest, which Ezekiel considered an abomination. The church also has the authority to change its teaching and pastoral practice in relation to same-sex couples who choose to commit to each other for life in a faithful, monogamous, and loving relationship. If it feels, in accordance with Article XX of the Articles of Religion, that it mustn't "ordain anything that is contrary to God's Word written"—as indeed it mustn't— it can join with a wide range of scholars and ethicists who are prepared to say: Scripture only condemns same-sex relationships in the context of idolatry, prostitution, and rape. A loving and faithful, monogamous and life-long same-sex relationship is capable of receiving the support and blessing of the church. "Against such as this there is no law" (Gal 5:23).

But isn't this something about which the whole church—not just The Episcopal Church or even the Anglican Communion—should reach a decision?

Some of the changes I've mentioned have not been universally adopted by the whole church—for example, the Eastern Orthodox Church still recognizes the apostolic prohibition on eating blood. Closer to our present concerns, the Episcopal Church has so interpreted the teaching of Jesus as to allow for divorce and remarriage—and it did this before many of the other provinces of the Anglican Communion had taken that step, to say nothing of the wider church..

The present question is whether the church should recognize the goodness inherent in reasonable and holy same-sex relationships, the values of fidelity and love manifest in those relationships, and find a way to support those relationships both liturgically and within the structures of the church—whether by the name of marriage or another name.

We will not, even as it is, be alone or the first among Christian bodies in taking that step: others have already gone before. But it seems that the time has come for us to take a step, and to take a stand.

It is a serious step and a serious stand—to uproot a teaching that has been so long planted, even if its roots are not as deep as at first they seemed and even if the tree has failed to produce much apart from bitter fruit. But it is within the power of the church to depart even from a biblical teaching if it can be shown to be in conflict with an even more important truth, and for the good of the people of God.

The Rabbis understood this to have taken place in the case of Esther, who violated the law that no daughter of Israel was to marry a Gentile (Deuteronomy 7:3–4). This was, and is, one of the most important laws concerning the identity of the Jewish people, and in most circumstances is marked with mourning as if for a death. But in a circumstance in which the Jewish people might be destroyed, the law was set aside—and Esther married King Ahasuerus. As her uncle Mordecai said to Esther, "Perhaps you have come to royal dignity for just such a time as this."

The Episcopal Church did not choose to find itself in this position. But it has come to just such a time as this, perhaps to lead and encourage not only its own members, but to help other churches see that God's grace is not to be limited on the basis of anatomy or gender; but that wherever the virtues of fidelity and love are found, there God is pleased to dwell.

In all of this I am not speaking to the prosecutors but to the jury—the membership of our church and of the Anglican Communion and of the wider Christian fellowship—who I believe are capable of learning to see as God sees, in looking at the heart of the matter; and that it is reasonable and holy to allow this development in Christian teaching, even if it means a departure from tradition, even a departure from a former scriptural understanding—for surely a deeper scriptural truth is here: "So we have known and believe the love that God has for us. God is love, and those who abide in love abide in God, and God abides in them" (1 John 4:16).

Some works cited or consulted

CERTAIN WELL-KNOWN DOCUMENTS ARE REFERRED TO BY THEIR USUAL INITIALS OR abbreviations. BCP indicates the 1979 Book of Common Prayer, unless otherwise indicated. Hooker's *Laws of Ecclesiastical Polity* is given here with modern spelling, and referenced by book and chapter, as are earlier classical and patristic writings. (For the most part, the translations from patristic sources are those of the Ante- and Post-Nicene Fathers series reprinted by Eerdmans. Where the book, chapter, and paragraph numbers in that edition differ from other versions, two listings may be provided.) Citations from rabbinic sources use the traditional lowercase *m* for Mishnah, *b* for the Babylonian Talmud, and *p* for the Yerushalmi. *Journals* of General Convention are referenced by year. The URLs for documents available online appear in brackets.

Bell A.P., and M.S. Weinberg. *Homosexualities: a study of diversity among men & women.* New York: Simon and Schuster, 1978.

Bagemihl, Bruce. *Biological Exuberance: Animal Homosexuality and Natural Diversity.* New York: St. Martin's Press, 1999.

Barth, Karl. *Church Dogmatics.* London: T&T Clark International. Reprinted 2004 in several volumes.

Bonhoeffer, Dietrich, ed. by Eberhard Bethge. *Ethics.* New York: Collier Books, 1955.

Boswell, John. *Christianity, Social Tolerance, and Homosexuality: Gay People in Western Europe from the Beginning of the Christian Era to the Fourteenth Century.* Chicago: The University of Chicago Press, 1980.

———. *Same-Sex Unions in Premodern Europe.* New York: Villard Books, 1994.

Brooten, Bernadette. *Love Between Women: Early Christian Responses to Female Homoeroticism.* Chicago: University of Chicago Press, 1996.

Brundage, James A. *Law, Sex, and Christian Society in Medieval Europe.* Chicago: The University of Chicago Press, 1987.

Childress, James F., and John Macquarrie. *The Westminster Dictionary of Christian Ethics*. Philadelphia: The Westminster Press, 1986.

Cross, F.L., ed. *The Oxford Dictionary of the Christian Church*. London: Oxford University Press, 1971.

Culbertson, Philip. *New Adam: The Future of Male Spirituality*. Minneapolis: Fortress Press, 1992.

Dorff, Elliot N., Daniel S. Nevins & Avram I. Reisner. "Homosexuality, Human Dignity & Halakhah: a Combined Responsum for the Committee on Jewish Law and Standards." New York: CJLS, 2006.

Dover, K.J. *Greek Homosexuality*. New York: Vintage Books, a Division of Random House, 1980.

Duberman, Martin B., Martha Vicinus and George Chauncey, Jr. *Hidden from History: Reclaiming the Gay and Lesbian Past*. New York: Meridian Books, 1989.

Eskridge, William N., Jr. *The Case for Same-Sex Marriage: From Sexual Liberty to Civilized Commitment*. New York, London, etc.: The Free Press, 1996.

Finnis, John. "Law, Morality and 'Sexual Orientation,'" in John Corvino, *Same Sex: Debating the Ethics, Science, and Culture of Homosexuality*. Lanham-New York-London: Rowman and Littlefield, 1997.

Gagnon, Robert A.J. *The Bible and Homosexual Practice: Texts and Hermeneutics*. Nashville: Abingdon Press, 2001.

——. *Does Jack Rogers's New Book "Explode the Myths" about the Bible and Homosexuality and "Heal the Church"*? 2006. [www.robgagnon.net/JackRogersBookReviewed.htm]

——. *How Bad Is Homosexual Practice According to Scripture and Does Scripture's Indictment Apply to Committed Homosexual Unions?* 2007. [www.robgagnon.net/HowBadIsHomosexualPractice.htm]

——. *Notes to Gagnon's Essay in the Gagnon-Via "Two Views" Book*. 2003. [www.robgagnon.net/2VOnlineNotes.htm]

——. "Response to Countryman's Review of *The Bible and Homosexual Practice*." 2003. [www.robgagnon.net/RevCountryman.htm]

——. *Why the Disagreement Over the Biblical Witness on Homosexual Practice*. *Reformed Review* 59.1 (Autumn 2005): 19–130. [www.westernsem.edu/files/westernsem/gagnon_autm05_0.pdf]

Geller, Myron S., Robert E. Fine, and David F. Fine. "The Halakah of Same-Sex Relations in a New Context." CJLS, 2006. [www.uscj.org/empire/Geller_Fine_Fine_Dissent_Final.doc]

Goldin, Hyman E. *Hebrew Criminal Law and Procedure: Mishnah Sanhedrin—Makkot*. New York: Twayne Publishers, Inc., 1952.

Greenberg, David F. *The Construction of Homosexuality*. Chicago: The University of Chicago Press, 1988.

Halperin, David M. *One Hundred Years of Homosexuality: And Other Essays on Greek Love*. New York: Routledge, 1990.

Hasbany, Richard, ed. *Homosexuality and Religion*. New York: Harrington Park Press, 1989.

Hefling, Charles, ed. *Our Selves, Our Souls and Bodies: Sexuality and the Household of God*. Cambridge, Mass.: Cowley Publications, 1996.

Hertz, J.H. *The Pentateuch and Haftorahs*. London: Soncino Press, 1965.

John, Jeffrey. *"Permanent, Faithful, Stable": Christian Same-Sex Partnerships*. London: Darton, Longman & Todd, 1993, for Affirming Catholicism.

John Paul II. "By the Communion of Persons Man Becomes the Image of God." General Audience, November 14, 1979, from what was later collected into *The Theology of the Body: Human Love in the Divine Plan*. (Boston: Pauline Books and Media, 1997.)

Lawler, Michael G. *Marriage and Sacrament: A Theology of Christian Marriage*. Collegeville, Minn.: The Liturgical Press, 1993.

Lewis, C. S. *Mere Christianity*. New York: Macmillan Company, 1943.

———. *Surprised by Joy*. New York: Harcourt, Brace and World, 1955.

Macquarrie, John. *A Guide to the Sacraments*. New York: Continuum, 1998.

McCarter, P. Kyle, Jr. *I Samuel: A New Translation with Introduction and Commentary*. Garden City: Doubleday and Company, Inc., 1980. (The Anchor Bible 8).

———. *II Samuel: A New Translation with Introduction, Notes and Commentary*. Garden City: Doubleday and Company, Inc., 1984. (The Anchor Bible 9).

Milgrom, Jacob. *Leviticus 17–22*. New York, London, etc.: Doubleday (The Anchor Bible 3A), 2000.

Meyendorff, John. *Marriage: An Orthodox Perspective*. Crestwood, N.Y.: St. Vladimir's Seminary Press, 1970.

Miller, James. "The Practice of Romans 1:26: Heterosexual or Homosexual?" *Novum Testamentum* 87, 1995, 1–11.

Murray, Stephen O., and Will Roscoe. *Boy-Wives and Female Husbands: Studies of African Homosexualities*. New York: St. Martin's Press, 1998.

Neuner, J, S.J., and J. Dupuis, S.J., eds. *The Christian Faith in the Documents of the Catholic Church*. New York: Alba House, 1982.

Neusner, Jacob. *Song of Songs Rabbah: An Analytical Translation, Volume Two — Chapters Four through Eight*. Atlanta: Scholars Press, 1989.

Norvell, M.K., G.I. Benrubi, R.J. Thompson, "Investigation of microtrauma after sexual intercourse." Journal of Reproductive Medicine 1984 (4), 269–71.

Pakaluk, Michael. "Why is Homosexual Activity Morally Wrong?" in *Homosexuality: Challenge and Change and Reorientation, Journal of Pastoral Counseling* 28. New Rochelle: Iona College, 1993.

Plaut, W. Gunther, ed. *The Torah: A Modern Commentary*. New York: Union of American Hebrew Congregations, 1981.

Pope, Marvin H. *Job*. Garden City: Doubleday & Company, Inc., 1965. (The Anchor Bible 15).

———. *Song of Songs: A New Translation with Introduction and Commentary*. Garden City: Doubleday & Company, Inc., 1977. (The Anchor Bible 7C).

Rouselle, Aline. *Porneia: On Desire and the Body in Antiquity*. Translated by Felicai Pheasant. Oxford: Basil Blackwell Ltd., 1988.

Scanzoni, Letha and Virginia Ramey Mollenkott. *Is the Homosexual My Neighbor? Another Christian View*. San Francisco: HarperSanFrancisco, 1978.

Schmidt, Alvin John. *Veiled and Silenced: How Culture Shaped Sexist Theology*. Macon, Ga.: Mercer University Press, 1989.

Scroggs, Robin. *The New Testament and Homosexuality: Contextual Background for Contemporary Debate*. Philadelphia: Fortress Press, 1983.

Siker, Jeffrey S., ed. *Homosexuality in the Church: Both Sides of the Debate*. Louisville: Westminster John Knox Press, 1994.

Some Issues in Human Sexuality: A Guide to the Debate. London: Church House Publishing, 2003.

Smith, Martin. *Cowley Sermons 2*. Cambridge, Mass.: Society of St. John the Evangelist, 1983.

Stanley, Keith with Mary Borhek. *Christian Spirituality and Same-Gender Relationship: A Moravian Perspective*. Bethlehem, Pennsylvania: Sanctuary, 2000.

Stott, John. *Homosexual Partnerships: Why Same-Sex Relationships Are Not a Christian Option*. Downers Grove, Ill.: InterVarsity Press, 1984.

Stuhlman, Byron David. *Occasions of Grace: An historical and theological study of the Pastoral Offices and Episcopal Services in the Book of Common Prayer*. New York: The Church Hymnal Corporation, 1995.

Stuart, Elizabeth, ed. *Daring to Speak Love's Name: A Gay and Lesbian Prayer Book*. London: Hamish Hamilton, 1992.

Webber, Christopher. *Re-Inventing Marriage: A Re-view and Re-vision*. Harrisburg, Pa.: Morehouse Publishing, 1994.

Weil, Louis. "'The Church Does Not Make a Marriage,'" *Anglican Theological Review* LXXII No. 2 (Spring 1990), 172–174.

White, Edwin Augustine, and Jackson A. Dykman. *Annotated Constitution and Canons for the Government of the Protestant Episcopal Church in the United States of America otherwise known as The Episcopal Church*. New York: The Seabury Press, 1981 in two volumes; with a *Supplement*, New York: The Domestic and Foreign Missionary Society, 1989.

Winston, David. *The Wisdom of Solomon: A New Translation with Introduction and Commentary*. Garden City: Doubleday and Company, Inc., 1979. (The Anchor Bible 43)

Via, Dan O., and Robert A.J. Gagnon. *Homosexuality and the Bible: Two Views*. Minneapolis: Fortress Press, 2003.